Consciously Created Cinema

Consciously Created Cinema

The Movie Lover's Guide to the Law of Attraction

Brent Marchant

Copyright © 2014, by Brent Marchant.

ISBN: 978-1495976643
ISBN-10: 1495976645

All rights reserved. No part of this book may be reproduced or transmitted in any form or by any means, electronic or mechanical, including by photocopying, recording, or any other information storage and retrieval system, without permission in writing from the copyright owner, except by a reviewer, who may quote brief passages for review purposes.

Cover design: Paul L. Clark, www.inspirtainment.com

Text design and manuscript conversion:
Lisa DeSpain, www.ebookconverting.com

Author photo: Jill Brazel Photography, www.jillbrazel.com

To Trevor

"Understanding the world before our eyes requires us to first understand the world behind them, how our thoughts, intents and beliefs function to create the reality we each experience. *How* we go about that is the subject of Brent Marchant's inventive new book, *Consciously Created Cinema: The Movie Lover's Guide to the Law of Attraction*, which effectively illustrates the process at work through contemporary film. Whether you're a movie lover looking for inspiring cinema, a truth seeker in search of enlightening examples to follow, or both, you're sure to find a wealth of useful, perspective-changing ideas in this engaging new book."

> Betsy Chasse
> Co-creator
> "What the Bleep Do We Know?!"
> Author
> *Tipping Sacred Cows*

"If you love movies and have even an inkling of interest in self-awareness and the meaning of your life beyond just simple existence, like I do, then Brent Marchant's book, *Consciously Created Cinema*, is an absolute must read and a great reference tool—not only to learn about, and from, movies that matter, but also to learn something deeper and more profound about yourself. Read this book, watch every film he discusses, and I promise you will emerge from the experience a deeper, brighter and better person."

> Austin Vickers
> Writer and Producer
> "People v. The State of Illusion"

"In this book, Brent Marchant provides a spiritual road map to fully embracing the movie experience and its relevance in modern-day life. In our breakneck-paced society, movie watching gets us to slow down for an hour or two, forget our troubles, spend time with friends and family, and, most importantly, *to use our imaginations* and *engage our consciousness*.

"In the larger sense, Brent's film essays are about the intersection of the art form of the motion picture and process of how human beings are exploring the mystery of who we truly are and why we are here and alive. *Consciously Created Cinema* goes farther and deeper than his first book, *Get the Picture*, in helping us to appreciate how movies have become the primary culturally shared practice showing us the dreams, visions, nightmares and longings that are the human experience.

"*Consciously Created Cinema* is an important and seminal work on motion pictures that I hope will be referred to for a long time to come by the movie lover, the movie writer and the spiritual explorer looking to expand their mind while being entertained."

> Randall Libero
> Senior Executive Producer
> VoiceAmerica/World Talk Radio Networks

"I'm thankful that someone like Brent is actually looking at what lies beneath the glittering flashes of light, as much more is communicated with the nuance of symbology, story, color and sound than what a viewer first recognizes. A feeling state precipitates all cognition, and a good filmmaker knows how to work this in their medium. We do not need another person telling us how to live our lives; we require personal realization that comes from authentic and honest depictions of new thought. I appreciate Brent pointing us to these films."

> Ri Stewart
> Director, Bluedot Productions
> "The Quantum Activist"
> "Creativity: A new thought won't kill you"
> "What the Bleep: Now What?!"
> "Capoeira: Fly Away Beetle"

"I'm very excited about *Consciously Created Cinema*. In this enlightening work, Brent Marchant takes us to the movies and, in the process, teaches us how to use the law of attraction to manifest our desires. If you love movies and if you would love to live the life of your dreams, you are going to love this book!"

> James Goi Jr.
> Author
> *How to Attract Money Using Mind Power*

"In an age of instantly accessible movies, Brent Marchant offers a valuable, articulate and insightful guide to those connected with conscious creation. Marchant's ability to give the reader a taste of the plot and insight into the underlying reality creating principles makes for a fascinating read and resource. *If you want movie reviews that you can use for intelligent entertainment, get this book. Highly recommended.*"

> Robert Waggoner
> Author
> *Lucid Dreaming: Gateway to the Inner Self*
> Co-editor
> *Lucid Dreaming Experience* magazine

"Brent Marchant has done it again. In *Consciously Created Cinema*, he shows with great clarity, detail and insight how the tenets of 'conscious creation' are one of the most important tools of post-modern storytelling reflected with increasing frequency and depth in contemporary cinema."

> Paul M. Helfrich, Ph.D.
> Author
> *Seth: the Ultimate Guide*

"Hooray! A critic who shares his joy and enthusiasm! Not only does Marchant love movies, he has a solid command of the principles of conscious creation. He's highly skilled in writing about both with insight and humor, which adds up to a uniquely informative and entertaining guide. Check it out before you pop the popcorn!"

> Irene O'Garden
> Off-Broadway playwright
> Author
> *Goodbye Fat Girl*
> *Glad To Be Human*

"Just as we have the opportunity on an individual level to recognize how the laws of creation are manifesting in our personal lives, Brent is able to brilliantly do so within the construct of the movies. *Consciously Created Cinema: The Movie Lover's Guide to the Law of Attraction* provides another tool to empower us in the quest of understanding how we create our reality. The movies and reality have a lot in common as they are both stories we tell ourselves."

> Gregory Zanfardino
> President
> Moniker Entertainment

"I overheard a grownup say once, 'Well, it depends on how you look at it.' Fascinated, I turned that over and over in my little boy mind and still couldn't figure it out. What is *it*, anyway? Now Brent Marchant comes to my (and our) rescue. As I read his book (go slow, by the way), I realized that I was not only *seeing* movies I thought I had already seen a long time ago in a new light, I was being helped to see my life in a new light as well. It really does depend on how you look at it, and the *it* is the joy of feeling like a powerful creator or feeling like a victim.

"If you read Brent's book, as he recommends, in order, you'll get that he is taking you on a guided meditation, which will help you to internalize the principles of conscious creation, not just read about them. Of course, another joy of this book is that you will discover movies you had never *heard* of that you're now desperate to put on your Netflix queue. So you can use this book to change your view of life, or just to read some provocative movie reviews. It all depends on you!"

>   Paul Giurlanda, Ph.D.
>   Author
>   *Vistas: A Theologian in Past-Life Therapy*

"In *Consciously Created Cinema*, author Brent Marchant eloquently illustrates how the art of contemporary cinema reflects the subtle concepts and forces (such as the much-touted 'law of attraction') that are embroiled in the momentous shift in human development that's now occurring. By combining his love for the cinematic arts with his profound knowledge of the esoteric and metaphysical literature that describes our shifting mentality, he has produced a book that is both reassuring and motivational for the reader. Collectively, the films profiled in this book can be viewed (metaphorically and literally) as the current state of play in our game of 'awakening' to an altogether more altruistic approach to life."

>   Christopher W.E. Johnson
>   Author
>   *It's About You! Know Your Self*

"Film and law of attraction expert Brent Marchant deserves countless accolades for his new release, *Consciously Created Cinema: The Movie Lover's Guide to the Law of Attraction*. Marchant siphons the chaff from the wheat for film buffs who want not only good entertainment but also relevant insight into how the law of attraction works. The book eloquently introduces the novice and connoisseur to movies of every genre, with in-depth research providing background details one normally wouldn't delve into. His integration of the storylines and the law of attraction inspires you to see the movies *and* practice the principles involved.

"The book is a pleasure to read. Marchant's grasp of the written word is impeccable. He has honed his craft, making each movie review essential to how anyone can improve their life and contribute to creating a better world in which to thrive and reach the fulfillment we all desire."

>Mary Barton
>Author
>*Soul Sight: Projections of Consciousness and Out of Body Epiphanies*
>*Everyday Telepathy, Clairvoyance and Precognition*
>*Experience Tomorrow Today: Dreams that come True*

"I can literally think of dozens of ways to use Brent Marchant's creative gem of a book: As a guide for a monthly movie club discussion group; a personal tool for psycho-spiritual development; an ice breaker at parties—the list goes on and on. Build upon the principles step by step as you read through it, or just flip through the pages and let your finger choose tonight's feature from the lines of probabilities; the opportunities for exploration are indeed endless!"

>Kerstin Sjoquist
>Creator
>*Bliss Trips* guided meditation products

"Brent Marchant's brilliant and innovative insight into movies invites readers to awaken inner wisdom, reach into the realm of all possibilities and 'choose' the kind of future that will arise from chaos of the present. To understand the power of conscious creation principles, buy the book, and move through change with most ease."

>Doreen Agostino, I.P.
>Radio Show Host
>*Align Shine Prosper*

"Brent Marchant bestows another gift on cinemaphiles with his 2014 release, *Consciously Created Cinema: The Movie Lover's Guide to the Law of Attraction*. As he did for films pre-2007 in *Get the Picture: Conscious Creation Goes to the Movies* (Moment Point Press, 2007), Marchant covers plot summaries, relevant conscious creation themes and full cinemagraphic details, including notations and major awards, on over 60 movies released 2006-2012. Each chapter opens with a thoughtful examination of a theme, ranging from 'Faith and Beliefs' to 'Integrity' and 'Transformation.' With a thoughtful approach to the many underlying tenets of conscious creation, *Consciously Created Cinema* provides readers with many insights on how they can learn from the films examined, and, with Marchant's delightful writing and humor, every movie lover will find something new to ponder about their favorite, or perhaps previously undiscovered, films. Students in film studies will find this title and Marchant's previous work to be extremely valuable in their research of contemporary films."

Dodie Ownes
Editor
SLJTeen

"Having been in broadcasting for 35 years, I've seen a lot of changes, such as the rise of 'on-demand' *everything*. And, in light of that development, to have *Consciously Created Cinema: The Movie Lovers Guide to the Law of Attraction* available as a resource is absolutely fantastic. To be able to call up any movie from the 13 categories in the book on any of the Internet on-demand services, and then watch something that can inspire, uplift and encourage, is one of the most incredible opportunities each one of us has as a spiritual being on this planet. I can watch what I want when I want and find the kinds of movies that will coincide with my life's choices and purpose. And, ever since I discontinued cable and satellite services (making me subject to the whims of the networks), I have seen more movies and documentaries that I had never heard of before, films that really opened my eyes to even more 'new paradigms for a new world.' So, whether you get this book for yourself or for someone else, what an incredible *gift* it will be."

Richard Dugan
Radio Show Host
Tell Me Your Story

"Brent Marchant has the brilliant and unique talent of being able to show how films are able to tap into experiences that set examples of what viewers can do to attract the life they desire. His new book, *Consciously Created Cinema: The Movie Lover's Guide to the Law of Attraction*, magically draws upon films to explain how probabilities, quantum physics, science and metaphysics are melded to create the reality their characters experience, even when they don't realize it. His book reveals how it's about time movies have begun exploring what is *really* going on in the lives of their characters, conditions that might also be found in the scientific and spiritual, physical and metaphysical realms of viewers. This book may help readers and moviegoers see beyond the cinematic experience and into the next realm, relating how to solve their problems through the use of the law of attraction and the power of imagination."

> Daya Devi-Doolin
> Author
> *The Only Way Out Is In: The Secrets of the 14 Realms to Love, Happiness and Success!*
> *If You can Breathe, You CAN Do Yoga: for Beginners and the Young at Heart*
> *Grow Thin While You Sleep: Go Figure!*
> CEO, The Doolin Healing Sanctuary

"*Consciously Created Cinema* is a modern-day *Think and Grow Rich*, in which movie sage Brent Marchant introduces spiritual laws and teachings through the art of film, played out in stories. This book will not only become a treasured resource, but it will certainly transform your life."

> Katana Abbott
> Founder
> MidlifeMillionaires.com
> Radio Show Host
> *Smart Women Talk*

TABLE OF CONTENTS

ACKNOWLEDGMENTS 1

FOREWORD 3
By Mary Giuffre

INTRODUCTION 5

CHAPTER 1: PROBABILITIES 15
In Pursuit of a New Science: "The Quantum Activist"
Figuring Out What Matters: "Greenberg"
Finding Our Way: "Away We Go"
Quantum Physics Goes Mainstream: "Source Code"
City of Enlightenment: "Midnight in Paris"

CHAPTER 2: FAITH AND BELIEFS 33
In Search of an Elusive Truth: "Doubt"
Something To Believe In: "The X-Files: I Want to Believe"
Putting Faith to the Test: "Higher Ground"
Believing the Dream: "The Other Dream Team"
A Temporal Leap of Faith: "Safety Not Guaranteed"

CHAPTER 3: PERSPECTIVE 57
The Perception Paradox: "World's Greatest Dad"
Lessons in Perspective: "A Serious Man"
Defining One's Life: "Another Year"
What Truly Nourishes Us: "*Malos Hábitos*" ("Bad Habits")
What Do We *Really* Believe?: "Sound of My Voice"

CHAPTER 4: CHOICE AND INTENT 81

Minding Our Motivations: "Julie and Julia"
Going with One's Gut: "The Ghost"
Explorations of Intent: "Please Give"
Rogue Intents: "Game Change"
Conjuring Kismet: "Ruby Sparks"

CHAPTER 5: FEAR AND COURAGE 97

The Courage To Create: "Mao's Last Dancer"
Stepping Into the Unknown: "The Intouchables"
Taking Chances: "Hitchcock"
Beating the Odds: "The Impossible"
Finding One's Voice: "The King's Speech"

CHAPTER 6: INTEGRITY 119

A Visionary Hero: "Milk"
'Express' Intent: "The Express"
Challenging Spiritual Assumptions: "We Have a Pope" ("*Habemus Papam*")
Hungering for the Truth: "Fair Game"
Living in Harmony: "Avatar"

CHAPTER 7: POWER 141

Conceding One's Power: "Never Let Me Go"
The Power of Belief: "The Social Network"
When Beliefs Become Addictions: "The Hurt Locker"
The Responsibility of Power: "Watchmen"
A Fable for Our Times: "Alice in Wonderland"

CHAPTER 8: CONNECTION 157

The Connectedness of All Things: "Cloud Atlas"
Celebrating the Power, Beauty and Glory of Creation: "Samsara"
Unlocking the Mysteries of Existence: "Something Unknown Is Doing We Don't Know What"
What's Right and Wrong with the World: "I Am"
Looking for the Links: "Babel"

CHAPTER 9: CHANGE 179
Like Ants Making Thunder: "Taking Woodstock"
To Boldly Go Where We've Been Before: "Star Trek"
Catalysts for Change: "The Kids Are All Right"
Fresh Starts: "The Best Exotic Marigold Hotel"
The Power of Love: "*Amour*" ("Love")

CHAPTER 10: MISFIRES 197
An Unmitigated Disaster: "2012"
A Missed Opportunity: "Inception"
Travelogue Spirituality: "Eat Pray Love"
Tearjerker Metaphysics: "Rabbit Hole"
Trimming the Branches: "The Tree of Life"

CHAPTER 11: REDEMPTION 219
Redeeming One's Reality: "People v. The State of Illusion"
Getting Off the Couch: "Shrink"
Trial by Belief: "Conviction"
It's Never Too Late: "Crazy Heart"
Reconciling One's Life: "Get Low"

CHAPTER 12: TRANSFORMATION 237
A Stranger No More: "The Visitor"
Where One's Heart Is: "*Amreeka*" ("America")
What You Don't See Coming: "The Blind Side"
Packing a Punch: "Poor Boy's Game"
Becoming More Human Than Human: "District 9"

CHAPTER 13: TRANSCENDENCE 255
Moments of Clarity: "A Single Man"
On Life's Transitions: "*Biutiful*" ("Beautiful")
The Eternal Frontier: "Infinity: The Ultimate Trip—Journey Beyond Death"
Meditation on a Common Fate: "Hereafter"
By Default or Design: "The Adjustment Bureau"

EPILOGUE 275
INDEX OF ARTISTS 277

ACKNOWLEDGMENTS

So many people play such a valuable role in the creation of a book that their contributions absolutely must be recognized, and this title is no exception. It is with profound thanks that I extend my sincere gratitude to those who have been so helpful in bringing this work into being:

* First and foremost, to my partner, Trevor Laster, for his unconditional love and support through the many long hours that went into the creation of this book.
* To Lynda Dahl, Kat Andrews, the late Stan Ulkowski, Cathy Aldrich, Susan M. Watkins, Mary Dillman and Sue Ray for the inspiration and catalytic sparks they each provided in their own way for helping to get me started in writing about conscious creation in the movies.
* To Mary Giuffre for a generous, heartfelt and thoughtful foreword, as well as for her ongoing support of all of my writing projects over the years.
* To Betsy Chasse, Austin Vickers, Gregory Zanfardino, Randall Libero, Ri Stewart, Daya Devi-Doolin, Robert Waggoner, Paul Giurlanda, Mary Barton, Christopher W.E. Johnson, James Goi Jr., Dodie Ownes, Paul Helfrich, Doreen Agostino, Irene O'Garden, Kerstin Sjoquist, Katana Abbott and Richard Dugan for their endorsement of this project and for their ample support in helping to spread the word about it.
* To Catherine Bradford, Shayne Traviss, Kyle Paterson and Suzanna Gratz for their assistance in helping to spread the word

about conscious creation in the movies in general and my writings on the subject in particular.

* To my many friends and fellow seekers in the conscious creation community, both in Chicago and worldwide, for their inspiration, suggestions, film recommendations and ongoing backing, particularly Karen Sanders, Dana Beardshear, Jim Gilbert, Cyndi Safstrom, Del Potos, Patt Timlin, Sue Seggeling, Steve Martin, Nancy Kraft, Elena de la Peña, Jane Erie, Jobi Harris, Georgie Norene, Beverly Nelson, Jim Funk, Joe Webb, Judy Ewing and Trina Hoefling.

* To Jill Brazel Photography (www.jillbrazel.com) for superb portrait work, Paul L. Clark (www.inspirtainment.com) for an outstanding cover design and Lisa DeSpain (www.ebookconverting.com) for excellent book production work, as well as to everyone who has aided in the creation and distribution of this title.

* And, finally, to my many friends and colleagues for their zealous encouragement and support over the years, most notably Linnaea Burkett, Patti Schuldenfrei, Gary Castine, David Boyd, Rolf Pelkey, Dion Tillmon, Susan McCormick, Darrick Coleman, Mike Evans Jr., Dave Gan, Kevin Keys, Kevin Haynes, Mark Sullivan, Marsha Evans, Rob Kruss, Bubba Smith, Barb Helfman, Nick Palumbo, Sue Zyrkowski, Laure West, Elena Lockhart, Yolanda Griffin, Michelle Moen, John Chaffin, Laura Harrington, Pervaiz Ladhani, Chuck Spady, Barbara Blum, Thom Juul, Tommy Johns, Kelly Courtney, Mostapa abd Sukor, Nathan Wilson and Walter Winston.

I truly thank you all from the bottom of my heart.

FOREWORD

In the early days of my television career as a promo producer/editor for national and international broadcasters, I spent many hours viewing an endless number of fabulous (and, if I'm to be completely honest here, lots of dreadful) films. It was my task to put myself in the place of the average viewer, choose the juiciest parts of a given movie, then arrange those clips in a way that would draw the biggest TV audience. Several awards from the New York festivals suggest I was pretty good at my job, too!

My husband/business partner Paul L. Clark and I have since left the big city in favor of more fulfilling artistic pursuits. We love the cozy nest where we live and create, but here in our one-store town in rural Canada, the DVD selection has always been seriously lacking, and our irregular satellite Internet makes movie downloads next to impossible, so the only thing I truly miss about my crazy life in Toronto is having those movie reels delivered directly to my office.

Over time, I found the best way to keep up with the movies was by reading about them, and Brent Marchant's conscious creation online reviews became my regular movie connection. The bonus was that his expansive insights introduced me to a new side of big screen storytelling I'd never considered, which, in turn, opened me up to viewing films in a whole new way! I was truly inspired and became an enthusiastic fan.

In the months that followed us sidestepping mainstream media, Paul and I founded a variety of creative initiatives, including a heart-centered online magazine, and we were very excited when Brent found us and proposed writing original reviews for our site! Thus began a wonderful friendship with one of the most consciously aware individuals I have had the privilege of collaborating with, and I'm delighted to have been asked to write the foreword for this outstanding piece of work.

Brent's interpretations in *Consciously Created Cinema* allow us to recognize that movies can serve a larger purpose. This exceptional volume is filled with rational and fanciful cinematic examples of how life—real or imagined—could progress. Brent's insights point out instance after instance of relatable ways for us to put ourselves in a character's shoes while he describes in detail how behavior creates circumstance. He then explains what's been accomplished and how conscious creation will always influence the most satisfying outcome—all valuable, relevant examples for setting conscious creation in motion in our own lives.

With this *Movie Lover's Guide*, where each chapter builds one concept to the next as one moves through the book, Brent provides a clear picture of how the conscious creation process actually works: Probability (Chapter 1) first requires Belief (Chapter 2). Our Beliefs take shape because of our personal Perspective (Chapter 3), which then provides opportunity for us to make our own Choices (Chapter 4). Our Choices often require us to be Courageous (Chapter 5), which provides us with the opportunity for lessons in Integrity (Chapter 6) and ... well, you get the picture.

Inspiring and thought-provoking, this book is packed with suggestions that illustrate heart- and mind-engaging conscious creation/law of attraction principles. *Consciously Created Cinema: The Movie Lover's Guide to the Law of Attraction* is perfect for movie lovers like me who (1) don't get to the theater as often as we'd like and (2) want a meaningful movie experience, whether we're viewing on the silver screen or in the comfort of our own homes.

I will use Brent's words from Chapter 2 to encourage you to devour his book from cover to cover: "... you'll be amazed at how much you can glean from it, information that will stand you in good stead when times get tough and help elevate you to unimagined heights of enlightenment ...."

Sage wisdom, Brent. Thank you!

From the Heart,
Mary Giuffre
Producer, Director, Editor, Writer
www.inspirtainment.com
Co-Author: *Scribble & Grin - 53 Rhymes for Inspiring Times*
www.ScribbleAndGrin.com

INTRODUCTION

Most of us are no doubt familiar with the expression, "Life is what you make of it." It's an adage that offers comfort in the face of disappointment and inspiration when undertaking new endeavors. Yet, as readily as we embrace the good feelings this saying imparts, how many of us *truly* take it to heart? Do we seriously believe the sentiment expressed by these words? And is the essence of this idea even possible, or is it oh so much warm fuzzy New Age hype?

For my part, I believe it really *is* possible for life to become what you make of it, thanks to the practice of *conscious creation*. This highly empowering approach to living maintains that we each create our own reality in conjunction with All That Is (or God, Goddess, Source, the Universe or whatever other term best suits you). This is accomplished by combining the thoughts, beliefs and intents we each formulate for ourselves with the power of our divine collaborator, thereby creating the conditions for manifesting the physical world that surrounds us. It applies to all areas of life, too, from romance to vocation to spirituality and everything in between. And, when the process is applied skillfully, it results in the life we crave.

While some may not be familiar with the term "conscious creation," the concept is anything but new. Students of the ancient esoteric practice of alchemy, for example, will readily recognize the underlying similarities between that discipline and this one. Likewise, followers of the law of attraction, the personal empowerment concept popularized through the immense success of the book and DVD "The Secret" (2006), will see conscious creation's uncanny resemblance to that practice. And those with a scientific bent will note the likeness between the principles of quantum physics and this metaphysical practice. But, no matter what one calls it or how one uses it, the process ultimately yields the same result, namely, that thoughts become things.

A number of important principles provide the foundation for this practice, and many excellent reference sources on them are available. They are perhaps best covered in the writings of author and consciousness pioneer Jane Roberts (1929-1984), who, together with her noncorporeal channeled entity, Seth, produced volume upon volume of material on the subject. But, as eloquently as these concepts are presented in prose, they are also brilliantly portrayed through an entirely different medium—the movies.

In many respects, movies are essentially the modern-day equivalent of storytelling, the time-honored practice that has long been used for instructing students in various philosophical, spiritual and metaphysical traditions. But, because motion pictures enhance their storylines with the high-tech wizardry of striking visuals and state-of-the-art sound, they bring their messages to life in ways that mere words often can't. Their messages carry enormous impact, evoking strongly felt responses among viewers and conveying their messages with palpable degrees of substance and meaning. This is particularly true when it comes to cinematic portrayals of conscious creation principles; they leap off the screen at us with the vigor of the great white star of "Jaws."

As a lifelong movie lover, I've found that films of all genres are capable of accomplishing this, too, including everything from comedies to dramas to science fiction and even documentaries. In fact, over time, I've come to discover that movies even can be organized into a sort of road map or outline for explaining the key concepts of conscious creation. Such an outline provides the basis for my previous book on the subject, *Get the Picture: Conscious Creation Goes to the Movies* (Moment Point Press, 2007, ISBN 978-1-930491-12-0). It's also the focus of my online movie reviews for *VividLife magazine* (www.VividLife.me) and my web site's ongoing blog (www.brentmarchant.com).

Many fundamental conscious creation concepts may seem like practical, commonsense guidance for everyday living, and that's true, to be sure. But, when the principles are viewed *collectively* (with the concepts building upon one another and working synergistically) and applied with a heightened sense of awareness (a truly "conscious" outlook), they work together to provide a powerful means for approaching life. They generate a heightened sense of self-empowerment and self-awareness to help us shape our existence more to our liking. They enable us to address life's opportunities, and to confront its challenges, more effectively and with a greater sense of fulfillment. Here's a look at some of those key concepts and films that exemplify them:

1. **Becoming aware of how we formulate beliefs.** Since beliefs are the starting point in conscious creation, it's important to know how they form in the first place. This involves becoming aware of the roles that our intellect and intuition play in this process. They provide the input that our consciousness evaluates and then uses to shape the beliefs we hold based on such assessments. Awareness of this overall process, as well as the individual beliefs we form through it, is crucial for one's conscious creation proficiency; the better we are at this, the more effective we can be at making use of it. Movies that show this include the romantic comedy "Under the Tuscan Sun" (2003) and the ballet world drama "The Turning Point" (1977).

2. **Going beyond surface perceptions.** Because we tend to put more reliance on intellect than we do on intuition, we also tend to put a lot of stock into surface perceptions, those that we perceive with our five outer senses. But sometimes these impressions don't tell the whole story. Looking *beneath* the surface provides a fuller picture, helping us to see that things aren't always what they seem. It also helps us sharpen our intuitive sense, which, as noted above, is a key element in belief formation. These ideas are explored effectively in the family drama "Ordinary People" (1980), the French farce "King of Hearts" (1966), the riveting character study "A Beautiful Mind" (2001), the biting satire "Wag the Dog" (1997) and the heartfelt father-and-son fable "Big Fish" (2003).

3. **Understanding the relationship of science and spirit in our lives.** In many ways, the harmony between these two forces is a metaphor for the relationship between intellect and intuition. Grasping the one aids our comprehension of the other, and

a number of pictures illustrate that, including the aforementioned law of attraction DVD "The Secret" (2006), the eclectic conscious creation treatise "What the #$*! Do We (K)now!?" (2004), the engaging sci-fi drama "Contact" (1997) and the metaphysical talkfest "Mindwalk" (1991).

4. **Drawing upon the power of choice and free will.** If we each create our own reality, then it would stand to reason that we also must be the ones making the decisions about how that reality materializes. This is where the power of choice and free will comes into play. Surprisingly, however, it's a power we often lose sight of. Maintaining an acute awareness of it is critical to formulating the beliefs that allow us to create the existence we want, no matter how outlandish or unusual those choices may seem. Examples of pictures that illustrate this are the gut-wrenching drama "Sophie's Choice" (1982), the edgy dark comedy "After Hours" (1985), the unconventional family drama "Housekeeping" (1987) and the futurist yarn "Brave New World" (1998).

5. **Making changes when needed.** When our beliefs don't pan out as we'd like them to, it's time to choose new ones. Being willing to evaluate our choices and to make changes to them (by rewriting the beliefs that underlie them) is essential to helping us achieve results more to our liking. Of course, we have to follow through on those changes in our choices to see them bear fruit; otherwise, we're likely to remain locked in place, unsatisfied with our creations. Films that address such questions include the offbeat comedy-drama "The Truman Show" (1998), the gender-bending comedies "All of Me" (1984) and "Switch" (1991), the romantic fantasy "Peggy Sue Got Married" (1986), the quirky Woody Allen comedies "Zelig" (1983) and "The Purple Rose of Cairo" (1985), and the never-ending saga of "Groundhog Day" (1993).

6. **Facing fears and living heroically.** This is precisely what's called for when making changes in our beliefs and in our lives. Without the courage to do this, we really *will* stay stuck in place. Many movies delve into this subject beautifully, but some of my favorites are the soul-searching sci-fi drama "Signs" (2002), the

courageous leap of faith character study "An Unmarried Woman" (1978), the Alfred Hitchcock classic "Vertigo" (1958), the otherworldly romantic comedy "Defending Your Life" (1991), and a trio of contemporary heroic tales (all from 2005) "The Constant Gardener," "Syriana" and "Good Night, and Good Luck."

7. **Assessing the evolution of our beliefs.** Looking at how our beliefs change over time gives us a sense of how far we've come with regard to achieving a particular goal. By taking stock of our beliefs in this way, we can see where further changes may be needed. Films in the road trip genre are especially effective at illustrating this principle, and some great examples include the cinematic classic "The Wizard of Oz" (1939), the screwball comedy "Flirting with Disaster" (1996), the action adventure "Indiana Jones and the Last Crusade" (1989) and the Frank Capra fantasy "Lost Horizon" (1937).

8. **Appreciating the connectedness of all things.** If we each truly create our own reality, then we indeed create the *totality* of that reality, including all its component parts. When we consider how intricately all of the various elements of our existence are interwoven with one another, it becomes clear just how careful we must be when making choices, formulating beliefs and effecting changes to them, for the implications can be far-reaching and unexpected. A number of movies explore this idea well, including the ironically titled "Six Degrees of Separation" (1993), the dysfunctional character study "American Beauty" (1999), the engaging gay drama "Hard Pill" (2005), the angst-ridden L.A. sagas "Grand Canyon" (1991) and "Crash" (2005), and the heartwarming charitable tale "Pay It Forward" (2000).

9. **Exceeding our personal limitations.** A chief aim of conscious creation is to create the reality we desire, something frequently achieved through spurts in our personal growth. Such advances can be realized by thinking the unthinkable, envisioning possibilities never before dreamed of, and imbuing ourselves with skills we never knew we had or thought possible. Also, it can involve allowing ourselves to wander the uncharted territories of alternate states of consciousness, such as those experienced in dreams, meditation and other unconventional states of mind.

Imagine what's possible with outlooks like that! Sci-fi and fantasy films are especially good at helping us see such possibilities, because they inherently push limits as part of their storylines. Some great examples are "What Dreams May Come" (1998), "Phenomenon" (1996), "Resurrection" (theatrical version, 1980; made-for-TV version, 1999), "K-PAX" (2001), "The Lathe of Heaven" (1980), "Brainstorm" (1983), "Eternal Sunshine of the Spotless Mind" (2004) and "Pleasantville" (1998).

10. **Experiencing the joy and power of creation.** As self-evident as this may seem, becoming more conscious of this state of being is tremendously uplifting. It allows us to experience being our own best, truest selves, living up to our potential for the betterment of our own lives and those of others around us, a notion sometimes known in conscious creation circles as *value fulfillment*. It's a state of being that begs the question, "Who wouldn't want to live a life like that?" We can see such sublime joy and tremendous power made manifest through such pictures as the gentle comedy "Being There" (1979), the Christmas classic "It's a Wonderful Life" (1946), the inspiring, high-flying historical adventure "The Right Stuff" (1983) and the dreamy fantasy world of "Wings of Desire" (1987).

Consider what's possible when all of these steps are put together, not only for achieving the existence we want to lead for ourselves, but also for the greater world in which we dwell. The satisfaction and rewards of such a life are truly worth experiencing. And to think it can all stem from the inspiration that movies provide us.

Now that's quite a creation, if I do say so myself.

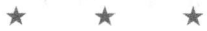

As noted earlier, I explored the foregoing principles in considerable detail when I wrote *Get the Picture*, so I won't belabor them here. My purposes in writing this book are to reiterate the significance of some of the most important notions (like the roles of beliefs, choice, fear, courage, connection and change) and to introduce a number of new ones, concepts that complement those outlined above (such as the importance of probabilities, faith, integrity, power, redemption, transformation and transcendence). And, in the course of addressing all of these ideas, I also elaborate on some specific conscious creation precepts that I covered in passing in *Get the Picture*, including the following:

* The notion that we're all in *a constant state of becoming*, a reflection of the evolutionary idea noted above. This is crucial to our personal growth and to the development of our greater, spiritual selves of which we, as individual physical beings, are part.

* The principle that we're innately *multidimensional beings*. This applies both to the many aspects of our individual character, as well to the multiple selves that comprise our greater being, both in the reality we experience firsthand and in the many other dimensional planes in which other parts (or "fragments") of our selves dwell.

* The idea that we live in a *Safe Universe*, one that has the best interests of our growth and development at heart. Under such conditions, our divine conscious creation collaborator provides us with the circumstances most conducive to that aim, no matter how seemingly unlikely (or even "undermining") they may appear at the time of their manifestation. Such conditions nearly always lead us to fortuitous connections and synchronicities that make the realization of our goals possible.

* The concept that, for better or worse, we've all chosen to incarnate to learn specific *life lessons*. This notion helps to explain a lot about why things happen as they do, for all of our incarnations are intended to provide us with exposure to and experience in all aspects of the human condition and physical existence. We'd serve ourselves well by doing whatever we can to make ourselves as aware of this as possible.

* The principle that the manifestation process involves acts of *co-creation*, those that we engage in with our divine collaborator, as well as those that we materialize with our fellow terrestrial beings. Those that we produce collectively with our peers are referred to as *mass events*, happenings that are generally made up of countless individual events occurring under common umbrellas but that likely wouldn't have materialized were it not for the mutually manifested conditions under which they arose.

* The principle that *the point of power is in the present moment*, the only one over which we have direct control. To achieve optimum results, we'd be wise to recognize this concept, for the past is behind us and the future has yet to occur. "Now" is what we have to work with, and we'd serve ourselves best by doing so.

* The idea that the manifestation process requires us to be *conscious* of what we're doing, as the philosophy's very name suggests. To do otherwise is to engage either in *creation by default* or *un-conscious creation* (where we manifest our reality without regard for the *responsibility* involved or the *consequences* that can arise) or in *semi-conscious creation* (where our focus on the *form* of an outcome often blinds us to recognizing the *spirit* of an intention when it materializes). The pitfalls of these practices can be considerable, to say the least.

* The notion that acts of creation are intended to promote our experience of *value fulfillment*, as discussed earlier. To do less is to shortchange ourselves, but to sincerely and consciously aspire to this aim is to truly fulfill our destiny.

All of these principles, when applied collectively, provide us with a powerful set of tools to create a meaningful existence. And movies provide us with powerful examples of how to make use of them. That is what this book is all about.

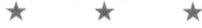

In many ways, I have employed the same general approach in this book that I used in *Get the Picture*. Each Chapter opens with a brief introduction to a basic conscious creation concept, providing an overview of its essence and its pertinence to the overall process. That's followed by five movie listings that illustrate the concept at work. Each listing includes a plot summary and discussion of the relevant conscious creation themes, as well as credits information on principal cast members, directors, writers, year of U.S. domestic release and notations on major awards (Oscars,[1] Golden Globes,[2] the Cannes Film Festival, and, in one case, Emmys[3]). However, unlike my previous book, which profiled films across the entire span of cinematic history, this work specifically looks at movies released since I wrote *Get the Picture*, from 2006 through the end of the 2012 awards season.

There's a logic to the order of the Chapters that will become apparent as readers go through the book. The concepts build upon one another, sometimes within a Chapter and sometimes from one Chapter to the next, showing how the different conscious creation principles fit together like the pieces of a puzzle. Due to the nature of this format, then, it probably wouldn't be practical to treat this book like a catalog to peruse for a movie to watch; the book's outline and contents don't readily lend themselves to that. Instead, the book functions more like a cinematic syllabus, taking readers through a course on conscious creation as depicted through recent film releases. So I'd strongly suggest reading it in order rather than jumping around at random.

The pictures I've selected for each Chapter are what I consider to be some of the best recent examples of films that portray the conscious creation concepts in question. Some selections could easily have fit into more than one Chapter, and good arguments could be made for organizing them differently, but I slotted them where I felt they best exemplified the ideas at hand. Some of these pictures may not have been purposely made with conscious creation or law of attraction principles in mind, but the ideas are present in them nevertheless. This isn't meant to give them revisionist treatment; rather, it's to show how good they are at portraying these particular notions, whether or not their creators intended them to do so.

With all that said, I'd like to add a few other comments about this book's nature and its contents:

* This is not an almanac of all of my personal favorite films of the past several years; that's not the intent of this book. Besides, some of my favorites wouldn't necessarily meet the criteria required to qualify for inclusion in this book.
* This is not an encyclopedia of all the pictures with metaphysical themes that have been made in recent years. Again, that's not what I'm striving for here, given the book's stated purpose.
* I have endeavored to avoid playing spoiler as much as possible. Although there may be hints at how the stories turn out (generally through the use of textual cliffhangers), I have done my level best to keep from blatantly divulging any endings. The only exceptions are entries involving biographies and pictures

based on historical events, storylines in which the outcomes are already known and in the public record. Otherwise, though, I'm not telling; you'll just have to see the pictures for yourself!

* With the specific exception of one Chapter's film listings, I *like* all of the pictures in this book. Since I'm not fulfilling the role of a traditional movie critic here, and considering my objective of providing readers with good examples of films that capably illustrate conscious creation principles, it seems counterproductive to devote a lot of space to pictures I don't like or wouldn't recommend. I *do* include criticisms of specific movie elements where warranted, but this is not one of my priorities in writing this book.

* One entry was originally made for cable television. I have always believed that relevant small-screen productions deserve recognition where pertinent and have never hesitated to write about them when relevant. I do so here again.

* As was the case in *Get the Picture*, certain movie genres are lacking almost entirely here, mainly out of personal preference. Some may think me cantankerous or prejudicial for saying that, and I'd respond that everyone is entitled to his or her opinion—including me. Consequently, you'll find no westerns (their testosterone-driven storylines rank about on par with professional wrestling), no horror flicks (their gratuitous, gore-dripping gimmickry makes me wish I'd skipped the concession stand on my way into the theater) and no musicals (most make me wish I'd been born heterosexual).

Conscious creation is truly a fascinating and empowering practice, and movies are great teachers of its key concepts (not to mention being a lot of fun, too). So sit back, pop some popcorn, fire up the DVD player and enjoy the show!

---

[1] Oscar(s)® and Academy Award(s)® are registered trademarks of the Academy of Motion Picture Arts and Sciences.
[2] Golden Globe(s)® is a registered trademark of the Hollywood Foreign Press Association.
[3] Emmy(s)® is a registered trademark of the Academy of Television Arts & Sciences and the National Academy of Television Arts & Sciences.

1

PROBABILITIES

It's often been said that "anything's possible." And, to those who actively employ the conscious creation process in their lives, this notion is practically a mantra.

At any given moment, thanks to the law of attraction, we're each capable of using our beliefs to materialize virtually any line of *probability* (*i.e.*, any expression of existence) we can imagine. When the power of our intents joins forces with the energy of our divine collaborator, we can bring forth into being almost any manifestation conceivable. That puts a tremendous palette of creativity at our disposal at any time, and we can work wonders with it, our imagination being the only limitation. It can be used for everything from solving problems to producing stunning works of art to manifesting a parking space in a crowded neighborhood. Indeed, no matter how the process is used, conscious creation is capable of making even the improbable possible.

Interestingly enough, those well-versed in quantum physics will no doubt recognize the similarities between that scientific discipline and the conscious creation process. In fact, they're often considered to be two sides of the same coin. So even those who possess a scientific, rather than a metaphysical, background are likely to understand how this practice fundamentally works.

The films profiled in this Chapter examine the notion of probabilities from a variety of perspectives. One of them explores probabilities in terms of the aforementioned scientific and metaphysical similarities. Another looks at the basic need of understanding how we employ probabilities as a means for getting through everyday life (and what can happen when we fail to grasp or employ the concept). And others examine the process of exploring probability options for choosing which one ultimately best serves our needs.

All too often, we look upon our circumstances convinced that we don't have any choice in what happens. But, as the infinite range of available probabilities makes clear, we truly have countless options open to us at any given time, more than most of us can probably imagine. All we need do is take a look at the probabilities and pick one that suits us. And, if that one doesn't work, there's plenty more where that one came from, all of which are capable of being birthed into being thanks to conscious creation.

In Pursuit of a New Science

"The Quantum Activist"
Year of Release: 2009
Cast: Amit Goswami
Directors: Renee Slade and Ri Stewart
Screenplay: Ted Golder

Every cause needs its activists. Be they political, social, artistic or philosophical, movements don't materialize without advocates to move them forward. One such initiative that's currently attracting ever-increasing ranks of proponents is the exploration of the relationship between science and spirituality. It's a bold undertaking with wide-ranging implications, one that's prompting us to take a new look at who we are and the place we occupy in the Universe. And, with our fundamental view of reality at stake, it's crucial that we seek out sources of wisdom and enlightenment to help guide us along the path of this brave new territory. That's why films like "The Quantum Activist" are so important.

This engaging documentary explores our evolving knowledge of the relationship between science and spirituality and how that understanding, in turn, affects our take on the nature of existence. It does so through the teachings of Indian-born quantum physicist Amit Goswami, a longtime professor of theoretical physics at the University of Oregon, Eugene, and the author of numerous books on the subject. Those outside the scientific and educational communities may best know him as one of the featured commentators in the conscious creation primer "What the #$*! Do We (K)now!?" (2004).

Having been born into a traditional Hindu upbringing, Goswami looked beyond the limitations of what conventional religion had to say about the nature of reality by taking up the study of quantum physics, a subject in which he would eventually become an expert. Ironically, however, the further Goswami explored this subject, the more he began to see uncannily clear parallels between its theories and the lessons taught in established spiritual practices, including those of his own religious background. Over time, Goswami (and a select group of peers, such as Fritjof Capra) began coming to the conclusion that many time-honored spiritual and religious writings were, in actuality, metaphorical texts for illustrating the principles of quantum physics. Granted, the language in those ancient writings may be more flowery or esoteric than what one typically finds in contemporary scientific literature, but the underlying principles are, in many respects, the same.

As Goswami became more convinced of this connection, he also became an active proponent for the advancement of a new science, one committed to exploring the links between the two long-separated disciplines of traditional science and conventional spirituality. His willingness to embrace this view was a bold move, too, since professing such ideas often meant professional suicide for many of Goswami's predecessors and peers. However, because he was unable to ignore the compelling body of evidence in support of his ideas, Goswami and like-minded colleagues forged ahead, steadily drawing bands of followers, including many fellow scientists.

"The Quantum Activist" chronicles the path Goswami took to reach this point and details his teachings in clips from interviews and filmed lectures. Through this narrative, Goswami covers a wide range of topics, including how spiritual teachings can be seen as illustrations of the principles of quantum mechanics (and vice versa) and how consciousness and beliefs are thought to affect the unfolding of the quantum process. But, perhaps most importantly, Goswami explores how the quantum process makes all conceivable probabilities possible (regardless of whether or not we experience their manifestation firsthand) and the implications of this in areas as diverse as human biology, the materialization of our physical world and the inherent connectedness (quantum entanglement) of everything in the Universe. These concepts are inventively illustrated using clips from vintage movies, glossy graphics, and innovative fusions of film and animation, all accompanied by Goswami's articulate voice-over narration. Topics that potentially could be thought of as painfully tedious are made engaging by this effective combination of cinematic techniques and Goswami's warm, gentle humor.

This film is a must-see for conscious creation practitioners, because it shows how quantum physics principles drive this process on an underlying "mechanical" level. Since these concepts are inherently at work in all probabilities (most obviously those through which we manifest our respective realities), it's essential that we be aware of them in order to become ever more proficient in this practice (and, one would hope, to produce results more to our liking). Knowledge of this subject truly opens up the infinite range of options available to each of us and enables us to achieve a deeper understanding of what Goswami so eloquently calls "the physics of possibility."

Albert Einstein once observed that "Science without religion is lame; religion without science is blind." Today's growing legions of quantum activists, like Amit Goswami, are building upon Einstein's insight to show us the veracity of that wisdom in the hope that ultimately we may create better lives—and a better world—for us all.

Figuring Out What Matters

"Greenberg"
Year of Release: 2010
Cast: Ben Stiller, Greta Gerwig, Rhys Ifans, Mark Duplass,
Jennifer Jason Leigh, Merritt Wever, Chris Messina, Susan Traylor,
Brie Larson, Juno Temple, Dave Franco, Zach Chassler, Mina Badie
Director: Noah Baumbach
Screenplay: Noah Baumbach
Story: Jennifer Jason Leigh and Noah Baumbach

As we wend our way through life, many of us face numerous challenges for managing our daily existence. Each of the tests we encounter can be difficult enough in themselves, but imagine what it would be like if we were fundamentally incapable of getting a handle on what's truly vital in life or how to materialize those essentials. Such is the lot of the title character in the disquieting comedy-drama, "Greenberg."

Roger Greenberg (Ben Stiller) is a seriously lost soul. The former musician-turned-carpenter has trouble with everyday existence. He spends much of it adrift in life's minutiae, an obsession that regularly launches him into incoherent stream of consciousness ramblings or angry rants, either verbally or in letter form. It's a pattern of behavior that probably helped land him in the mental institution from which he recently emerged. But now that Roger's back in mainstream society, his challenge is to figure out what's next, a daunting prospect for a 40-year-old who feels that life and its infinite probabilities are pointlessly passing him by.

As a start, Roger agrees to leave his New York home and travel to Los Angeles to house-sit for his brother Phillip (Chris Messina), who's embarking on a lengthy trip abroad with his family. While in L.A., Roger's told he can call upon Phillip's capable but somewhat spacey twenty-something personal assistant, Florence Marr (Greta Gerwig), if he needs anything, an offer that quickly spawns an often-awkward rollercoaster romance. Roger's visit also allows him to reconnect with his former band mates, Ivan (Rhys Ifans) and Beller (Mark Duplass), as well as an old flame, Beth (Jennifer Jason Leigh), all of whom have moved on with their lives while Roger has stayed emotionally and psychologically stuck in place, a realization that reinforces (and sometimes even empowers) his sense of isolation and inability to progress. Nothing seems to give Roger the inspiration he needs to get on with his life, but, given his scattered and perpetually discontented state of mind, there's no guarantee he'd even be able to recognize said spark if it were to appear. So what's someone to do as the years pile up and life marches ever forward? That's Roger's burden as he grapples with the life he wasn't expecting (nor wanted).

Taken at face value, "Greenberg" might seem like a frustrating film to watch, mainly because it comes across as an unfocused story about a self-absorbed misfit. But, if viewers go beyond its surface qualities, they'll find a very different—and very engaging—picture, one that's effective at conveying an important (and potentially unsettling) message: If merely *seeing* a character engaging in a life of apparent futility makes one squirm, then imagine what it must be like *to be* someone who lives out such an existence. That might be an especially uneasy prospect if it hits close to home, particularly given the degree of authenticity with which it's depicted here.

The movie thereby illustrates just how crucial it is to have an understanding of conscious creation principles for managing the basic functioning of day-to-day existence. If we were to lack such an innate awareness about the workings of life, we'd likely wander through it just as aimlessly and embittered as Roger does. And, since he seems unable to grasp even the rudiments of the process, he's consequently unable to assemble the most basic belief platform necessary for creating the foundation of a meaningful existence. Choosing a suitable line of probability becomes a virtually impossible task. Instead, he defaults to his inability to work the law of attraction process (a viable, if frustrating, line of probability in itself), which only brings him more of what he's already accustomed to, as well as peers (like Florence) who seem to be just as intrinsically clueless as he is. What's worse, these circumstances even lead him to frequently proclaim that he's *intentionally* seeking to create nothing out of his life, a defensive reaction to this fundamental failing. It's almost as if he's creating a *Seinfeld*-esque existence, only without the laugh track. It's all so very sad.

Viewers who grasp these notions should be able to see the debilitating difficulty involved in a condition like this, and that, in turn, should help increase awareness of the need for compassion for those so affected. Recall what I noted previously about trying to imagine what it might be like if the shoe were on the other foot: If you were to find yourself in the thick of such circumstances, wouldn't you want compassionate souls in your life to help show you the way out of your dilemma rather than to simply label you as demented, maladjusted or pathologically narcissistic? (I sure would.)

"Greenberg" is definitely *not* everyone's cinematic cup of tea. Those who prefer pictures that are plot-driven, rather than character-driven (as is the case here), are likely to be disappointed. What's more, those expecting a Ben Stiller comedy (as the film's somewhat misleading trailer would seem to imply) will likely be disappointed as well, for there are few genuine laughs in this picture.

With all that said, however, there's a lot here for moviegoers who enjoy the unconventional. Director/screenwriter Noah Baumbach shows us, rather than merely tells us, what he's trying to say, a rich, nuanced approach to filmmaking seldom seen in many of today's neat, tidy, formulaic productions. The overall style reminds me of the works of Robert Altman, many of whose pictures focused more on developing characters rather than playing out storylines, often with the same degree of quirkiness found here. Also, it's nice to see Stiller play a role where he isn't a walking punch line as has often been the case in many of his other movies. He turns in a capable performance in a rare dramatic turn, something I hope he attempts more of in the future.

"Greenberg" is the kind of movie that should help well-adjusted viewers be grateful for what they have. Seeing the greenery from the other side of the fence might be just what it takes to care for one's own lawn in the first place—and to be happy with the grass that's already growing there.

Finding Our Way

"Away We Go"
Year of Release: 2009
Cast: John Krasinski, Maya Rudolph, Catherine O'Hara, Jeff Daniels, Allison Janney, Jim Gaffigan, Carmen Ejogo, Maggie Gyllenhaal, Josh Hamilton, Chris Messina, Melanie Lynskey, Paul Schneider
Director: Sam Mendes
Screenplay: Dave Eggers and Vendela Vida

Journeys of self-discovery have long been staples of the movie industry, but they've nearly always been depicted through adolescent coming-of-age stories. Rarely has the notion been explored through the eyes of those who are a little older and, at least theoretically, a little wiser. Where are the tales of the twenty- and thirty-somethings who wonder whether or not they've missed the boat of life and are floundering about trying to find their way? Thankfully, there's a film for young adults who've experienced the uneasiness of feeling untethered and directionless, the comedy-drama "Away We Go."

Burt (John Krasinski) and Verona (Maya Rudolph) are a young unmarried couple expecting their first child. They live in what appears to be a pieced-together shack, yet they seem to be doing fairly well for themselves financially (Burt works in insurance futures, Verona's a medical illustrator). They live near Burt's parents, Gloria (Catherine O'Hara) and Jerry (Jeff Daniels), and they look forward to sharing the joy of their new arrival with them—that is, until the free-spirited grandparents-to-be announce that they're fulfilling their long-held dream of picking up and relocating to Belgium, a move scheduled to occur a month before the baby is born.

Needless to say, Burt and Verona are thrown for a loop; one of the few reasons underlying their current living arrangements is now gone. Gloria and Jerry's revelation thus prompts the young couple to wonder whether they've screwed up their lives and to question if there isn't something better for them out there somewhere else. And so they embark on a road trip to investigate other opportunities, a journey that's as much literal as it is metaphorical.

Burt and Verona's trip takes them to a variety of locations. Along the way, they have a chance to witness examples of how others live and whether they wish to emulate what they see. Specifically, their journey takes them:

* to Phoenix, where the couple meets Verona's former boss Lily (Allison Janney) and husband Lowell (Jim Gaffigan), an example of the American dream gone sadly awry in the tackiest of ways;
* then to Tucson, to visit Verona's younger sister Grace (Carmen Ejogo), whose successful but lonely life evokes sorrow and draws attention to issues of the past that her big sister is reluctant to discuss;
* then to Madison, Wisconsin, where Burt interviews for a new job and reconnects with an old friend, LN (Maggie Gyllenhaal), a flaky professor steeped in every New Age lifestyle cliché with her oh-so-sensitive squeeze Roderick (Josh Hamilton), a househusband so in touch with his feminine side that he'd make Alan Alda look like a chauvinist;
* then to Montreal, to visit Verona's old college friends, Tom (Chris Messina) and Munch (Melanie Lynskey), the proud

parents of a houseful of adopted children but whose seeming happiness is overshadowed by a painful secret;

* and then, quite unexpectedly, to Miami, where Burt attempts to comfort his brother Courtney (Paul Schneider), whose wife has just abandoned him and their young daughter.

But, even after all this travel and travail, Burt and Verona still don't find the model on which to base their new lives. They have plenty of examples of what *not* to do, but that still doesn't give them the template they need to create a happy existence for themselves. Maybe *their own* model would be the wisest line of probability to pursue, but what would that be? Coming up with such a prototype is the challenge for the questioning couple and, by doing so, maybe they'll find what they need (and discover some new things about themselves in the process). But, even more importantly, based on what they've seen in their journey, maybe they'll also find they're not as screwed up as they once thought they were.

This film aptly illustrates how we can sample probabilities for existence that have already manifested in physical form. But, since Burt and Verona are merely window-shopping at this point, they need not buy into any of them definitively. They're free to vicariously explore possibilities without the consequences that come with commitment. They very capably attract an array of options to consider on their way to making a decision.

This picture is also a prime example of showing how our beliefs evolve over time, and it does so fittingly through the road trip story model, one of the most effective means for examining this concept. The evolution of our beliefs often plays a major role in which probabilities we select for ourselves, and that idea is on full display as Burt and Verona sort out their options. In doing so, the picture also addresses the notion of *creation by default* (or *un-conscious creation*), the practice wherein we let life happen to us rather than assertively take the reins to figure out which probabilities serve us best. These unsuitable examples, ironically enough, enable Burt and Verona to rule out certain options, leading them to the inspiration they need to go out and create the tailor-made reality that's most appropriate for them.

One occasional criticism of the film has been that the character development is at times weak and/or inconsistent, that Burt and Verona are little more than undefined tour guides for carrying the story. However, I would contend that's what most journey of discovery films are all about—the emergence of self-awareness of one's beliefs and the creations that go with them. (After all, how can there be full development when that development is itself clearly in process?) In fact, I found it interesting that the protagonists actually seem to know themselves better than they often give themselves credit for; their self-awareness and their insights about what they want are often remarkably clear and incredibly specific, qualities that one could point to as healthy examples of character development (and in both on- and off-screen applications, too). Through this, Burt and Verona ultimately find that their lives may need mere tweaking than complete overhauls (we should all have it so good!).

"Away We Go" is an endearing story from start to finish, with excellent performances by the entire cast (props in particular to Janney, Gaffigan, Gyllenhaal and Hamilton). Sam Mendes's directorial efforts got back on track with this film, too, perhaps not up to the same level of achievement he attained in "American Beauty" (1999) but certainly a strong recovery from the disappointing "Revolutionary Road" (2008).

Find your way to this film. After seeing it, you just may uncover some enlightening revelations about your own way and the promise it holds for the future, leading you to probabilities that offer ever-greater degrees of personal happiness and fulfillment. And that's always worth the trip.

Quantum Physics Goes Mainstream

"Source Code"
Year of Release: 2011
Cast: Jake Gyllenhaal, Michelle Monaghan, Vera Farmiga,
Jeffrey Wright, Michael Arden, Cas Anvar, Russell Peters,
Brent Skagford, Kyle Gatehouse, Craig Thomas,
Gordon Masten, Frédérick De Grandpré, Scott Bakula (voice)
Director: Duncan Jones
Screenplay: Ben Ripley

The gap that has long existed between the worlds of science and spirit has begun narrowing in recent years through the rise of scientific disciplines like quantum physics and metaphysical philosophies like conscious creation. The popularity of those subjects has benefitted tremendously from the release of cinematic offerings like "The Quantum Activist" (2009) (profiled earlier in this Chapter), as well as "The Secret" (2006), "What the #$*! Do We (K)now!?" (2004) and "Mindwalk" (1991). As enlightening as those films are, however, they're primarily documentary in nature. So it's a real breath of fresh air to see pictures that effectively take a different approach and tackle this material from a fictional standpoint. One such film is the engaging thriller, "Source Code."

Pilot Colter Stevens (Jake Gyllenhaal) flies sorties for the U.S. military in Afghanistan. Or at least that's what he thinks he does. So it goes without saying that he's stunned when he inexplicably finds himself in civilian garb aboard a suburban commuter train headed for downtown Chicago one spring morning. Colter's flummoxed by his circumstances and by the comments of his apparent travelling companion, Christina (Michelle Monaghan), who's equally perplexed by the odd behavior of her fellow commuter (whom she calls Sean and with whom she's evidently been making the daily train trip for some time). But that astonishment is nothing compared to what Colter experiences when the train blows up.

After the explosion's fireball dissipates, Colter finds himself confined inside some kind of capsule surrounded by stacks of scientific equipment. On a nearby video screen, he sees a uniformed military officer named Goodwin (Vera Farmiga) who asks him cryptic questions about his experience on the train, all the while skillfully dodging his many inquiries about what's going on. Colter's initially frustrated by Goodwin's evasiveness, but he eventually settles down enough to answer her questions, at which point he's gradually given the answers he seeks.

Colter, it seems, is part of a test run for a top-level military project known as Source Code, the brainchild of quantum physicist Dr. Rutledge (Jeffrey Wright). Through this "time reassignment" experiment, the test subject's consciousness (in this case, Colter's) is infused with that of another person (in this case, the train passenger known as Sean (Frédérick De Grandpré)), a portion of which lingers energetically in the environment in the wake of the other individual's demise, like a sort of psychic echo or apparitional imprint. Goodwin and Rutledge explain that the purpose behind linking Colter's consciousness with the remnants of Sean's is so that he can find out who planted the bomb that blew up the train. He's told that discovering the identity of the bomber is not intended to prevent the train's destruction—that event has already happened—but to locate the suspect before more damage is done. The stakes are high, too; according to Goodwin and Rutledge, intelligence sources have uncovered evidence that the train incident was intended as just the first in a series of attacks leading up to the detonation of a dirty bomb in downtown Chicago.

So, with that knowledge in hand, and being the good soldier that he is, Colter allows his consciousness to be sent in search of the bomber. In true quantum physics/conscious creation fashion, Colter's consciousness can be launched multiple times, allowing him to explore different lines of probability with each transfer. There's just one catch—he only has eight minutes to work with in each iteration (that's as long as the imprint connection lasts). If he fails on one attempt, he needs to go back and begin again. And he has to work fast, for, while he may have multiple attempts to discover the bomber's identity in the "timeless" world of consciousness, the time frame to prevent a catastrophe in the physical world, where linear time prevails, is rapidly shrinking. Faced with the prospect of a nuclear explosion in a major urban area, Colter has no time to lose.

"Source Code" does a great job of illustrating how quantum physics and its metaphysical cousin, conscious creation, work. With unlimited lines of probability at his disposal in the world of consciousness, Colter is free to explore *any* of them on his way to completing his task. And, despite the belief limitations we often place upon ourselves about this, it's a capability we *all* possess as well—that is, as long as we're willing to believe in it and draw upon it accordingly when needed. At their heart, that's what quantum physics and the law of attraction are all about.

The film also reinforces the notion that our outer world creations originate from within, the realm of consciousness, ideas and beliefs. In doing so, it shows us how utterly magical the process ultimately is, a practice capable of spawning materializations that mesmerize and startle even the most ardent practitioners. And, as

Colter and his colleagues (and viewers) find out, its power is so great that it can exceed even the most inflated expectations (provided, of course, we allow it).

It's encouraging to see that films exploring subjects like this have become more "accessible." As noted above, overt explorations of such material, long limited to the ranks of little-seen independent pictures and documentaries, are now being supplemented with movies like "The Adjustment Bureau" (2011) (see Chapter 13), "Limitless" (2011), "Inception" (2010) (see Chapter 10) and "Déjà Vu" (2006), proving that there's a viable market for major studio releases that address these topics. While not all of these films have been carried off with the same level of skill, and while it certainly would be nice to see fictional movies about metaphysics that employ storylines other than thrillers, it's encouraging that pictures examining such subjects are increasingly not just for the art houses any more.

"Source Code" is a smart picture from top to bottom, well written and capably performed (despite Wright's occasional overacting tendencies). Its special effects, editing and cinematography are fine, too, beautifully showcasing Chicago in springtime (though, as a Windy City resident, I must admit to being somewhat partial on this). It makes for a rollicking Saturday afternoon at the show, an old-fashioned thrill ride with a New Age twist.

As we become increasingly aware of the idea that we create our own reality with all its myriad probabilities, it helps to have movies like "Source Code" available to remind us of that. It effectively illustrates our range of options and the means by which we go about accessing the possibilities. And, in the end, the results we get from that process might surprise us in ways we can't even imagine.

City of Enlightenment

"Midnight in Paris"
Year of Release: 2011
Cast: Owen Wilson, Rachel McAdams, Michael Sheen,
Marion Cotillard, Kathy Bates, Adrien Brody, Carla Bruni,
Kurt Fuller, Mimi Kennedy, Nina Arianda, Léa Seydoux,
Corey Stoll, Tom Hiddleston, Alison Pill, Yves Heck,
Marcial Di Fonzo Bo, Adrien De Van, Serge Bagdassarian,
Gad Elmaleh, Sonia Rolland, Daniel Lundh, David Lowe,
Yves-Antoine Spoto, Vincent Menjou Cortes, Olivier Rabourdin,
François Rostain
Director: Woody Allen
Screenplay: Woody Allen

The City of Lights has long stirred the creative juices of artists of all kinds. Its magical energy has helped birth the works of writers, painters and performers, giving rise to all manner of creative brilliance. But what is it about this inspiring locale that makes this possible? The mystique underlying this phenomenon is at last revealed in the delightful Woody Allen comedy, "Midnight in Paris."

Gil Pender (Owen Wilson) is lost and disillusioned. As a self-acknowledged Hollywood hack, he longs to escape his shackles and write serious literature in the same vein as his idols, most of whom came to prominence through the thriving literary scene of 1920s Paris. So, without hesitation, he jumps at the chance to visit the fabled city when he and his fiancée (Rachel McAdams) are invited to accompany her parents (Kurt Fuller, Mimi Kennedy) on an extended vacation to the iconic French metropolis.

Once in Paris, Gil is captivated by the city. He's in his element and wants to immerse himself in it to the fullest. But, while he finds himself increasingly in synch with the Parisian milieu, he also discovers he's becoming ever more *out* of synch with his fiancée, her family and her self-important friends (Michael Sheen, Nina Arianda). They behave like stereotypical Americans, treating their Parisian experience like they're visiting an overgrown theme park, seeing all the requisite tourist sights and purchasing overpriced souvenirs, rather than engrossing themselves in the city's rich, sophisticated ambiance. So it's not long before Gil abandons his traveling companions to go exploring on his own. What ensues is an urban adventure that leads him down an unexpected and enchanting path, a journey that begins with a simple midnight walk.

While returning to his hotel, Gil encounters a group of partygoers dressed in 1920s garb. He joins them for what he thinks is an invitation to a costume party, but he soon discovers that the festivities have an authenticity that's a little too realistic to be the creation of an overzealous party planner. It's then that he realizes he has somehow been whisked across time to the era he so adores.

As improbable as his circumstances might seem at first, Gil quickly embraces them, especially when he meets such luminaries as F. Scott Fitzgerald (Tom Hiddleston), Ernest Hemingway (Corey Stoll), Gertrude Stein (Kathy Bates), Pablo Picasso (Marcial Di Fonzo Bo), Salvador Dali (Adrien Brody), T.S. Eliot (David Lowe) and Cole Porter (Yves Heck), among others. He's quite taken by this new reality, particularly when he sees the favorable impact it has on his writing and his overall outlook on life. He also becomes smitten with the fair Adriana (Marion Cotillard), an aspiring fashion designer and intermittent mistress of Picasso, who becomes a sort of muse for the would-be novelist. Before long, Gil truly believes he's found the life he's meant to live. He plans to ditch his 21st Century existence for the Jazz Age—that is, until he learns Adriana also pines for an era different from the one into which she was born, the *Belle Époque* of 1890s Paris, a time she covets as much as the one that Gil has so long craved. A new temporal disconnect thus arises, prompting Gil to seriously ponder what he should do next.

Anyone who has ever been creatively blocked can certainly appreciate Gil's circumstances. The frustration that comes from being unable to express oneself, despite strong but undefined urges to the contrary, can lead to a desperate search for inspiration and enlightenment. And that's why the energizing effects that come from finding it—or even the *belief* that one has found it—seem so thoroughly satisfying.

Reaching that point may seem like an impossible task when we feel blocked, but it need not be. As long as we remain open to the idea that it's a probability attainable by shifting the beliefs we employ in creating the reality we experience, we just might find the inspiration we're looking for. Gil realizes his goal once he drops the limitations that hold him back, and the results are astounding; if it's possible to dissolve barriers seemingly as impenetrable as those associated with time, imagine what results are achievable when the walls impeding creative expression are felled. Through the example set by Gil's temporal shifts, it's apparent that the reality we create and experience need not be the fixed, rigid phenomenon we often expect it to be; instead, it's more fluid, malleable to our liking, depending on whatever beliefs we put into its materialization.

One can only begin to imagine what's possible once that happens. All sorts of probable new creative expressions are conceivable, including everything from the works of art we produce to the very conditions of our daily existence. Through our awareness and implementation of the law of attraction, we're also likely to find that we come into greater alignment with our lives, especially in crucial areas like *value fulfillment*, the concept concerned with each of us striving to be our best selves for our own and others' betterment. And, in that regard, the sky truly is the limit, depending upon how daring we're willing to be and what we'll allow ourselves to experience.

Of course, the realizations we come to while living out such experiences may surprise us as well, which can tell us much about the beliefs we *didn't* know we held. For instance, just when we think we've manifested our ideal expression of reality, we might find that it's not the be-all-and-end-all that we thought it would be. We may discover that a particular attainment is just one of *many* destinations along a continuous path of achievements, a stopover on the journey of reality creation. This circumstance thus aptly reflects the notion that *we're all in a constant state of becoming*, a key conscious creation concept with which its practitioners are so eminently familiar.

We might also find that a particular line of probability is disillusioning or even unsatisfying. This can be especially true for those who envision themselves living in other eras or alternate realities. In doing so, we may view such existences from overly romanticized perspectives, and these fantasies can come crashing down hard around us if they don't live up to what we hope for. Such realizations, however, can also open new doors. For example, paying a visit to an alternate reality may provide a measure of inspiration and enlightenment when it's lacking, but staying there is an entirely different matter. Visiting the past, for instance, is not the same as *living* there. Knowing how to draw from the inspiration such experiences provide, and then letting them go, rather than becoming trapped by them, is the key for making the most of them. Conscious creators are well aware of this, acutely cognizant that *the true point of power is in the present moment.* Those who have experiences where this realization becomes apparent—even if in a back-handed way—may ultimately discover a whole new sense of personal empowerment that they hadn't previously thought possible. (Now *that's* a creation.)

"Midnight in Paris" is easily one of the best films Woody Allen has made in years. It's charming, thoughtful and inspiring, going beyond the fluffy romantic comedy label that so many casually slapped on it. It's a well-crafted period piece, with fine production values and wonderful performances. It also shows off Paris beautifully, with its gorgeous cinematography doing for this French treasure what many of the director's pictures have long done for his native New York. Granted, like many of Allen's movies, the script of this film is a tad talky at times, but that's easily overlooked given everything else it has to offer.

The film was richly rewarded in awards programs, having won an Academy Award for best original screenplay, as well as three additional Oscar nominations, including best picture and best director. The picture matched those accomplishments in the Golden Globe Awards competition, winning top honors for best screenplay and earning nominations as best comedy picture, best director and best comedy actor for Owen Wilson.

All of us have our "Paris" moments, to be sure, and we should allow ourselves to experience them without reservation, for we'll never know what they'll yield until we plunge ourselves into them. This movie provides a superb example of what's possible if we follow that path, a probability that can lead us to our own shining City of Enlightenment.

2

FAITH AND BELIEFS

What we believe is what we create. In conscious creation terms, this is the core principle that explains how the process operates. And, as Chapter 1 illustrated, the range of *beliefs* open to us, like the range of probabilities they're capable of manifesting, is limitless.

Beliefs are immensely powerful forces for bringing our reality into being. That power is clearly observable in the results they produce, too. Look, for example, at how materializations like social networking, which were once mere intangible ideas in the minds of their creators, have subsequently grown into tangible, formidable manifestations. That principle is applicable across the board of creation as well, encompassing everything from physical constructions like buildings and mass transit systems to political and social movements like democracy and equality. And, in all cases, they get their starts as beliefs.

But what makes beliefs work? In essence, this is where the concept of *faith* comes in, the passion that fuels these notions and gets us behind them in heartfelt ways. The certainty of, and confidence in, our beliefs that faith engenders is what makes them work. In fact, faith is so crucial to their operation that, without it, beliefs would be little more than theoretical constructs, possibilities that are just as capable of becoming full-fledged materializations as they are of remaining dormant abstractions.

It should be noted that "faith" does not automatically equate to religion or some other formalized belief system (though it certainly can take that form if one chooses to go that route). More precisely, faith is something that arises within each of us *personally*, emerging with varying degrees of fervor and applied in many diverse ways, depending on what particular beliefs and what level of faith we each hold. That is essentially how we manifest our individual realities, existences that are tailor-made to whatever we each conceive of.

This Chapter's movies look at how our beliefs work to bring our reality into being in individualized ways. In several cases, the films feature characters who share mutual experiences but who go through them in their own unique ways, each developing their own particular take on them (based on their beliefs), despite the presence of common elements. In other cases, the pictures show us how the nature of our faith and beliefs contributes to shaping our overall worldview, as well as all of its various components. And, in nearly every case, this Chapter's entries illustrate how the power of our beliefs and faith can help us realize tremendous accomplishments—some that are even seemingly beyond belief.

It's been said that the pen is mightier than the sword, and that's no doubt true. But the beliefs that spring forth through that pen are even more potent than the writing implement that brings them into being, especially when delivered by a zealous scribe. Indeed, for an idea whose time has come, there's virtually nothing that can hold it back when it's fueled by the power of beliefs, and backed by the support of faith, that makes it possible.

In Search of an Elusive Truth

"Doubt"
Year of Release: 2008
Cast: Meryl Streep, Philip Seymour Hoffman, Amy Adams, Viola Davis, Joseph Foster II, Mike Roukis, Jack O'Connell
Director: John Patrick Shanley
Screenplay: John Patrick Shanley
Play: John Patrick Shanley, Doubt

We can trust everything we see, right? Our perceptions wouldn't deceive us, because they're accurate reflections of the beliefs we use to create the manifestations we experience. So how is it, then, that we may come to question what we witness? Is it due to faulty interpretations of events, or is it because they've been intentionally created with ambiguity as part of the mix? And how truly steadfast are we in our convictions? Are we thoroughly convinced of what we perceive, or is that alleged certainty based on beliefs involving what we think we're *supposed* to believe? Those are just some of the thorny philosophical and metaphysical questions addressed in the gripping religious school drama, "Doubt."

An ill wind blows through the Roman Catholic parish of St. Nicholas in the fall of 1964, and the troubles brewing there have to do with more than just the inclement November weather. The church, located in a working class section of the Bronx, is tended to by Father Brendan Flynn (Philip Seymour Hoffman), an outwardly kind, demonstrably compassionate pastor who cares deeply for his flock. In striking contrast, the adjoining parish school is administered by its hard-nosed, imperious principal, Sister Aloysius Beauvier (Meryl Streep), who carries out her duties with a ruthless efficiency and a cruel demeanor, an attitude destined to one day put the students she oversees into counseling for years.

So what's the source of the trouble? That's hard to say. In fact, it's not readily apparent that a problem even exists. In the end, figuring out what's wrong comes down to who one asks—and what they believe.

Sister Aloysius suspects that things aren't right with the priest to whom she reports. Based on passing observations and conversations with one of her teachers, Sister James (Amy Adams), she believes that Father Flynn may have engaged in an inappropriate relationship with one of the students, Donald Miller (Joseph Foster II). But did he?

Sister James, a young idealist who prefers to see only the good in others, is torn. She has considerable difficulty reconciling Father Flynn's overt displays of compassion with her fleeting glimpses of possibly questionable actions, particularly when he's in Donald's company. Are those suspect gestures what they really seem to be, or are they innocent acts that have been grossly misconstrued?

Father Flynn openly admits to taking an interest in Donald's well-being because he's the only African-American pupil in an otherwise all-Caucasian student body. He fears that Donald, a sensitive, thoughtful child, will be taunted, perhaps even victimized, by those less open-minded. He also encourages Donald's dream to one day become a priest himself. But Father Flynn isn't revealing everything he knows, and, when he's pressed for answers by Sister Aloysius, he recoils, asking his inquisitor to leave matters alone, which only raises her suspicions even further.

Needless to say, Sister Aloysius can't help but wonder what Father Flynn is hiding. Unsatisfied with his evasive answers, she turns to Donald's mother (Viola Davis) to find out if she can shed more light on things. Mrs. Miller's "disquieting" admissions fuel the Sister's speculation even more. Although nothing conclusively "damning" is revealed, Sister Aloysius is convinced she needs to act. But does she have enough evidence to bring a credible accusation? Or is there too much doubt to proceed? In true conscious creation fashion, how events play out will depend, of course, on what one believes.

In assessing the various characters' interpretations of events, one might be tempted to ask, "So who's 'right' about what *really* happened?" The short answer would be "Everybody," because the realities the characters each experience are *bona fide* representations of the beliefs they each hold. Since there's no faking how each of them ultimately sees things, it's impossible for their realities to be anything but faithful expressions of their metaphysical underpinnings. Even if their views of circumstances seemingly conflict with—or even blatantly contradict—one other, each resulting creation is intrinsically and undeniably "true" for each individual in question.

Many factors drive the formation of our beliefs, including our individual perceptions, personal experience and overall perspective (for more on Perspective, see Chapter 3). We draw upon each of these elements, as well as the input of our intellect and intuition, to fashion the beliefs that arise within each of us. This combination of influences not only leads to the particular beliefs we employ in the materialization process, but it also creates a customized "filter" through which all belief candidates are passed, a mechanism that assesses and shades their character to conform them to the configuration of the "instrument" through which they're evaluated.

In the context of this film's narrative, four distinct perspectives—and four distinguishable realities—emerge as a result of these foregoing principles. Sister Aloysius, for instance, has led a difficult life. Before becoming a nun, she was a married housewife. But, after losing her husband during World War II, the young widow adopted an embittered view of existence, one characterized by difficulty, tragedy and evil. She drew upon her religious beliefs to sustain her through her personal challenges, but her subsequent interpretation of those beliefs, as well as her approach to serving the institution they're associated with, were both likely shaped by her worldly experiences and prevailing secular outlook. And this development, in turn, continues to color the nature of her beliefs and her resulting reality.

Father Flynn, by contrast, maintains a far different view of life, and this is reflected through his beliefs and actions. He firmly believes in qualities like love, kindness and compassion, and he's convinced the Church must do all it can to embody them. To that end, he believes that the institution must become more approachable to retain parishioners and that those who minister to the masses must respond accordingly. Sister James and Mrs. Miller hold comparable views, believing in the inherent goodness of others and the need for establishing a world built on peace, compassion and understanding. And, naturally, the particular beliefs each of them holds contribute to the specific realities they subsequently experience.

However, no matter what Father Flynn, Sister James or Mrs. Miller may believe, their outlooks directly conflict with the worldview of Sister Aloysius, and her resolve only becomes *strengthened* when any of them behaves in ways that lend credence to her core convictions. For example, Father Flynn's reluctance to reveal everything he knows about Donald convinces Sister Aloysius that he *must* be harboring some sort of vile secret, a natural conclusion given her worldview. But is his hesitancy driven by guilt or by a sincere desire to preserve confidentiality? Father Flynn would naturally insist on the latter contention, while Sister Aloysius would zealously adhere to the former interpretation, and each, in their own mind, would be convinced as to the veracity of their viewpoints. And, in that regard, each of them could genuinely take comfort in the notion that they're "right" about their assessments of their circumstances.

The degree of support underlying our beliefs determines the extent of their power, and, when we provide them with a rock-solid foundation (as the protagonists each do here), we have the essence of *faith*. The relevance of this concept in the film's narrative applies, fittingly enough, both to the choice of its setting, as well as to the picture's exploration of it as a metaphysical principle. As the story unfolds, it becomes apparent that the characters each cling to their beliefs with a virtually unshakable fervor, providing them with the faith they need to create their tailor-made realities. Their experiences are each borne out of beliefs securely rooted in a foundation of faith, a condition that helps define the strength, persistence and viability of their respective manifestations.

So, in light of the foregoing, one might legitimately wonder why the film is titled "Doubt." Very simply, as alluded to above, it's because "doubt" is a quality that figures significantly into the picture's storyline, and, like all other aspects of existence, its presence also arises out of beliefs.

Interestingly, doubt (along with fear and contradiction) occupies a special place in conscious creation philosophy, because, even though its origins are belief-based, it generally serves to *undercut*, rather than validate, our intended manifestations. Doubt prevents outcomes from materializing, either at all or as hoped for, by seemingly "corrupting" our intentions. Since doubt arises through our beliefs, when intents behind this notion are paired with those aimed at manifesting particular outcomes, the result is confusion, because our divine conscious creation collaborator has difficulty accurately interpreting what we're trying to accomplish. In an attempt to reconcile matters, our divine collaborator either does nothing or does its level best to accommodate all of the competing beliefs, yielding results that often perplex or disappoint everyone involved.

Given the different (and conflicting) realities at play in this film, doubt factors into the plot frequently, especially since "conclusive" proof of suspected actions remains elusive. It's at such junctures in the story that either faith takes over or doubt creeps in, thereby affecting the functioning of the law of attraction process. The resulting manifestations arise, as always, from the beliefs (or, more precisely in this case, from the convoluted *combinations* of beliefs) in question. And, when the role of doubt becomes apparent in this mix, the revelation can be devastating, and the resulting impact can be considerable, for all involved, *especially* the intent's originator.

Despite the widespread acclaim and many accolades this film received, I sincerely believe it's one of the most underrated pictures of recent years. Its powerful writing examines a timely, highly controversial subject, but it does so sensitively and thoughtfully, without ever becoming sensationalist or exploitative. And the film's philosophical and metaphysical content is deftly handled, presenting its material in a practical, approachable manner that never becomes tedious, dogmatic or esoteric. What's more, the stellar portrayals of the four protagonists are some of the best performances to have graced the screen in quite some time, both individually and as an ensemble. For its efforts, "Doubt" garnered five Oscar and five Golden Globe nominations for its four principals and for its adapted screenplay, but, regrettably, it received no awards.

Doubt is a powerful force that can exonerate the innocent or enable the guilty to escape unscathed. But, no matter what outcome arises, the result will always depend on the beliefs that drive it. In that regard, then, it could be said that it's actually the *beliefs* behind doubt, as well as one's *faith* in those beliefs, that make it such a force to be reckoned with, as this film so aptly illustrates. So, in the search for an elusive truth, we must thus know *precisely* where to begin our inquiry—and be truly honest with ourselves in doing so—if we're ever to get the answers we seek.

Something To Believe In

"The X-Files: I Want to Believe"
Year of Release: 2008
Cast: David Duchovny, Gillian Anderson, Amanda Peet,
Billy Connolly, Xzibit, Mitch Pileggi,
Callum Keith Rennie, Adam Godley, Fagin Woodcock
Director: Chris Carter
Screenplay: Frank Spotnitz and Chris Carter
TV Series Source Material: Chris Carter, The X-Files

No matter what aspect of life we concern ourselves with, beliefs always factor in as the driving element. That's especially significant when we consider the big picture issues of life, such as our spiritual and metaphysical worldviews, because the core convictions we hold in these matters underlie the beliefs that support and create everything else. Coming to terms with those beliefs can be a seriously challenging task, particularly if we experience difficulty in defining them or even identifying their existence. One film that's exceptionally adept at this is "The X-Files: I Want to Believe."

This picture may seem an unlikely candidate in this context, given the franchise's reputation (first as a TV show, later as a movie) as a vehicle for tales of science fiction and horror. Yet the franchise has long had a metaphysical component associated with it, and its second big screen outing is so concerned with it that the notion of belief is even part of the title.

In a nutshell, former FBI special agents Fox Mulder (David Duchovny) and Dana Scully (Gillian Anderson) are coaxed out of hiding and retirement, respectively, to help solve a particularly troubling case involving several missing persons and a clairvoyant former priest (Billy Connolly) who was defrocked for being a pedophile. And, as far as the plotline is concerned, that's all one really needs to know, for that part of the story is largely unimportant, a mere pretext to what the film is really all about—the protagonists' search for meaning in their new lives and how to bring it into being.

After years of chasing monsters in the dark, a time when their purpose in life at least *seemed* fairly clear, Mulder and Scully are each left to wrestle with the question of what their mission is now. Mulder, who always had been an ardent believer in the magic of the paranormal and the extraordinary, suddenly sees himself in quite a pedestrian existence, wondering whether he can recapture the spark of his past beliefs and use them as a guiding principle for his new life. Scully, a scientist and fence-post Catholic who long toiled to find balance between the rational and the miraculous, finds herself still ensconced in this challenge, still struggling to determine whether reason or spirituality should guide her new existence (an internal conflict expressed metaphorically through her new calling in life—as a physician in a Catholic hospital). These core belief dilemmas, in turn, further affect the characters' search for answers in other areas of their lives, such as their relationship with one another, the future of their vocations and coming to terms with their morbid fascination with "the dark side."

Getting a handle on this is crucial for Mulder and Scully, not only for a sense of personal well-being and inner peace, but also for very *practical* purposes: If beliefs are the basis of conscious creation and the reality we manifest for ourselves, we had better grasp what it is we believe and the implications that accompany such thoughts, for they quite tangibly materialize what we ultimately experience. This may be easier said than done, especially if we *don't* know what to believe, as is acutely exemplified by some of the protagonists' experiences. But that task must be approached and addressed lest we spend our days wandering the metaphysical wastelands of our consciousness.

Circumstances like these can also be exacerbated by a tepid level of support for our beliefs, which could well be the case here. Mulder, for example, says he *wants* to believe in the veracity of the phenomena he investigates (a notion even reflected in the film's subtitle). But his repeated use of the word "want" implies that something is inherently lacking, and the more we believe in the want of something, the more we fuel intents perpetuating that innate lack, bringing us no closer to the fulfillment of what we say we're attempting to manifest. Getting clear about what we *truly* wish to materialize and then backing it with impassioned belief support is thus essential if we hope to see our objective realized. This even includes the wording we use to formulate the beliefs underlying those goals. Mulder, for instance, would serve himself well by replacing the expression "I want to believe" with "I *do* believe," an affirming example we'd all be wise to follow.

This picture, unfortunately, wasn't well-received by viewers, critics or many fans of the franchise, but that may be due to some preconceived notions, coupled with misleading marketing. The film was plugged as a thriller in the tradition of the franchise; however, it's clearly anything but. It's principally a character study, cerebral and introspective, rarely if ever suspenseful except for how Mulder and Scully each respond to and resolve their respective belief challenges. Those seeking to be scared will likely be disappointed (and rightfully so), but those looking for something more profound than a simple horror story will be rewarded beyond their expectations.

"I Want to Believe" is a picture that demands close viewing, requiring audiences to delve beneath its surface qualities to see what's *really* going on. The spiritual and metaphysical symbolism is subtle but often clever and quite witty, served up through images that embody law of attraction principles in their most basic, yet most eloquent and poetic expression.

Some have speculated about the prospects of additional films in this franchise, and, as much as I'd love to see the further exploits of this divine duo, I'd prefer that the producers forgo them. In many ways, this picture provides a satisfying end point for the series, one that needs no further elaboration. Some mythologies are best left undisturbed once they've run their course, and I would certainly argue that such should be the case here.

At a time when so many films are long on style and short on substance, it's refreshing to see releases like this amidst the throngs of high-gloss extravaganzas. Of course, to fully appreciate what this film has to say, one must open one's eyes—and heart—just as Mulder and Scully must do, to figure out what's transpiring, not only outwardly but also inwardly in the world of beliefs. In the end, viewers, like the protagonists, must realize that the responsibility for the development of our life paths, both spiritually and otherwise, rests with *us* (after all, why do you think this film is subtitled "*I Want to Believe*"?). The inspiration and courage offered by Mulder and Scully, as illustrated through their individual quests, provides ample fuel for the spiritual flames in all of us. And that's truly something to believe in.

Putting Faith to the Test

"Higher Ground"
Year of Release: 2011
Cast: Vera Farmiga, Joshua Leonard, Dagmara Dominczyk,
Michael Chernus, Norbert Leo Butz, Donna Murphy,
John Hawkes, Nina Arianda, Sean Mahon, Bill Irwin,
Taissa Farmiga, Boyd Holbrook, Kaitlyn Rae King,
McKenzie Turner, Taylor Schwencke
Director: Vera Farmiga
Screenplay: Carolyn S. Briggs and Tim Metcalfe
Book: Carolyn S. Briggs, *This Dark World*

Often in life we're asked to take things on faith, a practice for which we're given no handbook at birth, leaving us to find our own way. That frequently makes for an intriguing journey, one that tests us on many fronts, especially when it comes to understanding and embracing the core issue of faith. But, no matter what path we choose, it always helps to have inspiration to draw from, and one particularly thoughtful example of this is offered up in the spiritual drama, "Higher Ground."

Corinne Miller (Vera Farmiga) is a woman on a mission to find herself. Unfortunately, she spends much of her decades-long journey seemingly lost in a fog, often sincerely believing that she's found the answers she seeks only to discover later—and repeatedly—that "truth" can be a rather elusive commodity.

Corinne's odyssey is a largely spiritual quest. Having grown up in a household without much of a religious compass (her parents, Kathleen (Donna Murphy) and CW (John Hawkes), show little interest in the subject, especially after her mother suffers a heartbreaking stillbirth), Corinne is left to fend for herself spiritually. She grapples with church-related issues, first as a child (McKenzie Turner) and later as a teen (Taissa Farmiga), hoping that they'll somehow magically fill the void in her life. She looks to the teachings of an affable local minister, Pastor Bud (Bill Irwin), for inspiration, but her enthusiasm is often lukewarm at best, as if she's just going through the motions and not really grasping what she's supposed to get out of the experience. Her efforts are further sidetracked by a healthy curiosity of worldly matters, such as interests in rock 'n roll, "questionable" literature and boys, particularly her teenage beau, Ethan (Boyd Holbrook), who eventually becomes her husband (Joshua Leonard).

Corinne's journey takes a dramatic turn, however, when a potentially disastrous personal tragedy produces an unexpectedly miraculous outcome, prompting her and Ethan to commit themselves wholeheartedly to a life of devotion, a vow that culminates in their initiation into a fundamentalist Christian community. Through this sacred indoctrination, it appears Corinne has finally found true happiness and contentment in her life. Or has she?

Sometimes Corinne seems genuinely filled with the spirit of Jesus and the Divine Creator, but, at other times, she appears utterly perplexed, as if she's missing out on something she believes she's supposed to be experiencing. This is especially true when spending time with her friend Annika (Dagmara Dominczyk), who frequently lapses into tongues, a spontaneous personal prayer language that fills her with bliss. Needless to say, Corinne feels left out, longing for the same elation her friend so thoroughly enjoys.

But things don't stop there. Over time, Corinne increasingly becomes filled with doubt about her faith. She recalls past tragedies, like her mother's stillbirth, and then lives through new ones of her own, such as witnessing the anguish of a dear friend who suffers a debilitating brain tumor. She can't help but wonder where God is when such dire circumstances arise, especially since He was there for her when she suffered her own misfortune. Reconciling this glaring contradiction causes her much confusion and heartache. Just what is she supposed to believe?

Learning how to balance secular issues and spiritual considerations in her daily life becomes a growing challenge, too. While glimpses of this arise during her adolescence, they grow more pervasive with age. What's more, her attempts at addressing these matters come under heightened scrutiny by other members of the community, sometimes involving things as trivial as her clothing choices. But the fellowship's scrutiny doesn't stop with Corinne's worldly acts; it carries over into her spiritual practices as well. She becomes puzzled, for example, when she's criticized for freely expressing her own religious fervor, an act viewed by the congregation as sermonizing, something reserved exclusively for the men of the community. She wonders why she's not allowed to openly share her joy and epiphanies with others; after all, would a truly loving God really instruct followers to restrict such acts on the basis of something as limiting, arbitrary and ultimately inconsequential as gender?

While the film overtly deals with religious and spiritual considerations in a Christian context, many of its underlying themes are applicable to other sacred and metaphysical traditions as well. Chief among them is the issue of faith, that steadfast trust we each place in our relationship with God/Goddess/All That Is (or whatever other term best suits you). It's a subject that raises a host of questions, such as how committed must we be to it? Can we implicitly trust the deity in whose hands we pledge our devotion? What are we to make of situations in which our prayers seemingly go unanswered or manifest in "distorted" ways? And what are we to do if disillusionment sets in?

These questions are not exclusive to Christianity. Practitioners of other belief systems often grapple with these issues in their own particular spiritual or philosophical milieus. It's not unheard of, for example, for conscious creators to find their intents going awry, either materializing in unexpected forms or not at all, making them wonder what their divine collaborator is up to. These incidents are not unlike what Corinne experiences, and such episodes sometimes are enough to evoke questions about the nature of one's beliefs and the strength of one's faith, no matter what tradition that devotion is based upon.

In these instances, if we have concerns about the path we find ourselves on, it's a sign that we must examine the beliefs we're putting out, for they drive what we experience. To that end, are we being clear with the Universe about what we really want? Are we allowing secondary considerations, like doubt or fear, to undercut the manifestation process by sending mixed signals to our divine collaborator? Or, perhaps most importantly, are we inherently mistrustful of our collaborator, believing that it's behaving capriciously or not in our best interests? The presence of thoughts like this will invariably affect the character of the outcomes we experience and the satisfaction we get from them.

Those who *truly* understand this divine relationship, be it in a conscious creation, Christian or other context, ultimately *know* that we dwell in a *Safe Universe*, one that operates with our best interests at heart, even if we don't always readily recognize that as such. This is where the issue of faith really comes into play, something that frequently requires considerable effort to fully grasp and embrace. In fact, getting to this point is often a *process*, something that we grow into over time as our trust and understanding deepen, making it ever easier to recognize, acknowledge and accept the character of this intimately collaborative relationship. Indeed, as noted in Chapter 1, it's often said that we're each in a constant state of becoming, a notion that aptly sums up the progressive nature of this revelatory journey. Corinne experiences this for herself firsthand in the film, personifying a process that many of us will likely go through during our lifetimes, no matter what religious, spiritual or metaphysical tradition we're engaged in.

Corinne's saving grace in this is that she's cognizant enough to know when to raise questions about her faith and not to follow it blindly, especially when being cajoled by others who insist that her thoughts and practices must follow prescribed forms. Anyone who *genuinely* understands the nature of faith realizes that the Universe provides us with the means to fulfill our intents in the ways *It* deems most expedient, even if we don't always comprehend Its methods or if Its manifestations don't match our preconceived notions. Yet those who zealously subscribe to established religious traditions often demand strict, unquestioning adherence to their dogmas, liturgies and even costuming, insisting that their way is the only "right" way, a conviction that, ironically enough, flies squarely in the face of how All That Is fundamentally operates.

For her part, Corinne isn't afraid to raise questions about her community's spiritual and secular requirements and even her own personal faith. She seeks the truth, with her ultimate goal being an understanding of her relationship with God, not those who claim to speak for Him. In fact, it's through such questioning that her own understanding deepens, showing her that spirituality is something more than just what happens in church or a closed-off community; it's about how one chooses to live one's life *in the world*, the one that she and All That Is have co-created in both its secular and spiritual aspects, and not about adherence to the arbitrary preferences of a group that believes its answers to life are the only ones anybody needs. In this sense, then, Corinne comes to discover that secular and spiritual questions are not mutually exclusive, as many would contend, but instead are intrinsically intertwined, a realization that comes from true faith and not from rigorous obedience to subjectively adopted theological trappings. Any notion of separation between the two is an illusion (and a manmade one at that).

It would have been easy for the characters in this film to be portrayed as caricatures, but, thankfully, that temptation was effectively resisted. Credit the writing and, especially, the skillful direction of first-time filmmaker Vera Farmiga for that. The movie depicts its characters as individuals, not stereotypes, allowing their layered, complicated natures to shine through. This balanced approach makes the story and its players engaging to watch, in both moments of drama and humor, drawing viewers into the characters' spiritual sojourns and warmly welcoming them to come along for the ride (and what a ride it is).

Faith is something we're all tested on at some point, and "Higher Ground" provides an effective guide to help prepare us for such occasions. Watch closely; you'll be amazed at how much you can glean from it, information that will stand you in good stead when times get tough and help elevate you to unimagined heights of enlightenment, no matter what your spiritual or philosophical leanings.

Believing the Dream

"The Other Dream Team"
Year of Release: 2012
Cast: Arvydas Sabonis,
Šarūnas Marčiulionis, Rimas Kurtinaitis,
Jonas Valančiūnas, Vytautas Landsbergis, Jim Lampley,
Alexander Wolff, David Remnick, Bill Walton, David Stern,
Chris Mullin, Donnie Nelson, Mickey Hart, Greg Speirs
Director: Marius Markevicius
Screenplay: Marius Markevicius and Jon Weinbach

Movies with sports themes are often some of the corniest, most predictable and yet also most inspiring films that find their way into release. Their outcomes seldom surprise us, but we watch them all the way through, if for no other reason than the ample good feelings they fill us with. Pictures that recognize the efforts of underdogs, like "Hoosiers" (1986), "Cool Runnings" (1993), "Breaking Away" (1979) and "Secretariat" (2010), easily get our attention. But those that celebrate unlikely champions competing under extraordinary extenuating circumstances, such as "Glory Road" (2006), "The Express" (2008) (see Chapter 6), "A League of Their Own" (1992), "Miracle" (2004) and "The Blind Side" (2009) (see Chapter 12), captivate us. Such is the case with the entertaining and informative sports documentary, "The Other Dream Team."

The world was a rapidly changing place in 1992. The Cold War had recently ended, the Berlin Wall had just fallen and the U.S.S.R.

was in the process of breaking up. Several once-occupied nations, such as the Baltic states of Lithuania, Latvia and Estonia, had declared their independence and emerged from Soviet domination. Indeed, the global geopolitical stage was shifting in ways no one would have thought conceivable just a few years before.

The implications of these changes were seen in many aspects of life. One of the most visible areas was in the world of sports. This became most apparent at the 1992 Summer Olympics in Barcelona, Spain, where a number of new nations competed for the first time or after protracted absences. Among the new entrants were the aforementioned Baltic states, countries that, although small geographically, were formidable as competitors. This was particularly true for Lithuania in the sport of basketball.

Lithuanians have long loved basketball, and the tiny nation had been a powerhouse in the sport in European tournaments as far back as the 1930s. However, when Lithuania was annexed by the Soviet Union in 1944 and vanished as a sovereign state, so did much of the world's awareness of the country, its culture and its traditions, including in the world of sport. What's more, because of this loss of independence, Lithuanian athletes were prohibited from competing internationally under their own flag; they now had to do so under the Soviet banner.

Lithuanians contributed significantly to Soviet sports accomplishments in the five decades that they competed for the U.S.S.R. This was perhaps most obvious in the basketball tournament at the 1988 Summer Olympics in Seoul, South Korea, when the Soviets beat the heavily favored U.S. team on their way to winning the Gold Medal, and they did so by fielding a team on which four of the five starters were Lithuanians. However, despite such success, Lithuanian competitors resented having to represent themselves as "Soviets" rather than as "Lithuanians." They grew especially irate when erroneously referred to as "Russians," particularly since only two members of the 1988 medal-winning team actually fit that cultural label.

When Lithuania gained its autonomy, its athletes were anxious to compete under their own flag at the Barcelona Olympics. They wanted to show the world what they could do. They were also anxious to settle scores with representatives of their former occupiers on a leveled playing field. But getting to the Olympics took money, something the bankrupt fledgling state seriously lacked. Raising funds to pursue this goal thus became a priority.

After achieving only meager results in its initial fundraising efforts, the team got a big boost from a very unlikely source, the American rock band, the Grateful Dead. The band members were big fans of both basketball and underdogs, so, when they heard about the team's struggles, they wrote a huge check to support its efforts. They also supplied the players with tie-dyed tee shirts featuring the band's infamous skeleton logo and printed in the colors of the Lithuanian flag. Grateful for the Dead's support, the team enthusiastically embraced the band's assistance, ubiquitously sporting their donated gear both before and during the Olympics.

As colorful as the Lithuanians' odyssey had been, however, the overarching story of the Barcelona tournament was the U.S. team. The 1992 Olympics marked the first time that professional players were allowed to compete, and so the Americans assembled a team featuring such NBA all-stars as Michael Jordan, Scottie Pippen, Magic Johnson, Larry Bird, Charles Barkley and David Robinson, a lineup that became better known as "the Dream Team." It was a team that lived up to every bit of its billing, too, handily defeating all of its opponents (*including* the Lithuanians in a semifinal game) on its way to nabbing the Gold Medal.

But the Lithuanians were not to be denied their moment of glory. Despite their loss to the Americans (which honestly came as no surprise), the Lithuanians, as one of the tournament's final four teams, qualified to compete in the Bronze Medal game against the Unified Team, a squad made up of players from the remaining Soviet republics at the time. The Lithuanians would thus get an opportunity to redeem themselves against representatives of their nation's former occupiers, an event whose ramifications clearly went beyond just sports.

The story of the Lithuanian basketball team was one of more than just its proficiency on the court. It was a tale of personal and national pride, the significance of which becomes apparent in the film's back story about life in Lithuania under 50 years of Soviet domination. The picture presents detailed documentation on the harshness of everyday life, as well as the rigidly regimented routines imposed on Lithuanian members of the Soviet national team, during that period. It's easy to see how such pervasive oppression took its toll—and how anxious Lithuanians, from all walks of life, were to pursue the dream of freedom when the opportunity finally presented itself.

Viewers are thus treated to a moving tale of courage, character, justice and inspiration, as well as the inherent power of beliefs. We witness the resolve of a team—and a nation—that *knows* what each is truly capable of manifesting for itself, a hallmark of conscious creation expertise. The film also documents the lasting legacy of such valor on contemporary Lithuanians, as told through the experience of NBA center Jonas Valančiūnas, who, at the time of the picture's filming, was an aspiring professional prospect. Valančiūnas, born in 1992, grew up with the legend of his national team's Olympic success, and its accomplishments inspired the young player (and many of his basketball-playing peers) to pursue a career in the big leagues.

"The Other Dream Team" is a thoroughly engaging documentary, conveying its material with heartfelt emotion and uplifting vision in both its political and sports-related narratives. It successfully avoids the pitfalls of getting too technical or resorting to empty platitudes. It incorporates a wealth of archival footage and a wide variety of recent interviews, including team members Arvydas Sabonis, Šarūnas Marčiulionis and Rimas Kurtinaitis, as well as sports journalists Jim Lampley and Alexander Wolff, basketball analyst Bill Walton, Dream Team member Chris Mullin, NBA commissioner David Stern, former Lithuanian head of state Vytautas Landsbergis, Grateful Dead band member Mickey Hart, and tee shirt designer Greg Speirs.

On the surface, a documentary about a basketball team from a little-known European nation might not sound like an especially noteworthy topic for a feature-length movie, but "The Other Dream Team" defies such thinking. It shows us how one need not be famous to be a superstar, that greatness is something we're each capable of achieving—as long as we believe we can and have sufficient faith in our abilities to see things through.

A Temporal Leap of Faith

"Safety Not Guaranteed"
Year of Release: 2012
Cast: Aubrey Plaza, Mark Duplass, Jake Johnson,
Karan Soni, Mary Lynn Rajskub, William Hall Jr.,
Tony Doupé, Xola Malik, Jenica Bergere, Kristen Bell
Director: Colin Trevorrow
Screenplay: Derek Connolly

Time travel is a notion that has intrigued readers and writers for ages, and its depiction on the big screen has offered viewers a host of interpretations over the years. But temporal excursions can have both advantages and drawbacks, some of which carry loaded consequences, implications explored in the quirky indie comedy, "Safety Not Guaranteed."

This film was inspired by a cryptic classified ad that read as follows: "WANTED: Someone to go back in time with me. This is not a joke. You'll get paid after we get back. Must bring your own weapons. I have only done this once before. SAFETY NOT GUARANTEED". The ad first appeared in the survivalist magazine *Backwoods Home* in the mid '90s. It later garnered widespread attention when featured in a "Headlines" segment on *The Tonight Show with Jay Leno* and on the Internet, eventually becoming a viral sensation. It's not clear if the original ad was placed merely as an enigmatic prank or if there was something more significant behind it. In any event, regardless of the intent, the ad provided intriguing fodder for the cinematic tale it inspired.

"Safety Not Guaranteed" follows the adventures of a reporter and two interns from an alternative Seattle-based magazine who are assigned to get the story behind the ad. The trio of investigators includes Jeff (Jake Johnson), a hard-partying veteran reporter who delegates most of the work while taking most of the credit for the results unearthed by his two industrious associates, Darius (Aubrey Plaza), a detached, live-at-home recent college grad searching for herself, and Arnau (Karan Soni), a bookish biology major seeking to diversify his background through his internship. In conducting their inquiry, the investigators have only one clue to go on—a post office box number in the tiny resort town of Ocean View, Washington. And so, armed with this single scrap of information, they set off in search of the mysterious would-be time traveler.

While staking out the local post office, Darius spies her target, the ad's box holder, when he comes to collect his mail. She tails him when he drives off, following him around town, eventually ending up at his job. As it turns out, the prospective temporal tourist is a mild-mannered but brainy clerk at a local supermarket named Kenneth (Mark Duplass), whose impassioned ramblings about the potential of quantum physics lead most of his co-workers to believe that he's delusional. But, despite the mystery man's quirky demeanor, Darius is intrigued by Kenneth and proceeds to present herself as a candidate to become his time-traveling companion.

Kenneth is initially a bit skeptical, concerned that Darius might be an operative of the government agents that he believes have been clandestinely pursuing him. But he quickly relents and begins indoctrinating Darius into the training program that he's developed to prepare himself and his companion for their journey across time.

As things progress, Darius becomes ever more involved in Kenneth's plans, slowly losing sight of her original intent—to get the story behind the ad. She's pressured by Jeff and the magazine's no-nonsense publisher, Bridget (Mary Lynn Rajskub), for progress reports, but she becomes so wrapped up *in* the story that she begins to lose sight of her pursuit of it as a journalist. Disillusionment begins to set in as well, especially when she uncovers evidence indicating that Kenneth's co-workers might have been correct, that he really is seriously delusional. But then that revelation is offset when she discovers that Kenneth's claims of being followed by government agents are correct, too, especially when she meets them (Tony Doupé, Xola Malik) in person. All of these developments leave Darius's head spinning as she tries to figure out what to believe about what's really going on—and how it will all eventually play out.

Most of us have undoubtedly given thought to reliving a pleasant time from our past, perhaps even going so far as wishing we could return to it—literally. That's something all the characters in this film wish for, too. We witness this most notably through Kenneth, who is so preoccupied with the idea of revisiting his past that he actually wants to bring that possibility into being (and, based on his knowledge of quantum physics, the scientific explanation for how conscious creation essentially works, he genuinely believes it's feasible, too). Meanwhile, after listening to Kenneth's theories at length, Darius also finds the notion desirable, if a bit far-fetched, to bring about a return to a more pleasant time in her own life. And, in a storyline parallel to the picture's main narrative, Jeff seeks to do the same when he looks to reconnect with Liz (Jenica Bergere), an old flame with whom he spent his youthful summers while vacationing in Ocean View with his family.

As conscious creators are well aware, rescripting the past can produce worthwhile results, a notion explored in films like the sci-fi comedy "Men in Black III" (2012). But is *retreating* into the past the best idea, even if it's possible? That's something with which Kenneth, Darius and Jeff must all come to terms, each in their own ways, especially when they find that it's a process often full of pitfalls. Attempting to jump back into that prior period will likely yield skewed results, for the mere presence of our "current" selves in that "prior" timeline would automatically place us in a fundamentally different line of quantum probability from the one that we recalled having been in. The beliefs we held about our past before escaping into it thus might not line up with the reality we experience once we find ourselves in the midst of it, if for no other reason than we would no longer be the same person in that past as we had been when we were there once before. While that rediscovered past might seem substantially *similar* to the one we recall, it wouldn't be *identical*, and that disparity may ultimately be just different enough to keep us from realizing the hoped-for outcome. What's more, even if it *were* essentially the same, who's to say that the beliefs creating such familiar circumstances ultimately wouldn't play out roughly the same way *again*? That could leave us, for all practical purposes, right back where we started from, as if we were caught in a sort of temporal loop.

Perhaps an even bigger question, though, is why would anyone want to escape into his or her past in this way? The protagonists are each under the impression that returning to their past will take them to a more pleasant (*i.e.*, "safer") time in their lives, one free of the hardships they seek to flee. But, as the film's title and narrative suggest, "safety's not guaranteed," not only in terms of time travel, but also of life in general, something about which Kenneth, Darius and Jeff are perplexed, if not naïve. Indeed, our lifetimes are often replete with challenges in which "safety" (*i.e.*, the alleged freedom from difficulty) seems noticeably lacking, but such situations usually amount to nothing we can't handle, even if appearances suggest otherwise. Such instances, in fact, are often beneficial, if not integral, to our personal growth, even if we believe them to be "unsafe" at the time we encounter them.

Ironically, and at the risk of appearing to contradict the foregoing, conscious creation maintains that we all live in a Safe Universe (as discussed earlier in this Chapter), one that lovingly and whole-heartedly supports us in our personal evolution and development. However, this doesn't mean we'll never escape challenges to be surmounted, that we'll never be free from the *seeming* lack of safety described above. Guarantees to the contrary don't exist in the lines of probability most of us draw to ourselves through the law of attraction, and the sooner we understand this, the less likely we'll engage in the kind of delusional avoidance tactics that this film's protagonists seek to pursue.

As an alternative, we would be wise to follow the conscious creation principle that maintains the true point of power is in the *present*. Ultimately, this is the only moment over which we have any direct, meaningful control, and we should focus our beliefs and consciousness in it, not in some past that has come and gone or in some future that is full of variables and is as yet to transpire. Who knows what we might manifest for ourselves by doing so! And, through the proper focus of their beliefs, the protagonists just might come to discover the same for themselves, attracting outcomes far preferable to those that they might have originally envisioned.

The foregoing qualifications notwithstanding, one still can't help but admire Kenneth's sheer gumption for what he's attempting to undertake. Only by placing unwavering faith in new ideas can any of them ever be brought about. Think of the many inventions that never would have seen the light of day had it not been for advocates who passionately believed in the possibility of their successful manifestation. Time travel technology might seem like an unrealistic concept for many of us, but I'm sure the same was once said of the brainchildren of Thomas Edison, the Wright Brothers and Steve Jobs. Nothing materializes without adequate belief support, and, regardless of the motivations that inspire such conceptions, the faith placed in the manifestation of these ideas is something to be admired, no matter how outrageous they might seem.

While the film plays largely as a quirky quasi-romantic comedy, "Safety Not Guaranteed" has a lot to say metaphysically, but it does so without ever getting heavy-handed or overly serious. Its leads are exceptionally well cast, and they fit their roles perfectly. The writing is generally solid, though the main narrative is clearly handled better than its parallel story track, which, at times, becomes a bit tedious. Overall, it's a fun piece of indie filmmaking, an ideal selection for when you're in the mood for something a little out of the ordinary.

Visiting the past, and looking to relocate there, are two very distinct options, and the wise would-be temporal traveler is the one who knows the difference. "Safety Not Guaranteed" helps to shed light on that distinction—and takes us on a fun-filled ride in getting there.

3

PERSPECTIVE

What distinguishes the beliefs of one individual from another? When you come down to it, it's largely a matter of *perspective*.

Perspective plays an enormous role in how our beliefs take shape. To a great degree, it serves as a sort of template, made up of core elements that color *all* of our beliefs across the board, no matter which aspect of life it's applied to. But, just like beliefs, we're each capable of adopting a wide variety of perspectives, an ability that allows us to view a particular set of circumstances from an array of vantage points, each highly personalized.

Perspective is thus what makes it possible for two or more individuals to perceive the "same" circumstances in different ways. For instance, is a room with a particular illumination level lit too brightly, too dimly or just right? Ask different people, and you're likely to get a range of responses, even though logic would dictate that the answers seemingly "should" be the same. No one's response is intrinsically "right" or "wrong," either, since our individual perspectives and perceptions account for the differences, and each of them is equally valid in its own right.

Variances in perspective apply not only to different individuals; sometimes we're each capable of viewing situations in multiple, or even myriad, ways ourselves. The ability to see circumstances from different vantage points better enables us to assess how we respond to the prevailing conditions. The beliefs we form in response thus determine how our reality subsequently unfolds. We have multiple options for belief formation available to us under such circumstances, but our perspective helps to determine which *specific* beliefs we select and, ultimately, what transpires from them as a result.

To illustrate how all of this works, this Chapter's entries profile films in which various situations are capable of being viewed from different perspectives, depending on the outlook of the individual doing the perceiving. These pictures also examine instances where one individual is capable of viewing his or her circumstances in a variety of ways, enabling multiple options for response. In all of these cases, though, how things play out rests with how the characters choose to view their circumstances.

Perspective, like beliefs, makes a wide range of options possible. Which one we end up with depends on us.

The Perception Paradox

"World's Greatest Dad"
Year of Release: 2009
Cast: Robin Williams, Daryl Sabara, Alexie Gilmore,
Henry Simmons, Geoff Pierson, Evan Martin,
Jermaine Williams, Lorraine Nicholson, Tony V.,
Deborah Horne, Toby Huss, Mitzi McCall, Bruce Hornsby
Director: Bobcat Goldthwait
Screenplay: Bobcat Goldthwait

Ever form an opinion about someone that you later come to find out is far different—perhaps even the exact opposite—of what others have of the same person? Seems paradoxical, doesn't it? But what's even more puzzling is, what if *both* perspectives are accurate? Such is the metaphysical conundrum posed in the dark comedy, "World's Greatest Dad."

This little-known (and much-overlooked) gem is definitely worth a peek for many reasons, both for its entertainment value and its conscious creation themes. But don't let the title mislead you; it's not a warm fuzzy family flick. Rather, it's one of those wickedly cynical comedies where you frequently find yourself laughing at things you probably think you shouldn't be chuckling about. Of course, such questionable humor is what makes so much of this film so effective.

Chapter 3: Perspective

Poetry teacher and would-be author Lance Clayton (Robin Williams) desperately needs a life makeover. As a writer who's never published any of his works and a private school instructor whose dwindling class enrollment endangers its future (and his tenure), Lance is depressed about the bleak prospects he faces. But, if that weren't enough, he's also a single father, dutifully attempting to raise (or, more precisely, "manage") his teenage son Kyle (Daryl Sabara), an unappreciative, insolent, foul-mouthed brat who has a smart answer for everything. He attends the same school where Lance teaches, routinely making life difficult for his old man when not busy offending his classmates or irritating dad's colleagues. Lance clearly needs for things to change if he's ever to find any enjoyment—or peace of mind—in his life.

Sadly, though, things go from bad to worse one evening when Lance discovers his son dead at home, the victim of a tragic accidental death (but one with potentially embarrassing connotations if the truth were ever to get out). Lance is devastated, of course, but, even in the midst of his sorrow, he remains composed enough to "clean up" the death scene, a final gesture designed to give Kyle some dignity and to protect his son's reputation (as well as his own). Lance makes Kyle's death look like a suicide, attending to all the associated details, right down to writing an eloquent suicide note. He composes an articulate message (he's a writer after all), using prose that allows Kyle to come across as an expressive but tortured, misunderstood soul. Even under such terribly trying circumstances, Lance is, without a doubt, an unquestionably devoted dad.

Ironically, when the contents of Kyle's note become public, his one-time detractors begin seeing him in a new light. The "we-never-knew" reactions flow freely, and Kyle is viewed with a newfound sense of sympathy, all thanks to "his" parting words. In fact, the public reaction is so overwhelming that Lance is asked if Kyle left behind any other writings chronicling his teenage angst. When faced with this request, Lance sees an opportunity to resuscitate his writing career, and so he jumps at the chance to give his dead son's audience what they want while simultaneously fulfilling his own need to create. He then sets about writing an alleged antemortem personal journal under Kyle's name, a treatise that quickly becomes a national sensation.

Lance relishes the attention initially, but, as time passes and the phenomenon grows ever larger, he begins to question his actions: In managing Kyle's legacy, is he doing right by him by manufacturing a trumped-up reputation, or is he being a genuinely protective parent who's acting out of love? Is he doing a public service by spotlighting the anguish associated with teen suicide, even if the "suicide" prompting such altruism is a total fabrication? But, most importantly, is Lance's primary motivation in all this protecting his son's memory, or is he simply cashing in on Kyle's demise to benefit himself (especially now that publishers are interested in Lance penning his own works, too)? Or are *all* of these motivations legitimate to some degree or another? Can *all* of these perspectives be true simultaneously? Those are some profound questions for Lance—and viewers—to address.

All of this takes us back to the aforementioned perception paradox. If viewing Lance from a single perspective, one might see only one dimension of his character, a genuine liability when relying on this criterion alone as the basis for belief formation and assessment. On a more detailed viewing, however, Lance might well be seen as the *multidimensional being* that he truly is. Like all of us, there are many aspects that go into the makeup of Lance's persona, some of which are very different from one another. But, despite these "discrepancies," they're all part of who he is as a consequence of the intentions that he puts forth to create them. The question for us in this situation (and in any others like it for that matter, both on and off screen) is, will we take the steps to see Lance for his intrinsic multidimensionality, or will we fall prey to the potentially illusory imprecision of the perception paradox? This film gives us much to ponder in that regard.

So why does Lance display such seemingly disparate dimensions of himself in this film? I believe it's because they're *all* part of who he really is, all facets of his true being and all related to different aspects of the value fulfillment he is attempting to live out. And, in that sense, he really *is* the "world's greatest dad" in *all* of the ways that designation can be applied in line with the themes explored in this film.

For example, by attempting to protect his son's sullied reputation and by imparting cautionary information about the perils of teen suicide, Lance is virtuous in his deeds, allowing him to live up to the supreme paternal honor in its most positive light. At the same time, by seizing upon the unexpected opportunity to help his own career, he could easily be labeled self-serving, justifiably earning him the aforementioned title in its most cynical of iterations. However, by jumping on this opportunity to provide for himself materially, he also makes it possible to support himself while engaging in the altruistic endeavors noted above, a practical approach to capturing the title that carries no especially laudable or derisive implications with it. Of course, juggling all this is a challenge for the protagonist, and he must decide to what degree he can live with any or all of these different aspects of himself (and the fallout that comes with each). Effectively managing our multidimensionality can be tricky business indeed. But then that's all part of the joy—and the challenge—in creating our own reality.

In the end, the sum total of our beliefs affects the overall perspectives we hold of ourselves, others and the circumstances surrounding us (which, in turn, contributes to the ongoing formation of beliefs that manifest all subsequent expressions of our reality). This is what makes Lance's inherent multidimensionality possible, for instance, because, to varying degrees, his fellow characters (and we, as viewers) collectively hold all of the diverse beliefs that give rise to his different attributes. Indeed, as distinct (and even dissimilar) as those qualities are, they're all still intrinsic parts of Lance, because there's underlying support for their materialization and existence.

The same can be said about Kyle, particularly after his demise, when "information" (no matter how intentionally fabricated it may be) comes to light that feeds into the formation of beliefs that others hold about him. As "erroneous" as those perspectives might seem, however, they're nevertheless legitimate, because they arose *sincerely* through the belief formation process, regardless of how questionable the input was that birthed them.

We should all bear the foregoing in mind if we attempt to beat ourselves up in the wake of finding out we've been deceived. If we genuinely trusted the content that fostered our beliefs, we shouldn't fault ourselves for our actions; instead, we should learn from the experience and draw upon the wisdom we glean from it for future reference should we ever be faced with comparable circumstances down the road. Situations like this, as difficult as they sometimes can be, are often invaluable *life lessons*, those that we incarnated to experience for our personal growth and spiritual development, teachings that go a long way to help us in the formation of our beliefs and perspectives, especially going forward.

"World's Greatest Dad" is a real sleeper of a film. It's progressively more captivating with each passing frame, smartly written and directed by Bobcat Goldthwait. Robin Williams turns in one of the best performances he's given in years, and he's backed by an excellent ensemble of supporting players, most notably Darryl Sabara, Alexie Gilmore, Henry Simmons, Evan Martin and Geoff Pierson.

"World's Greatest Dad" is an excellent option for alternative viewing. The title might not sound beckoning, but don't let that superficial consideration deter you; the movie's as multifaceted as its protagonist, and his character allows us to view him from the range of perspectives with which we'd all be wise to view ourselves. And there's nothing paradoxical about that.

Lessons in Perspective

"A Serious Man"
Year of Release: 2009
Cast: Michael Stuhlbarg, Sari Lennick, Aaron Wolff,
Jessica McManus, Richard Kind, Fred Melamed,
Peter Breitmayer, Amy Landecker, David Kang,
Simon Helberg, George Wyner, Alan Mandell,
Adam Arkin, Ari Hoptman, Allen Lewis Rickman,
Yelena Shmulenson, Fyvush Finkel, Michael Lerner
Directors: Ethan Coen and Joel Coen
Screenplay: Joel Coen and Ethan Coen

Pick a proverb: We must all endure a little rain to appreciate the sunshine; when life hands you lemons, make lemonade; a rolling stone crushes everything in its path (especially when big enough). Clichéd though at least some of the foregoing might be, these words of wisdom all provide us with opportunities for lessons in perspective, a core theme of the quirky Coen Brothers comedy, "A Serious Man."

Chapter 3: Perspective   63

Larry Gopnik (Michael Stuhlbarg) is a man beset by many problems. He's a hardworking Jewish everyman living in the Minneapolis suburbs in the late 1960s who diligently strives to support his family, do a capable job as a physics professor, and be a good friend and neighbor. But, no matter what Larry does, life always seems to dump on him. Whether it's due to the incessant whining of his ungrateful kids (Aaron Wolff, Jessica McManus), the freeloading of his ne'er-do-well brother (Richard Kind), the less-than-subtle bigotry of his next-door neighbor (Peter Breitmayer) or the unreasonable demands of his shrewish wife (Sari Lennick) (who unapologetically plans to ditch him for one of his best friends (Fred Melamed)), Larry ends up the butt of everyone's indignities. He gets stuck paying legal bills, funeral costs and bail bonds for things seemingly not of his making. And, when he consults three rabbis (Simon Helberg, George Wyner, Alan Mandell) for guidance on the meaning of these seemingly unjust acts, he's met with cluelessness, irrelevance or indifference.

However, as unfair as these circumstances may appear, there are compensating factors that help to tilt the balance back in Larry's favor, such as the unsolicited acts of "kindness" offered by his neighbor, Mrs. Samsky (Amy Landecker), a sort of Mrs. Robinson-in-training. What's more, not all those who would perpetrate untoward acts against Larry wind up succeeding. (Things *can* get better, it would seem.) But, even when all is apparently going well, that doesn't mean the other shoe still can't drop, reversing circumstances yet again—and in far more devastating ways.

Or, then again, perhaps not.

So, in light of all this, what is Larry to think about life? Most of the time, he feels justifiably put upon; others, meanwhile, somehow feel he owes them. So who's right? And what's Larry to do about it to make things "right"? Ultimately, it's a matter of perspective.

Anyone who employs conscious creation practices knows that we each co-create our own reality through our beliefs and intents with the assistance of our divine collaborator. That includes both the positive and negative manifestations we experience. How we *respond* to these outcomes, however, is what matters most, for those reactions form our subsequent beliefs and shape our overall perspective, which, of course, contribute to the formation of future beliefs and color the nature of our reality going forward.

But, even knowing that, one still can't help but wonder, if we supposedly have a choice in the reality we create, why would anyone purposely use the law of attraction to manifest anything negative? (Larry would certainly appreciate a clear answer to that question.) In part, it has to do with how the materialization process plays out.

In achieving the results we seek, we can't always predict how we'll reach them, even when we've stated our intents clearly and honestly. Sometimes the Universe needs to take us down an unlikely path, perhaps to arrange for an unforeseen but highly fortuitous synchronicity. Similarly, sometimes we need to experience a supposed "setback" to rid ourselves of a hindrance that's preventing forward movement, because it no longer serves us, no matter how attached we may have become to it.

Both of the foregoing explanations call to mind the proverbial silver lining in the cloud metaphor. But then, just because we successfully see such a silver lining materialize doesn't mean that we can't experience further challenges subsequently, often of an even greater magnitude (just ask Larry). Of course, such circumstances also raise the possibility of even greater rewards for surviving these later tests. (Think of this as metaphysically upping the ante, enabling the attainment of fulfillment beyond our expectations.)

As noted above, how we get through such transitions depends greatly on how we respond to them. When things go "wrong," we can allow our perspective to become tainted, thereby giving ourselves license to wallow in self-pity. Or we can approach such situations by realizing that everything that happens is all part of the plan, that our divine collaborator is guiding us in the direction we need to go to get the results we seek, even if the means and methods don't seem beneficial, sound or plausible. That requires faith and trust on our part, lessons that can sometimes be very hard to come by (something Larry can certainly attest to eloquently). But, if we're ever to keep ourselves from becoming permanently stuck, this is a lesson in perspective that's positively essential to our forward progress.

Letting go of our preoccupation with "how" we believe circumstances should unfold is crucial. Holding on to such preconceptions can deter us in shifting our beliefs, perspectives and outcomes.

Overcoming this tendency is understandably difficult for many of us, but it can be especially challenging for an analytical type like Larry, a physics professor who believes everything—even the essence of reality—can ultimately be understood from a purely mechanistic standpoint. Nevertheless, if we close ourselves off from embracing a more open-minded perspective about how the Universe works, we potentially saddle ourselves with the prospect of unfulfilled or less-than-satisfying results.

Indeed, our perspective often makes all the difference in interpreting prevailing conditions, especially the meanings behind unenvisioned occurrences. This, again, comes down to a matter of the beliefs associated with it, particularly those that relate to matters of perception, choice and openness to change.

Consider, for example, the film's opening segment, a fable sequence (unrelated to the main story) that sets the tone for the film's central narrative. A husband and wife (Allen Lewis Rickman, Yelena Shmulenson) living in an Old World *shtetl* are visited by a mysterious stranger (Fyvush Finkel). The husband sees the stranger as a Samaritan for having helped him out of a jam on his way home, while the wife believes the stranger is a *dybbuk* (a malicious possessory spirit) and unhesitatingly stabs him. Because of his wife's actions, the husband is convinced the family's life and reputation have been ruined; the wife, on the other hand, believes her actions have protected the family against a walking evil. So who's right? Similarly, in the main story, Larry continuously feels justifiably put upon; others, however, somehow feel he owes them. Once more, who's right? In either instance, it ultimately depends on one's perspective—and how one accepts and applies it to the circumstances at hand.

Despite the picture's critical acclaim, "A Serious Man" didn't fare as well with the viewing public. But the lack of popular appeal was compensated for by two Oscar nominations, one each for best picture and best original screenplay, and a Golden Globe nod for Stuhlbarg for best actor in a comedy. Personally, I can't speak highly enough about this movie. It was my favorite film of 2009, and I've thoroughly enjoyed it each time I've screened it. It's striking in every respect, and it's a movie that could be examined from a multitude of perspectives far beyond what I've discussed here. So my advice regarding this movie is simple—*see it*.

Lessons in perspective can sometimes be compared to the act of attempting to swallow the proverbial hard pill. Yet such acts, difficult though they may be, also often reveal the disguised blessings we're so anxious to embrace once they become apparent. "A Serious Man" effectively pays homage to these notions and does so in a lighthearted, humorous way.

So, the next time you're tempted to exclaim "*Oy vey!*" in response to one of life's foibles, think about what that foible might be leading you to. By holding fast to a perspective of being willing to accept circumstances for what they are, you just might find that silver lining quicker—and more lustrous—than you thought possible.

Defining One's Life

"Another Year"
Year of Release: 2010
Cast: Jim Broadbent, Ruth Sheen, Lesley Manville,
Oliver Maltman, Peter Wight, David Bradley, Martin Savage,
Karina Fernandez, Michele Austin, Imelda Staunton
Director: Mike Leigh
Screenplay: Mike Leigh

For better or worse, we all have our limits in various areas of our lives. We might not always like to admit that we have them, either, perhaps seeing them as selfish or uncharitable. But boundaries *do* have their place, for they help to define how we handle the assorted elements that make up our lives. Maintaining a healthy perspective on such matters is crucial for our personal happiness and stability, as evidenced in the gentle drama, "Another Year."

Tom (Jim Broadbent) and Gerri (Ruth Sheen) live a happy, fulfilling life. As an aging middle class London couple, they've managed to forge rewarding careers (he as a geologist, she as a counselor), raise a bright, successful son, Joe (Oliver Maltman), and, above all, stay madly in love with one another after many years of marriage. They approach life with an optimistic but practical outlook that affords them much happiness and active engagement with the lives they've made for themselves, both individually and collectively. One could say they're contentment personified.

In fact, Tom and Gerri have been so successful in creating such fulfillment that they freely share their abundant blessings with others who have been less fortunate at creating the same in their lives, such as Tom's brother Ronnie (David Bradley) and their longtime friend Ken (Peter Wight). But the person who receives the lion's share of their attention is Gerri's friend and co-worker Mary (Lesley Manville), an often-spacey, somewhat boozy, middle-aged clerical who spends much of her time lost. Mary desperately looks for happiness in all the wrong places and invariably seeks to shift blame elsewhere when things don't pan out as hoped for, a perspective that makes her increasingly embittered, and pitiable, as time passes. But, despite their tremendous capacities for compassion, empathy and understanding, even Tom and Gerri have their limits, and, as Mary pushes those boundaries, their friendship gets stretched and strained, threatening the very existence of their relationship. Over time it becomes apparent that something has to change if the friendship is to survive.

As physical beings, we're innately accustomed to living life in a reality where nearly all of its elements—like us—have defined physical parameters. Those inherent boundaries give shape, definition and limitation to everything we encounter within this existence. But, strange though it may seem to some of us, boundaries are not limited to just the physical aspects of our world; they also provide limits to things of a nonphysical nature, like our emotions and the frameworks of our interpersonal relationships. However, given our almost dogmatic preoccupation with physicality, most of us are probably less familiar with the boundaries associated with our reality's nonphysical components, not only in terms of establishing them but of even recognizing their existence. Consequently, it can be quite easy for borders to be crossed that shouldn't be, creating havoc and mayhem, even in situations where we thought we knew where things stood, ultimately yielding emotional pain, suffering and heartache.

Those who are skilled in recognizing and setting such parameters realize their necessity. Even though those boundaries may not apply to items of a physical nature, their existence provides buffers against unwanted intrusions by those who, wittingly or unwittingly, would disregard the limits of another's personal sovereignty. Indeed, poet Robert Frost probably said it best when he wrote in his poem *Mending Wall* that "good fences make good neighbors," sound advice that applies whether the boundaries in question are physical or otherwise.

Those who are effective at establishing these kinds of limits are undoubtedly effective conscious creation practitioners, for they recognize that *definition* is an intrinsic part of the materialization process, no matter what canvas of existence they create upon. And it's also quite understandable that those who are skilled at developing such a perspective might eventually lose patience with, or even grow resentful of, others who are unable—or unwilling—to respect boundaries when their limits are reached.

So it is with Tom and Gerri in their relationship with Mary when she starts to cross lines that are off limits. Ultimately she fails to respect the healthy borders that define the nature of her relationship with her friends and their family. This is most apparent when Mary meets Joe's girlfriend, Katie (Karina Fernandez), for the first time. Mary, who had long had an unrealistic crush on the young man, becomes unabashedly snippy with everyone after being introduced to Katie, clearly angering those who had been so giving to her for so long, even when they didn't always need to be. Mary fails to realize that Tom and Gerri's tremendous compassion and generosity of spirit in dealing with her doesn't automatically give her the right to trample all over them as a means to help her solve her problems (problems, by the way, that, by their nature, are of *her own* creating, based on how she's employed the law of attraction).

These circumstances, in turn, speak to another of the film's major themes—the idea that we're each ultimately responsible for creating our own happiness. While it's true that others may come along to help us out in a pinch, such assistance doesn't automatically equate to a license to lean on those compassionate souls completely for helping us attain fulfillment in life. In the end, it ultimately comes down to each of us to develop the perspective that we're each responsible for choosing our own happiness (and fashioning beliefs in line with that notion).

It's indeed sad that there are so many lost souls in the world who experience this these days, and their ranks are amply represented in this film by the likes of Mary, Ken and Ronnie, as well as one of Gerri's patients, Janet (Imelda Staunton), who appears at the picture's beginning and sets the tone for this theme. They sit idly by, watching yet "another year" pass without any resolution to their unrelenting despair, all the while hoping that something will miraculously alleviate their sadness and grant them new lives. By embracing such a perspective, however, they miss the point that it's up to *them*, and not some outside savior, to create that result. Those who lack this perspective, and who try to milk salvation out of others who, in the end, are not directly responsible for creating their contentment, will pay an even greater price for such ignorance and irresponsibility. Clearly, developing a healthy perspective about life begins with each of us.

"Another Year" is a thoughtful, introspective piece of filmmaking. Some may find the pacing a bit slow at times, an argument I wouldn't totally disagree with, but its character-driven nature nevertheless manages to keep viewer attention quite effectively. The writing is subtle (perhaps even a little too understated at times) but substantive, attributes that helped earn it an Oscar nomination for best original screenplay. The performances are all solid, too, especially Manville, who's very convincing as the troubled lost soul, a portrayal that, sadly, was largely overlooked for consideration in most of the major awards competitions. The film was also a *Palme d'Or* nominee at the Cannes Film Festival (the event's highest honor), as well as the recipient of the Festival's Prize of the Ecumenical Jury.

The ties that bind us can also become ensnaring, especially when the limits of those bonds are breached. If we approach life expecting others to help us achieve happiness and fulfillment, that perspective could easily become the source of our own undoing. Respecting those boundaries is crucial for maintaining significant interpersonal connections, for failing to do so could result in long-lasting disappointment and irreparable harm, damage that, without proper remediation, can easily last for many years to come.

What Truly Nourishes Us

"Malos Hábitos" ("Bad Habits")
Year of Release: 2007
Cast: Jimena Ayala, Elena de Haro,
Marco Treviño, Aurora Cano, Elisa Vicedo,
Emilio Echevarría, Patricia Reyes Spíndola,
Raúl Cardós, Alma Sofía Martínez,
Milagros Vidal, Victor Rivera
Director: Simón Bross
Screenplay: Ernesto Anaya and Simón Bross

Sustenance is essential to our continued existence, and the perspectives we hold about the nature of that nourishment determine the quality of life we experience. As conscious creators, we're free to choose from a wide range of options in that regard, but we'd be wise to choose carefully, as illustrated in the mesmerizing Mexican comedy-drama, *"Malos Hábitos"* ("Bad Habits").

"Malos Hábitos" is, arguably, one of the most unusual, yet most captivating, films to come out in a long time. Its interwoven storylines revolve around members of the Soriano family, all of whom are affiliated in one way or another with a Catholic university and convent in Mexico City. The narrative's various strands weave an intriguing tapestry of ideas that examine two seemingly unrelated, but fundamentally essential, aspects of our lives—spirituality and food. As unlikely as this pairing might seem, however, there is a common thread that binds them: They both nourish us, one feeding our bodies and the other feeding our souls. And, in the spirit of conscious creation, the film eloquently explores the beliefs underlying our relationships with these life-sustaining forces.

The film opens at a family gathering hosted by Ramón Soriano (Emilio Echevarría). All of the relatives have assembled to meet Elena (Elena de Haro), the new girlfriend of Gustavo (Marco Treviño), Ramón's brother. However, not long after the family sits down to dinner, Ramón begins to choke on his food, prompting his daughter, Matílde (Alma Sofía Martínez), to begin praying desperately. As a deeply spiritual young girl, she promises to devote her life to God if her father is spared, a prayer that's quickly answered.

Flash-forward several decades to a time when a now-older Matílde (Jimena Ayala) receives her medical school degree. Everyone is thrilled for her. Yet no sooner is the ink dry on her diploma when she announces her intention to become a nun, proudly proclaiming that she's keeping her promise to God for sparing her father's life so many years before. Ramón is somewhat baffled by her decision, but Matílde contends that religious faith can do as much to heal the body as anything that medicine can, and she's eager to prove that, doing whatever she can to spiritually facilitate miraculous recoveries.

However, as Matílde sees it, becoming a successful healing intercessor requires personal sacrifice, particularly regarding anything worldly, including even basics like food. She willingly abides by her vow but struggles to live up to it; she's torn between sustaining the needs of the body and fulfilling the sacrificial obligations she believes are required of her. The beliefs driving this internal conflict cause her much pain and strife, eventually jeopardizing both her physical health and psychological well-being.

Meanwhile, in the years while Matílde toiled to fulfill her promise, Gustavo and Elena married and started a family. As an architect and university professor, Gustavo has managed to provide handsomely for his wife and their young daughter, Linda (Elisa Vicedo). By all accounts, one would think the upscale couple's life should be happy, but nothing could be further from the truth, at least for Elena. She wrestles with a number of control issues, most notably her preoccupation with her daughter's growing waistline.

As a chubby (though certainly not obese) little girl, Linda is a constant (albeit grossly exaggerated) source of embarrassment to Elena, who'll go to almost any lengths to get her daughter to slim down. She's particularly upset that Linda struggles to fit into her First Communion dress, prompting her to pursue assorted weight loss tactics with a vengeance. Elena's fixation saddens Linda, who clearly doesn't understand or share her mother's fanatical views. Ironically, Linda eventually seeks guidance from—of all people—her Aunt Matílde, who counsels her niece that eating is not a sin, advice that positively infuriates *Madre dearest*.

But Elena's fanaticism doesn't stop with Linda. She's become so preoccupied with *her own* body image that she virtually stops eating altogether, getting by on little more than bottled water and cigarettes. She becomes so emaciated that her bones protrude everywhere. Her obsessive behavior, sickly appearance and hostile attitude about others' eating habits eventually cause Gustavo to turn away from her. He seeks solace in the arms of a buxom, voluptuous Peruvian woman (Milagros Vidal), who unapologetically indulges her love for life and all its carnal and gastronomic pleasures. Gustavo willingly goes along with her, enthusiastically embracing everything that his wife so inexplicably denies herself.

Given their fundamentally different perspectives on life, it should come as no surprise that Elena and Gustavo drift far apart. But that mutual isolation quickly proves to be the least of their troubles with the rise of events that force them to examine some of life's bigger questions, such as the quality and meaning of existence, topics directly impacted by the twin sources of nourishment that are at the heart of this film's narrative. *How* those sustaining elements affect them (and us), though, is what's most important, and "*Malos Hábitos*" probes their impact (and the beliefs that drive them) from a variety of angles.

At the risk of oversimplifying matters, the characters who hold fast to "healthy" perspectives about these sources of physical and metaphysical sustenance, such as Gustavo and his girlfriend, are happiest, while those who embrace "unhealthy" views, like Matílde and Elena, experience a host of challenges, ranging from frustration to ill health to despair. And then there are those in between, like Linda and her friend Lalo (Victor Rivera), who struggle to find their way with their beliefs and end up experiencing manifestations reflective of both extremes. For each of these characters, the combined beliefs they hold color their overall perspectives, which, in turn, shape their realities extensively.

So why do the characters embrace such distinctly different perspectives? To a great degree, it has to do with the life lessons they've chosen to experience. The beliefs and perspectives associated with those lessons lead them to attract the conditions that make such teachings possible. Those conditions shape their subsequent beliefs and frame their overall perspectives, *reinforcing* the prevailing paradigm of ideas and experiences in their respective lives. And that reinforcement "feeds" those circumstances, perpetuating them until they become played out (by which time, one would hope, the lesson in question is learned).

The impact of perspective reinforcement makes its presence felt repeatedly throughout the film. Linda, for example, is often dismayed by her circumstances, especially when she's regularly subjected to Elena's extreme weight loss "treatments" and bombarded with her insensitive "advice," which includes such statements as "No one likes a fat person" or (even more shockingly) "I'd rather my daughter be dead than fat." Yet, on some level, Linda truly doesn't believe her mother's obsessive actions and judgmental statements, that her life choices and creations are just fine as they are. She thus quietly yet routinely draws contrary manifestations into her reality to counter (and confound) her mother's relentless onslaught of criticism, such as Aunt Matílde's heartfelt advice, a doctor's reassuring prognosis and the warmth of Lalo's friendship, all of which support and reinforce Linda's alternative outlook. How this life lesson eventually plays out for Linda will naturally depend on which viewpoint she chooses to embrace—and which form of reinforcement ultimately proves more compelling.

Reinforcement manifests in many ways, too. Besides the foregoing illustrations, it also arises by way of inspiring personal examples, something Matílde regularly draws upon in shaping her beliefs. For instance, she believes her spiritual and intercessory callings parallel those personified by historical religious figures. The development of a spiritual sense early on in life, for example, calls to mind the experiences of a youthful St. Francis of Assisi. Similarly, as a healing intermediary, Matílde identifies with the sacrifices of St. Nicholas, a benevolent figure who willingly took on the lion's share of his followers' penance burdens so that they needn't suffer as greatly, an example she sincerely believes she can follow. In fact, she's so convinced she can succeed at working miracles that she believes she might one day even be able to emulate the works of Jesus himself, a notion revealed to her in a vision in which she literally follows in his footsteps—and atop a body of water at that.

As should be apparent from the foregoing, the film's storylines deal extensively with issues of denial and indulgence. Those who adhere to the perspective of sacrifice, be it in a spiritual or culinary context, seem to believe that they're traversing a moral high road, that denial is a noble, enlightened pursuit and that indulging our appetites is something about which we should feel guilty. But, considering the impact such a perspective has on the health and well-being of those characters, is their path really one to which we should aspire? After all, by incarnating in this reality, we've chosen to be *physical* beings with *physical* needs for our continued existence. And, given that, one can't help but ask, why would anyone intentionally deny themselves what they need to survive? Isn't our attraction to life's physical pleasures something that's fundamentally meant to keep us alive and healthy? Compare the experiences of the picture's principal characters, and draw your own conclusions.

The impact of these perspectives is also apparent in the experiences of both individuals *and* en masse. For instance, the archaic, often-dour perspective held by Church traditionalists (like the aging convent residents depicted in this film) has contributed greatly to declining support for the institution, even in a heavily Catholic country like Mexico. Many former and would-be followers have turned away, looking upon the Church as rigid and irrelevant. So, when the convent faces a financial crisis, it desperately needs to do something to raise funds. The Sisters' inventive solution is to sell the delicious food they create in the convent's kitchen, an idea that goes over big with the public and gives the facility a much-needed infusion of cash. The Sisters' experience thus shows that, when you have something substantial to offer, people will flock to you. Indeed, even if the Church's message fails to nourish, at least its culinary offerings do, thanks to the practical, life-affirming beliefs underlying their creation (maybe the Church should apply the same perspective in the pulpit that it uses in the kitchen).

Interestingly enough, all of this is set against an intriguing mass-created backdrop—a city besieged by incessant rain, an image that can be interpreted in multiple ways. For instance, the rain can be viewed as "God's tears," a physical manifestation of our divine collaborator's despair over the state of a world we've asked it to help us co-create. Similarly, the rain could also symbolize God's tears in response to how we've grossly misinterpreted the gifts our celestial partner has bestowed upon us, sadness over how we've come to misconstrue as vices the blessings that we *should* regard as pleasures. But, in yet another interpretation, the rain could be seen as a baptismal symbol, a divinely initiated sacrament aimed at cleansing us of our "sins," which conceivably could apply to the circumstances noted in either or both of the foregoing analyses. In all of these instances, though, the resulting materialization is a mirror of the creative beliefs that invoked it, no matter which perspective is at play or from what source the manifesting intents originated.

There is *so* much more I could say about this film that I could easily go on for many pages. So, to simplify matters, as I wrote about "A Serious Man" earlier in this Chapter, let me just say *see it*. Admittedly, that may be easier said than done, since this film is, regrettably, rather hard to find. It played mostly at film festivals in the U.S. (which is where I first saw it), having never received a general release domestically, either in theaters or on cable TV. The best bet for finding it is to look for it on DVD from specialty movie sellers. The picture is definitely worth it, however. Its thoughtful writing, expert direction, superb performances and skillful editing make for a movie that will hold your attention during every single frame.

It's been said that "we are what we eat." That's true enough, but I'd like to expand on that to say "we are what we *believe*," for the beliefs and perspectives we maintain about what sustains us serve to shape the general state of our health and well-being, both physically and psychologically. "*Malos Hábitos*" shines a brilliant spotlight on those notions, providing us with a clear, concise and illuminating guide to what truly nourishes us.

What Do We *Really* Believe?

"Sound of My Voice"
Year of Release: 2012
Cast: Christopher Denham, Nicole Vicius,
Brit Marling, Davenia McFadden, Kandice Stroh,
Richard Wharton, Christy Meyers, Alvin Lam,
Constance Wu, Avery Pohl
Director: Zal Batmanglij
Screenplay: Zal Batmanglij and Brit Marling

What we believe makes up who we are. Much of the time we take that for granted, too, never giving our beliefs a second thought.

But every so often we undergo profound experiences that prompt us to examine our beliefs, perhaps even our overall perspectives, to see how they form the basis of our individual realities, a notion explored in the intense drama, "Sound of My Voice."

Intrepid documentary filmmakers Peter Aitken (Christopher Denham) and Lorna Michaelson (Nicole Vicius) are so eager to make a movie about cults that they're willing to secretly infiltrate one to conduct research. Besides the investigative journalism value, Peter has a personal stake in making the film: Having been orphaned at age 13, when his mother, a longtime follower of a New Age movement that eschewed the merits of modern medicine, died of cancer, Peter now seeks retribution for the "brainwashing" inflicted upon her by documenting and exposing the alleged fraud and false hope he believes such charlatan-esque organizations peddle to gullible followers. It's a crusade to which he's fervently committed—and one that's eminently more fulfilling than the day job he holds as a substitute teacher at a private elementary girls' school.

After successfully surviving a period of recruitment and scrutiny, Peter and Lorna are indoctrinated into the inner circle of a secret fellowship led by an enigmatic guru named Maggie (Brit Marling). The charismatic, soft-spoken leader offers up her singular pearls of wisdom to a small group of disciples in informal gatherings in the basement of an undisclosed residential location somewhere near Los Angeles. And what's the basis underlying Maggie's philosophy/theology? She claims to be a time traveler from the year 2054, having come back to the past to share information about what lies ahead with a select handful of followers, people whom she claims to know and care about in her own future life.

Peter initially sees Maggie's claims as the pinnacle of lunacy, becoming quietly angered whenever he thinks about how she's preying on a band of weak-willed, vulnerable followers, not unlike what happened to his mother years before. However, the more involved he becomes with Maggie and her minions, the more he loses his focus—and himself—in the mindset of the group. He's particularly captivated by Maggie's insights about him personally, revelations that involve information she couldn't possibly know about him without some kind of foreknowledge—the kind that would come about only from intimate personal interaction. And, since Peter has never met Maggie before, the only way she could possibly have come into possession of such facts would be from interaction that hasn't yet happened but that *could* conceivably happen at some other time—like the future.

Ironically, such incidents cause Peter to question his own skepticism. As he's increasingly drawn into the workings of the group, he finds himself ever more willing to comply with the questionable tasks asked of him by Maggie and her lieutenants. At the same time, Lorna grows concerned that Peter is losing his perspective, especially when she witnesses some of the dubious activities that Maggie's closest advisors, like Joanne (Kandice Stroh) and Klaus (Richard Wharton), engage in. More red flags get raised when Lorna learns that Maggie is the target of a Department of Justice investigation led by special agent Carol Briggs (Davenia McFadden). But, given the uncanny disclosures that continue to stream forth as part of Maggie's cryptic pronouncements, doubt persists about the real truth of what's going on. Is Maggie who she claims to be? Or is she a flagrant and potentially dangerous fraud? Or is "the truth" even more incredible than either of these possibilities? In the end, it would seem, it all comes down to one's perspective.

But, then, when it comes to assessing the reality we experience, it *always* comes down to the beliefs we employ in manifesting our existence, and that point is driven home subtly yet repeatedly in this film. For the followers of her group, Maggie becomes *exactly* whoever each of them needs her to be. In doing so, she assumes a chameleon-like persona reminiscent of the unassuming gardener Chance (Peter Sellers) in the whimsically delightful comedy, "Being There" (1979). For those who need Maggie to be a prescient time traveler, she's a prescient time traveler; for those who need her to be a New Age con artist, she's a New Age con artist; and for those whose personal uncertainty calls for her to be an inscrutable enigma who ambiguously seems to embody qualities alluding to both of these characters, she once again complies accordingly. In each instance, though, the beliefs of those perceiving her govern which permutation appears in each of their respective individual realities, for better or worse and regardless of whether seemingly contradictory qualities are involved. Such is the fundamental nature of the law of attraction at work.

To some, this may sound like a notion devoid of credibility. But, if we assume that our individual beliefs shape all of the other elements of the existence we each experience, why should it be any different for the beliefs we associate with the people who populate our realities? In fact, we already do this, often unwittingly and even if we don't readily associate the "creation" aspect with it. Why, for example, would one person perceive another individual as a paragon of virtue while another perceives that "same" individual as an unmitigated jerk? In both instances, the characterizations are defined by the beliefs of those doing the perceiving/manifesting. So it is also with Maggie.

In this film, however, the characters' beliefs have implications far more significant than just what version of Maggie crosses their paths. They delve into much deeper subjects, such as the concept of time travel and whether it's possible. That, in turn, raises other profound questions, such as would Maggie's appearance in her past alter the course of the timeline going forward? Could her presence in contemporary Los Angeles potentially have a temporal "butterfly effect" for the events leading up to the time from which she claims to have come? Would such alterations affect her alone or all involved? Again, it all turns on one's beliefs and perspective, for they dictate what manifestations arise.

This, of course, raises questions related to the notion of choice and how what we choose determines what we ultimately experience. It also underscores the importance of personal responsibility, for each of us is accountable for what we choose to believe and what we each materialize as a result of those choices. Exercising care and caution would be a wise course in this pursuit, for embracing the "wrong" choices can potentially carry consequences that fly in the face of hoped-for expectations. Indeed, whether our choices involve matters as seemingly innocuous as what to have for breakfast or as seemingly life-changing as whether to join a cult, in each case we should all strive to choose wisely. (For more on Choice, see Chapter 4.)

"Sound of My Voice" is a thoughtful exploration of the foregoing considerations, going far beyond the surface attributes of its narrative. Much of the picture's action takes place in the aforementioned basement, shot close-up, creating an intimate, almost claustrophobic feel that closes in on the characters (and, by extension, the viewers), effectively emphasizing the intensity of an experience that impels serious examination of oneself and one's beliefs. The crisp writing and fine performances serve to bring all of this to life, making for a gripping viewing experience one soon won't forget.

Beliefs are powerful forces that can frame our existence or shake us to our very core, as the characters in this film find out for themselves in many different ways. What we do with those beliefs, and how we respond to the materializations that they birth, impact what we experience, both now and in the future that lies ahead of us. "Sound of My Voice" draws these ideas sharply into focus, giving us pause to think about who we are, where we are and, perhaps most importantly, where we're going. We'd be wise to give serious thought to such notions; after all, our future depends on it.

4

CHOICE AND INTENT

Knowing that we have an infinite range of probabilities available at any given moment, we're free to choose from among *any* of the options open to us. Imagine what that can afford! And, having the freedom to select as we will, that realization should fill us with a tremendous feeling of liberation, one that's open to all kinds of possibilities for personal and creative fulfillment.

But, because we have such an infinite range available to us, we must exercise our power of *choice* carefully. We must therefore scrutinize the *intents* we put forth, as well as the manifesting beliefs that result from them, for they will surely and inevitably yield the materializations they're destined to realize, for better or worse. Such conditions should thus encourage us to place emphasis on considerations like responsibility and consequences, because they're intrinsically wrapped up with whatever choices we make and intents we hold.

This Chapter's films urge us to judiciously examine our choices and intents, a process that's likely to prompt a host of significant, introspective questions: What exactly are our motivations behind our choices and intents? Should we always follow our impulses, even if the choices that stem from them ultimately produce outcomes with desirable but questionable results? Are we focusing our intents in the right direction, or are our efforts misplaced, either innocently or with malice? Is expediency of some sort factoring into our decisions, regardless of the consequences? Or are we making genuine choices that have the potential to fulfill us as creative beings in ways far more satisfying than we can possibly imagine? Regardless of the context in which we make our choices—be it our vocations, career opportunities, acts of altruism, political decisions or creative pursuits—these questions and their associated choices all come into play.

Choice and intent are essential birthrights. They're also precious and fragile gifts to ourselves. We should feel free to make use of them, but, like those cherished presents we open on Christmas morning, we must also handle them with the care and respect they deserve.

Minding Our Motivations

"Julie and Julia"
Year of Release: 2009
Cast: Meryl Streep, Amy Adams, Stanley Tucci,
Chris Messina, Linda Emond, Helen Carey,
Jane Lynch, Deborah Rush, Joan Juliet Buck,
Mary Lynn Rajskub, Frances Sternhagen,
Mary Kay Place (voice)
Director: Nora Ephron
Screenplay: Nora Ephron
Source Books: Julie Powell, Julie and Julia, and
Julia Child and Alex Prud'homme, My Life in France

Why do we do what we do? That's a question most of us have probably asked ourselves from time to time. In essence, it boils down to our motivations, the intents that drive us to create as conscious creation practitioners. To achieve authentic bliss in our lives, however, we must mind those motivations faithfully, following our true, belief-driven passions to achieve success. It's a principle that's illustrated effectively (albeit with varying degrees of engagement) in the comical biopic, "Julie and Julia."

The film presents two interwoven biographies. One is of the eccentric, iconoclastic doyenne of the kitchen, author and chef Julia Child (1912-2004) (Meryl Streep), whose books and television shows introduced the joys of French cooking to American audiences accustomed to the blandness of processed foods. The film chronicles Julia's initiation into the culinary world while living in Paris in the 1940s and '50s, followed by her initial forays into publishing, the means by which she exuberantly spread the gospel of good eating in unconventional, though always-heartfelt, ways.

The second story, set in 2002-03, is that of Julie Powell (Amy Adams), an aspiring, potential-laden New York writer stuck in what she sees as a dead-end job. Julie watches life passing her by while quietly (but enviously) witnessing her friends' successes. To alleviate the tedium and frustration of her daily routine, Julie seeks solace in one of her personal diversions, cooking. And, before long, it even provides her with a way to unlock her creative promise and escape her self-imposed funk: She decides to embark on a year-long odyssey of cooking her way through all the recipes in Julia Child's seminal cookbook, *Mastering the Art of French Cooking* (co-written with Simone Beck and Louisette Bertholle), with her experiences detailed in a daily blog that steadily develops quite a following.

The film thus parallels the experiences of these two women and how each achieved success in their own way by minding their motivations. It's interesting to see what motivations are actually at work in the two stories, too, for, while both deal with the joy of cooking (at least superficially), underneath the culinary exploits are two very different intents, and it's those core motivations that truly characterize the stories of the two protagonists.

For Julia, cooking was an outgrowth of her passion for eating, something for which she unapologetically acknowledged her love. Once enrolled in culinary school, she threw herself into this newfound pursuit with boundless enthusiasm and reckless abandon, the first step toward a life of numerous accomplishments and infinite self-satisfaction. Julie's underlying motivation, however, seemed to have more to do with keeping up with her friends' achievements than with an unconditional love of the kitchen. She thus comes across as being motivated more by a sense of competitive, ego-driven me-tooism than by an earnest passion for the gastronomic arts.

According to conscious creation principles, *all* options are equally valid when it comes to their expression in physical reality, and that would certainly be the case with these two stories. However, I ask you, which one would you rather watch on the screen for two hours? Julia's story is so much more engaging than Julie's that I was disappointed every time the film switched away from it. Seeing someone loving what they do, no matter what they might encounter through it (and heartily laughing off any letdowns that occur along the way), is much more compelling than watching someone trying to keep up with the Joneses (and who invariably reverts into a whiny brat whenever success eludes her). Julie's story may be intrinsically viable, but that doesn't mean it merits its own cinematic showcase.

As effective as both stories ultimately are in conveying their respective messages about minding one's motivations, viewing "Julie and Julia" is still like watching two films in one—one intriguing, the other tiresome. I could have watched Meryl Streep's phenomenal performance for hours; she captures Julia's persona so brilliantly that it's as if she were channeling her character's spirit, a portrayal that won her boatloads of accolades, a Golden Globe Award for best lead actress in a comedy and an Oscar nomination for best lead actress. Amy Adams, one of today's brightest young talents, does her best with what she has to work with, but, sadly, given her character's often-sniveling nature (and her co-star's towering portrayal), even her very capable performance is not enough to save her portion of the film. In addition to Streep's win at the Globes, "Julie and Julia" also received a nomination as best comedy picture.

It's unfortunate that this film suffers from such an inherent consistency problem, but here's my recommendation for how to view it: Savor Julia's story for every delicious morsel it serves up. And, while viewing Julie's story, remember that leftovers have their place, too.

Going with One's Gut

"The Ghost"
(originally titled "The Ghost Writer")
Year of Release: 2010
Cast: Ewan McGregor, Pierce Brosnan, Kim Cattrall,
Olivia Williams, James Belushi, Tim Preece, Timothy Hutton,
Tom Wilkinson, Jon Bernthal, Eli Wallach, Robert Pugh,
David Rintoul, Soogi Kang, Lee Hong Thay
Director: Roman Polanski
Screenplay: Robert Harris and Roman Polanski
Book: Robert Harris, The Ghost

We've all undoubtedly experienced situations in which we've had a powerful intuitive flash come our way that we've acknowledged and then promptly ignored, only to have it come back later to bite us you-know-where. That may be a little inconvenient or bothersome when the stakes are low, but, when they're high, it can mean the difference between life and death. Listening to one's gut, by paying attention to the intents it's attempting to convey, can prove crucial, as illustrated in the Roman Polanski thriller, "The Ghost."

As high-powered book publisher John Maddox (James Belushi) prepares to release the political memoir of former British Prime Minister Adam Lang (Pierce Brosnan), he foresees a hot seller for his company. There's just one problem, however: The manuscript sucks. What's more, one of Lang's longtime political aides, who had been entrusted with tweaking the text into readable form, has been found dead under mysterious circumstances. So, to bring the book up to industry standards, Maddox hires a ghost writer (Ewan McGregor) to apply the proper spit and polish. The hired gun has his reservations, mainly because political biographies are not his specialty and because the unusually tight deadline will make completing the job on time difficult. But, with the lure of a huge payday awaiting him for one month's effort, he ignores his gut and follows the advice of his agent (Jon Bernthal), who assures him that this is a good career move. Unfortunately, nothing could be further from the truth.

To carry out his mission, our hero leaves his London home and travels to the remote New England island of Martha's Vineyard, where Lang is residing between engagements while on a U.S. speaking tour. The idyllic maritime setting proves to be anything but, however; security is so tight, in fact, that it makes Ft. Knox look like easy pickings by comparison. What's more, our hero is seriously muzzled in terms of how he can go about his work. He can't help but wonder why such extreme precautions are necessary for the simple rewriting of a manuscript, but, as he becomes further involved in the process, he begins to see that there is much more going on than he ever imagined. He quickly finds himself embroiled in a web of intrigue centering on war crimes allegations against Lang, accusations that ultimately involve a lucrative defense contractor, a former British defense minister (Robert Pugh), a mysterious university professor (Tom Wilkinson), the father of a deceased soldier (David Rintoul) and even the former PM's wife (Olivia Williams).

By now, it would seem that following the intents prompted by one's gut would have been far more prudent after all.

So, if listening to our intuition is so important, why don't we do it more often? Most likely it's because its messages don't seem logical. They often run counter to what we would think of as rational or practical. And, because we tend to be so caught up in our intellect and the messages it provides, we consequently tend to summarily dismiss the insights our intuition affords us. That's a mistake; after all, if our intuition weren't meant to serve some kind of purpose, then why would we have it in the first place? It's an essential element in helping us shape our beliefs and, by extension, our reality. But, by ignoring our intuition, we leave ourselves vulnerable to the perils of *un*-conscious creation or creation by default, where we allow things to happen to us in seemingly random ways, often much to our shock or disappointment. Paying attention to our gut is thus not only important for us to make better choices and become more effective conscious creators; it's also sometimes essential to our very survival, as this film's protagonist clearly discovers for himself.

Going with our gut is also important when it comes to following our own sense of personal integrity and being truthful to our calling in life (for more on Integrity, see Chapter 6). This is apparent on a number of occasions in the film when our hero waxes philosophically and muses about the virtues of being "a real writer" rather than a hired gun cleanup man. It makes us think about the impact that comes from always lurking in the shadows of our true destiny—like a ghost—rather than stepping out fully formed into the brilliance of our own light of day. By failing to follow our intuition and our true intents, we hold ourselves back, never fully becoming who we can truly be, a circumstance that can pervade all aspects of our character—or even our very being. (And, if you doubt that, to illustrate this point, let's see if you can identify the ghost by name by the end of the picture.)

"The Ghost" is an excellent thriller from start to finish, tautly written and directed, with one of the most chillingly memorable closing shots I've ever seen in a movie. The storytelling style is reminiscent of the Polanski classic "Chinatown" (1974) in that the director reveals clues to solving the mystery slowly, piece by piece, tantalizing viewers with just enough information to intrigue them but without giving away the gist of the story until the very end. The film also features an array of fine performances, particularly by Brosnan, who turns in some of his best on-screen work here, and Williams, whose cold, calculating character is more ominous than any of us ever realizes.

Choices carry consequences in all we do and create for ourselves. Following our intuition and acting on the intents it engenders is sound advice for anyone under even the most mundane of circumstances, but it becomes positively essential when life's biggest issues are involved. "The Ghost" provides an excellent cautionary tale in that regard for those seeking to avoid the problems of conscious creation gone awry.

Remember, you've been warned ....

Explorations of Intent

"Please Give"
Year of Release: 2010
Cast: Catherine Keener, Oliver Platt, Rebecca Hall, Amanda Peet, Ann Guilbert, Sarah Steele, Lois Smith, Thomas Ian Nicholas, Josh Pais, Rebecca Budig
Director: Nicole Holofcener
Screenplay: Nicole Holofcener

Behind every consciously created materialization in our lives lies an intent. It's something that, at least superficially, takes on one appearance in our mind but often reveals itself outwardly as something entirely different, especially once the interactions of others become involved in its manifestation. As cryptic as that might sound, that premise provides the basis of the storyline of the unusual comedy-drama, "Please Give."

Kate (Catherine Keener) and Alex (Oliver Platt) run a trendy Manhattan furniture showroom that resells well-kept retro pieces acquired from estate sales. Their acquisition tactics are a bit questionable, though; they prey on the clueless, grieving survivors of deceased seniors who have no idea how much the merchandise is worth, snatching up the goods for a pittance and reselling them at exorbitant prices to upscale Gothamites. It's a practice that's earned them a pretty cushy existence, too, enough so that they and their teenage daughter, Abby (Sarah Steele), can live a comfortable city lifestyle. In fact, they've done well enough to purchase the apartment unit of their elderly, curmudgeonly next-door neighbor, Andra (Ann Guilbert), whose ailing health has put her near the top of the list in God's waiting room.

But the couple's ethics also carry a price, at least for Kate. She often feels guilty about the affluence she and her husband have amassed. To alleviate these feelings, Kate regularly engages in spontaneous acts of selflessness, such as handing out money to New York's homeless, a practice that seldom works out as intended (and never really gives her the relief or solace she seeks). Kate also feels uneasy each time she sees Andra, wondering what her real feelings are toward her elderly neighbor: Are they those of someone who genuinely cares about a senior citizen's well-being, or are they those of someone who can't wait for the old lady to kick off so she can snatch up her apartment? On top of all this, Kate often wonders what kind of example she and Alex are setting for Abby. All combined, these circumstances force Kate to come to terms with her innermost intentions, rightly or wrongly, for better or worse, and with or without the encumbrance of guilt.

But Kate's intentions aren't the only ones probed in this picture. We also see Andra's granddaughters, Rebecca (Rebecca Hall) and Mary (Amanda Peet), wrestling with their intents when it comes to caring, or not caring, respectively, for the welfare of their elder relation. Rebecca, in particular, also grapples with her intents underlying other issues, such as unraveling her feelings about grandma's neighbors and trying to understand the often-selfish ways of her self-absorbed sister. And, speaking of self-absorption, we see plenty of that with Alex and Abby as well; their self-centeredness is routinely expressed without hesitation, remorse, an awareness of what drives it or even an acknowledgement of its existence.

"Please Give" skillfully examines the subject of intent from a variety of angles and through a host of intricate interactions among characters. When all the threads of this colorful tapestry are interwoven, viewers are treated to a thoughtful exploration of the topic, one that provides much food for thought in helping us understand the choices behind our creations and the realities in which they arise. But what I like most about this film's narrative is its restraint in judging the characters' intentions. While there certainly are suggestions about which types of intentions might be preferable, the film is also careful not to slam those that might be considered less desirable. I believe that's because the creators of this picture recognize that, as human beings, we're all here to learn different life lessons and that *all* options are equally valid as part of that learning curve. The path to enlightenment has many stops along the way, and we need to visit them all to reach our ultimate destination.

Bearing that in mind, some of the intentions explored in this film might seem surprising. For instance, is Kate's altruism always the proper course for her to follow? Most of us would probably answer "yes" without a second thought. But what if her actions and intentions impede someone from learning a life lesson in something many of us would find unpalatable, like ingratitude, as is the case with Andra, for example? Kate's well-meaning intents in such a case might run counter to the experience Andra is attempting to obtain, and she thus shouldn't be surprised when her gestures of generosity and thoughtfulness are summarily rebuffed. Now, that's not to suggest that Kate's altruistic inclinations should be shelved; it just means that she needs to redirect her efforts to where they're genuinely most appreciated, which, ironically enough, may be toward those whom *she* believes are undeserving (there's a lesson in itself in that). Clearly, intentions have a wide range of expression, and sooner or later we need to experience them all, no matter how improbable or "wrong-headed" they might initially appear.

In true conscious creation fashion, the practice of examining our intentions once again brings us back to the question of getting clear with ourselves about our beliefs, the driving force behind our intents and, ultimately, the realities we choose to create. Nearly all the principals in this film are in need of doing that, and so, in that regard, the picture provides an in-depth look at how to go about that through the eyes of characters searching to understand themselves.

"Please Give" is an enjoyable piece of cinema, neither raucously funny nor tragically dramatic, but a nice way to spend a quiet afternoon watching a movie. The performances are all wonderful, but Guilbert's overlooked award-worthy portrayal is a real standout.

The writing is generally solid, though some elements of the picture seem oddly out of place, such as the opening credits sequence.

Intentions can seem like funny things at times, but the better we understand them, the better off we'll be in the long run. Greater insights in this area are bound to lead to better choices as we move forward in life. And, to that end, "Please Give" does a lot to help get us started down the right path.

Rogue Intents

"Game Change"
Year of Initial Broadcast: 2012
Cast: Julianne Moore, Woody Harrelson, Ed Harris,
Peter MacNicol, Jamey Sheridan, Sarah Paulson,
David Barry Gray, Austin Pendleton, Alex Hyde-White
Director: Jay Roach
Teleplay: Danny Strong
Book: John Heilemann and Mark Halperin,
Game Change: Obama and the Clintons,
McCain and Palin, and the Race of a Lifetime

Creating a reality that lives up to our hopes and expectations starts with the formation of beliefs and intents that infuse those hopes and expectations with honesty and integrity. However, when we allow those reality-generating elements to go astray, we can set ourselves up for disappointment and disillusionment. Such was apparently the case with the 2008 Republican presidential campaign, as pointedly portrayed in the made-for-cable docudrama, "Game Change."

When Senator John McCain (R-AZ) (Ed Harris) ran for president in 2008, he faced an uphill battle against his opponent, Senator Barack Obama (D-IL). In the run-up to the election, the young, articulate, charismatic Obama held moderate to sizable leads over the aging McCain in almost every demographic category of likely voters, and the Arizona senator was staring at certain defeat unless he took drastic steps to reinvigorate his campaign. McCain and his strategists decided that choosing a suitable running mate—one capable of shoring up his numbers in key demographic segments—would be the best way to bolster his efforts.

Chapter 4: Choice and Intent 91

While McCain favored the selection of an experienced peer politician, like Senator Joe Lieberman (I-CT) (Austin Pendleton), most of his preferred VP choices were not seen as being able to ignite enthusiasm among sought-after voters. So, to compensate, McCain's advisors, such as chief strategist Steve Schmidt (Woody Harrelson), encouraged their candidate to think outside the box and select a game-changing running mate, one who could effectively counter Obama's strengths. The campaign believed that a woman would make the best choice for the VP slot, and that decision ultimately led to the naming of a little-known governor from Alaska, Sarah Palin (R-AK) (Julianne Moore), as the other half of the Republican ticket.

The McCain campaign had high hopes for Palin. Her ability to whip up crowds, as in her acceptance speech at the GOP national convention, led the candidate and his advisors to believe that they were back in the race. However, those hopes were quickly dashed when it became apparent that the inexperienced Palin was in way over her head. Her lack of preparation for press interviews, for example, created PR nightmares. What's more, her unwillingness to cooperate with campaign staffers, her frequent withdrawals into isolation and her preoccupation with comparatively trivial issues, such as her post-nomination approval rating with Alaskan constituents, left the candidate and his handlers with a full plate of challenges to solve on an almost-daily basis. One staffer, Nicole Wallace (Sarah Paulson), reached such a level of frustration with Palin that she refused to work with her.

As the campaign wore on, McCain and company did their level best to hold things together. They took such drastic steps as teaching Palin how to memorize responses to likely questions, rather than allowing her to come up with answers on her own. However, these measures ultimately did more to bolster enthusiasm among *Palin's* most ardent followers rather than aid McCain's efforts. But, despite Palin's popularity among her core constituency, the hoped-for widespread appeal among voters at large never developed. Even many Republicans failed to rally around the VP candidate, with some seeing her as a liability to the ticket. And, in the end, McCain lost the election, the campaign's strategy having backfired.

From a conscious creation perspective, this result shouldn't have come as any surprise. The intent behind Palin's selection, as portrayed in the film, was based almost entirely on doing whatever it took to win the election, not necessarily selecting the candidate best qualified for the job. As hoped-for objectives failed to pan out, the campaign engaged in progressively more drastic measures to palatably package Palin for the voting public, with results that often went seriously awry. It was almost as if the campaign was trying to wedge the proverbial square peg into a round hole; McCain and company would have fared far better working with a round peg, but that wasn't possible because of the choice they made. The results of such a decision speak for themselves. They illustrate what happens when we practice *un*-conscious creation, where the law of attraction is employed to achieve a particular outcome without regard for the consequences.

It's interesting to note that, despite the picture's overarching narrative, the film successfully manages to portray Palin as more than a one-dimensional figure, accurately (and fairly) depicting the candidate's multidimensional nature, something we all share as conscious creators. Given how much the former VP candidate has been lampooned on TV shows like *Saturday Night Live* (several clips of which are featured in the picture), it would have been easy to cast Palin as a cartoonish, one-note character. However, "Game Change" resists that temptation, showing the protagonist as someone who is simultaneously ambitious yet out of her league, confident yet vulnerable, and a committed politician who also happens to be a devoted wife and mother. This balanced portrayal not only avoids an easy stereotype, but it also gives the film a level of credibility, both in terms of the believability of its narrative and its underlying metaphysics.

This is important considering some of the criticisms that have been leveled against the picture. Some have called "Game Change" nothing more than Democratic Party propaganda in light of its emphasis on Palin's and the McCain campaign's shortcomings, not to mention the fact that the film's teleplay focused on only one portion of the book on which the picture is based. While one could argue that these contentions have some merit, it's also significant to note that Nicole Wallace, the McCain campaign staffer who gave up on working with Palin, said in press reports that the picture was so uncannily on target that it made her squirm while watching it.

"Game Change" is an absolute knockout—smartly written, fair in its recitation of events, dramatic and funny, all at the same time. It also features terrific performances by Harrelson, Harris, Paulson and, especially, Moore, all of whom won well-deserved awards or nominations for their efforts. My only criticism is that this picture didn't play in theaters (it's that good). That said, however, HBO cable subscribers can still catch periodic re-broadcasts of the movie, while others can find it on DVD.

For its efforts, the film was rewarded with a boatload of accolades. It was nominated for 12 Primetime Emmy Awards in categories recognizing outstanding achievements in made-for-TV movies and miniseries, taking home five statues, including honors for best picture, best lead actress (Moore), best casting, best teleplay and best director. In addition, "Game Change" took home three Golden Globe Awards on five nominations, including best made-for-TV movie, best lead actress (Moore) and best supporting actor (Harris).

Clichéd though it may be, it always pays to be true to oneself, especially when invoking the powers of conscious creation. To do otherwise runs the risk of producing unpredictable, and often unsatisfactory, results, as "Game Change" so clearly illustrates. Going rogue may appear to have a certain appeal, but, where choices, intents and consequences are concerned, that allure may merit thorough scrutiny.

Conjuring Kismet

"Ruby Sparks"
*Year of Release: 2012
Cast: Paul Dano, Zoe Kazan, Chris Messina,
Elliott Gould, Annette Bening, Antonio Banderas,
Steve Coogan, Aasif Mandvi, Toni Trucks,
Deborah Ann Woll, Alia Shawkat
Directors: Jonathan Dayton and Valerie Faris
Screenplay: Zoe Kazan*

Wouldn't it be great to conjure up the ideal mate simply by writing one's beloved into being? Sounds easy enough, right? But, as with any consciously created manifestation, we must be careful about the choices we make to get the results we desire, a notion explored in the offbeat romantic comedy, "Ruby Sparks."

Novelist Calvin Weir-Fields (Paul Dano) suffers from severe writer's block. Having become a best-selling author at a tender age, the literary *wunderkind* has come under severe pressure to produce from his agent (Aasif Mandvi), from his readers and, perhaps most of all, from himself. It's become so serious, in fact, that he's sought the guidance of a psychiatrist, Dr. Rosenthal (Elliott Gould). But nothing seems to help, and the condition grows ever more frustrating with each passing day that he stares at the blank paper in his typewriter.

Inspiration finally arrives by way of an unlikely source—his dreams. Calvin begins having recurring nighttime encounters with a mystery woman who captivates his imagination, one whom he feels compelled to write about. Before long, Calvin builds a narrative around his dream girl, whom he's named Ruby Sparks. His passion for writing is thus reignited and subsequently soars. However, he also begins experiencing a variety of unusual, unexplained waking life anomalies, such as finding women's lingerie in his bedroom closet. But the biggest shock of all comes one day when he finds a stranger in his house—a personified version of his allegedly fictitious creation (Zoe Kazan).

Needless to say, Calvin is shocked to see his "character" come to life, even though Ruby seems perfectly comfortable being herself, oblivious to the notion that she's a manifestation of his imagination made flesh. Ruby exhibits all of the traits—including the personal history—that her creator has given her, and she seems intimately acquainted with the man who wrote her into being. It's all a bit much for Calvin, though, who seriously starts to question his sanity—that is, until he becomes aware that others can see Ruby, too. He's at last convinced that she's indeed real.

But now what? Since he created her, where does he go from here? And, perhaps most importantly, should he tell her who she really is?

Calvin soon realizes that, whenever he writes anything new about Ruby's character, her physical doppelganger begins exhibiting the same behavior. It thus dawns on him that he can make her do *anything* he wants, a quality that initially seems tantalizing but that quickly proves to be a challenge to manage, raising a whole host of questions he's ill-prepared to handle. (Comparatively speaking, writer's block suddenly doesn't seem so bad.)

Despite the film's seemingly lightweight storyline, "Ruby Sparks" is anything but frothy fluff; rather, it's a thoughtful meditation on conscious creation practice, particularly the power of choice we employ as part of it. Through Calvin's exploits, we see that the law of attraction is an all-inclusive process that carries with it tremendously potent power. With that power, however, comes a need to act responsibly, for *we* are the driving forces in it and what we ultimately draw to ourselves. And, because of that, we must be careful how we proceed with it, for we might easily end up with what appear to be "unintended" results, outcomes that arise from acts of either *un-conscious* or *semi-conscious* creation.

To make the process work, it's incumbent upon us to understand and acknowledge that the power of creation originates *from within us*, from the beliefs and intents we hold and the choices we make in materializing the reality we experience. In that regard, then, it's crucial that we know *what* we want to create, something that Calvin struggles with in almost every aspect of his life. His writer's block, for instance, stems from not knowing what to write about. Similarly, his personal life is so socially Spartan, virtually devoid of friends and fun, that he spends nearly all of his free time with his brother (Chris Messina) and his dog, Scottie. He has trouble not only managing his creations but even *conceptualizing* them in the first place, seemingly letting them unfold on their own, by default.

So, in light of the foregoing, is it any wonder that Calvin has difficulty with his romantic life and the manifested object of his desire? Perhaps that's because, like most other facets of his life, it's an area in which he has little experience, as an encounter with his one and only ex-girlfriend (Deborah Ann Woll) reveals. Through that "chance" meeting, we learn that he didn't have a good handle on what he was doing or what he wanted out of their relationship, a pattern that, sadly, has carried over into his romance with Ruby, despite the supposedly desired attributes he imbues her with. He consults others, such as his counselor, his brother, his mother (Annette Bening) and his mother's boyfriend (Antonio Banderas), about how to proceed, but their suggestions don't inspire him, so the ball just gets thrown back in his own lap. But, then, that shouldn't really come as any surprise, since creating *his* reality is *his* business (just as it is with each of us), and that's where the responsibility for making it work inherently lies.

Calvin's struggles in this regard shed significant light on the concept of free will, one of our most important birthrights. For his part, Calvin has been squandering his personal stockpile of this metaphysical capital, choosing, for whatever reason, to allow most of his life to unfurl without much personal input or apparent purpose. And, because of his lack of experience in this part of his life, he's unprepared for how to wield this power when he finally becomes aware of it (such as through his materialization of Ruby). He's like a kid with a new toy, trying it out to see what it can do and not always playing nicely with it, as becomes readily apparent in one rather unsettling scene in which he uses the process to manipulate Ruby as if she were a puppet come to life. Learning how to employ free will effectively, justly and responsibly is a difficult lesson for Calvin (especially when it comes to using it to *create* rather than *control*), but it's one he must master if he ever hopes to have happiness and contentment in his romantic dealings, his literary calling and his life in general.

This is not to suggest that "Ruby Sparks" is oppressively heavy or unduly serious; far from it. There are lots of great laughs in this film, reminiscent of those found in the delightful comedy "Stranger Than Fiction" (2006), and they effectively reinforce the movie's more substantive underlying themes. And, despite a somewhat slow opening half-hour, the picture quickly takes off and pulls in viewers, leading them through a thoughtful and entertaining narrative. Dano and Kazan are terrific in the lead roles, effectively fleshing out their characters and sharing a great chemistry as the seemingly mismatched lovers.

The conscious creation process can have its pitfalls when practiced with imprecision, indifference or willful carelessness. But, by employing it genuinely, with clear intent, the results can be miraculous. Calvin comes to realize this for himself when he observes that falling in love is like an act of magic, but it's one that results from deliberate choice and not random chance. Such is the kind of true beauty that can arise from the power of creation.

5

FEAR AND COURAGE

What good is it to possess the power to create if we're afraid to make use of it? That's a key question for anyone who practices conscious creation. *Fear* stifles us needlessly, a self-imposed, self-limiting hindrance that causes our innate materialization capabilities to stifle and deteriorate. What a sad state of affairs it is for those of us who squander such an inherently tremendous skill.

Amassing the *courage* to conquer our fears is perhaps one of the most daunting challenges—and yet also one of the most rewarding triumphs—that we experience in the development of our law of attraction capabilities. It makes forward movement and personal growth possible, enabling us to experience unknown wonders beyond measure—provided we allow that to happen.

The impeding effects of fear can impinge on us in almost any creative endeavor we undertake. The films in this Chapter illustrate that notion and show us how we can move past it, whether we're seeking free creative expression in the wake of political oppression, life fulfillment in the face of physical disability, artistic freedom in the wake of critical scrutiny, survival under extraordinary conditions or the ability to articulate ourselves under personally intimidating circumstances. In each case, we're presented with heroic figures, great and small, who have the courage to act on their convictions and forge ahead toward the satisfaction that comes with successful accomplishment.

As I have often written, those who stay locked in fear stay locked in place. This flies in the face of everything that conscious creation stands for, so the sooner we learn and act upon this teaching, the sooner we'll move toward the fulfillment that we were each born to experience.

The Courage To Create

"Mao's Last Dancer"
Year of Release: 2010
Cast: Chi Cao, Bruce Greenwood, Kyle MacLachlan,
Joan Chen, Shuang Bao Wang, Wen Bin Huang,
Chengwu Guo, Amanda Schull, Ferdinand Hoang,
Camilla Vergotis, Su Zhang, Gang Jiao, Xiu Qing Yue,
Steven Heathcote, Madeleine Eastoe, Penne Hackforth-Jones,
Aden Young, Suzie Steen, Chris Kirby, Jack Thompson
Director: Bruce Beresford
Screenplay: Jan Sardi
Book: Cunxin Li, Mao's Last Dancer

Our ability to create effectively depends greatly on having the freedom to do so—the freedom to choose what we want to manifest, the freedom to decide how we go about it and, perhaps most importantly, the freedom from limitations (self-imposed and otherwise) that could potentially block our path. All of these elements fuel our sense of personal power, contributing to the development of that all-important attribute, the *courage* to create, a capability that provides the focus of the captivating biopic, "Mao's Last Dancer."

The film tells the life story of world-famous Chinese ballet dancer Li Cunxin (Chi Cao). Selected by Communist Party officials at a tender young age to enroll in a prestigious ballet training program, the youthful Li (Wen Bin Huang) wasn't sure why he was chosen since he knew virtually nothing about the art form in which he was to be indoctrinated. In fact, he wasn't sure he even wanted to participate in the program, because it meant leaving his family in their rural village for life in Beijing. But Li's parents (Joan Chen, Shuang Bao Wang) saw this opportunity as a way for their son to escape his impoverished roots and to build a better life for himself. Of course, the officials who chose Li had more in mind than cultivating his dancing skills. With an aging but formidable Chairman

Mao still firmly in power and the opening up of China to the West still in its infancy, Li's development as a propaganda tool was just as crucial to the Party as any of the moves he would make on the stage.

Li struggled with his early training, a challenge that would persist for years. Abusive taskmaster instructors, like Teacher Gao (Gang Jiao), made life difficult for the sensitive young artist, hampering the growth and maturity of his abilities. But, thanks to the thoughtful and inspiring guidance of mentors like Teacher Chan (Su Zhang), the teenage Li (Chengwu Guo) eventually came into his own as a powerful performer with a dynamic stage presence, one clearly destined for greatness. However, those who made him also wanted to make sure that they got a proper political payoff from their investment, that his dancing would make an ideological statement equally powerful to its artistic merits.

As China began to play a more prominent role on the world stage in the early 1980s, its leadership was anxious to show off its assets in all their artistic and propagandist glory. Because of that, Li was chosen to participate in a student exchange program with the Houston Ballet. Before long, the dutiful, disciplined young star was off to America to study with the company's artistic director, Ben Stevenson (Bruce Greenwood). Little did anyone know what that would lead to.

Li arrived in America as a reserved, polite representative of his country and its ideology. And, just to make sure he toed the line, Li was strongly cautioned by the local Chinese consul (Ferdinand Hoang) to avoid the "decadent" temptations of the West, especially its women, who were not to be trusted. But, once Li got a taste of what life in the West was like, particularly the artistic freedom it afforded, his loyalties slowly began to shift. With the rapid ascendance of his star power and the blossoming of a new romance with an aspiring young ballerina (Amanda Schull), there was no going back—something Li would soon discover, both literally and figuratively.

Li initially sought an extension of his stay but was quickly turned down by Chinese officials, a ruling that prompted him to seek asylum—and that subsequently touched off an emotionally charged international incident with harsh consequences for all involved, including Li's family back in China. But, armed with the support of a sharp immigration lawyer (Kyle MacLachlan), a new marriage to a U.S. citizen to legally justify his stay and his personal commitment to the courage to create, Li fervently exercised his personal power to pursue his goal, despite the burdens involved.

Li's story is an excellent example of someone who's willing to take on the challenges associated with the pursuit of a dream of artistic freedom, arguably the noblest application of the conscious creation process, since its very aim is *to create*. In doing so, Li stares down his fears and overcomes the limitations that stand in his way, key objectives necessary for accomplishing such a goal. His experiences in America illustrate this most pointedly, but then that's because he was prepared for it, having endured similarly challenging conditions during his "training" in China, an education that clearly involved more than just learning his ballet routines. Some of Li's obstacles were startlingly difficult to overcome (and sometimes maddening to contemplate, given their self-imposed nature), but his struggle to beat them continually made him physically and emotionally stronger, enabling him to live up to the potential of which he was truly capable. Li's efforts thus illustrate his drive and desire to live out his value fulfillment, the conscious creation principle concerned with becoming one's truest, best self, an objective aimed at benefitting oneself and one's peers (and, in Li's case, the legions of ballet fans around the globe). Of his accomplishments one can genuinely say, "What an artist!"—and not just for his dance moves.

"Mao's Last Dancer" is a triumphant film, undoubtedly one of 2010's best releases, not only for its inspiring story, but also for its technical brilliance. The dance sequences are magnificent, easily in the same league as predecessor pictures like "The Turning Point" (1977). Its performances are solid across the board in both its on- and off-stage scenes, giving the film a wonderful sense of balance that could have easily been overshadowed by the sheer artistry of the ballet sequences (a pitfall that, thankfully, was avoided). The writing, which could readily have become trite and predictable, is crisp and free of cliché, quite a feat for a biopic, where a known storyline and a documented outcome provide the basis for the narrative.

Interestingly, the film is also an engaging period piece, depicting a 1970s version of China and a 1980s version of the U.S. that evoke feelings of nostalgia that simultaneously seem both foreign and yet strangely familiar. Given the many developments that have occurred in both cultures since then, it's hard to believe so much has changed in such a relatively short period of time. The portrayal of 1970s China in particular seems almost quaint with its ubiquitous bicycle riders and its self-important, revolution-themed ballet sequences, which, while faithfully depicted, come across today like exercises in tastefully restrained camp, a directorial coup for sure.

The courage to create is a powerful force that's eloquently depicted in this masterfully crafted film. Anyone seeking enlightenment in this vein should make a point to see it. Regardless of whether we're looking to improve our performance on the ballet stage or on the stage of life, the inspiration this picture provides will be sure to imbue us with the means to make our own masterpieces.

Stepping Into the Unknown

"The Intouchables"
Year of Release: 2012
Cast: François Cluzet, Omar Sy, Anne Le Ny, Audrey Fleurot,
Alba Gaïa Bellugi, Cyril Mendy, Thomas Solivéres,
Dorothée Brière Meritte, Clotilde Mollet, Absa Dialou Toure,
Grégoire Oestermann, Christian Ameri
Directors: Olivier Nakache and Eric Toledano
Screenplay: Olivier Nakache and Eric Toledano

Venturing into uncharted territory can be quite intimidating. Not knowing what to expect leaves us unsure of ourselves and feeling ill-equipped to respond or to determine how to plot a course of action. But, to get past some apprehensions, sometimes the only way to overcome them is to courageously step into the unknown, just as an unlikely duo discovers in the heartwarming, fact-based French comedy-drama, "The Intouchables."

When Philippe (François Cluzet), an affluent quadriplegic Parisian tragically crippled in a paragliding accident, seeks to hire a new caretaker, he's presented with an array of eminently qualified applicants. But, no matter how capable they come across on paper, Philippe seems unimpressed with all of them. In fact, strangely enough, the only candidate in whom he has any interest is Driss (Omar Sy), an unruly, untrained immigrant from Senegal with a criminal record who only showed up for the interview as a means to fulfill requirements for receiving government assistance benefits.

Despite Driss's lack of qualifications, Philippe is impressed with the unlikely applicant's unabashed moxie. In contrast to the other candidates, who wear their obsequious (and largely self-serving) attitudes on their sleeves, Driss naturally exhibits attributes to which Philippe is drawn—pragmatism, quiet confidence and a lust for the qualities that make life worth living. Philippe's handlers (Anne Le Ny, Audrey Fleurot, Grégoire Oestermann) are concerned when he hires Driss, given his lack of skills and his checkered past. But Philippe justifies his courageous decision by saying that he believes his new caretaker will give him what he wants most—no pity.

The unlikely duo gets off to a rocky start, but Philippe and Driss quickly develop a bond that gives rise to an unusual but remarkable, dynamic friendship, one that transcends the employer-employee relationship. As time passes, Driss gives Philippe the thing he needs most—a reason to continue living, despite his condition. This renewed sense of purpose, in turn, makes it possible for Philippe to give Driss what he needs most—a life of fulfillment that would have otherwise eluded him, one that exceeds his dreams and expectations. This arrangement thus makes it possible for the caregiver to allow his patient to live life without fear and for the patient to enable his caregiver to courageously broaden his horizons. Everyone wins.

It's been said that, when life hands us lemons, we should make lemonade, and that's certainly true when we look at our lives from a conscious creation perspective (especially once we realize we created those lemons, for better or worse, in the first place). That can be difficult, given the bitterness of such metaphysical fruit. But, even if Philippe isn't clear about the reasons why he created his own personal citrus (in most instances like this, some type of life lesson is usually involved), he's certainly well aware of the need to squeeze out the juice as passionately as possible, and that's where his relationship with Driss comes in.

For instance, even if Philippe can no longer directly participate in all of the joys he once did, he quickly learns he can compensate for that with Driss's assistance, partaking either with special accommodation or through vicarious experience. Likewise, Driss, a kid of the streets, comes to see unexplored possibilities for himself that he previously never envisioned or even considered, thanks to Philippe's support and guidance. Who would have thought, for example, that someone who once openly mocked the art world would himself come to be an accomplished painter? In the end, it all depends on what one does with one's own lemons, especially when it comes to being willing to take chances.

Of course, reaching this point requires us to get in touch with ourselves. This may not be the easiest of undertakings, especially if we're afraid of what we might find. Nevertheless, we must all become our own "in touch-ables," learning how to access the inner thoughts, beliefs and intents that we draw upon to manifest the reality we experience. In particular, we need to get in touch with the inherent connections that exist among the various elements of our realities, seeing the ties that bind them, their relevance and what they ultimately might lead to. Would Philippe, for example, be able to enjoy the richness of his life were it not for Driss helping to show him a new way to live it? Similarly, would Driss have come to appreciate the blessings of his existence if Philippe hadn't seen the untapped potential residing within his unorthodox caretaker? In this context, the giver benefits from the receiver as much as the receiver benefits from the giver. Indeed, conscious creation connects *everything*, and the more we become cognizant of this, the more joy and contentment we'll be able to realize from our existence. (For more on Connection, see Chapter 8.)

None of this would have happened, however, were it not for each character being willing to move past whatever was holding them back. Making the decision to forge ahead proves less daunting than anticipated, too, demonstrating that the fear of taking action is often more unnerving than taking the action itself. Once committed to their respective courses of action, Philippe and Driss move forward confidently, relishing their new experiences and all they afford. Had they not been willing to proceed, they each would have missed out on a lot, arguably more than they ever could have imagined.

"The Intouchables" is a delightful movie, full of warmth and gentle humor but never losing sight of the circumstances out of which its narrative arises. It has an occasional tendency to veer off on tangents that don't always receive their just due, but, thankfully, no unresolved or seemingly inexplicable threads are left hanging. The leads turn in solid performances, and they have great chemistry both with one another and with supporting players. The cinematography shows off Paris well, and the diverse soundtrack provides a nice musical backdrop.

The movie has been something of a cultural sensation in its native France, initially becoming the nation's most-watched film in 2011 after only four weeks in theaters and eventually becoming the second most-viewed picture in French history. It's also received its share of accolades, including Omar Sy's win as best actor in the César Awards competition, the French equivalent of the Oscars, even edging out eventual Academy Award winner Jean Dujardin for "The Artist" (2011) in that same category. In addition, the picture was a Golden Globe nominee for best foreign language film.

It's ironic that someone who can't walk is so willing to take such bold steps. But, when faced with the alternative, those daring measures may prove less frightening than anticipated. We'd be wise to remember that, for fear, like any other state of mind, arises from what we believe, and such limiting thoughts can be dismissed as readily as they are conceived, as long as we *allow* such transformations. "The Intouchables" illustrates this effectively, unmistakably revealing the rewards that come from being willing to chart new ground.

Taking Chances

"Hitchcock"

Year of Release: 2012
Cast: Anthony Hopkins, Helen Mirren, Scarlett Johansson,
Danny Huston, Toni Collette, Michael Stuhlbarg,
Michael Wincott, Jessica Biel, James D'Arcy,
Richard Portnow, Ralph Macchio, Kurtwood Smith, Josh Yeo
Director: Sacha Gervasi
Screenplay: John J. McLaughlin
Book: Stephen Rebello,
Alfred Hitchcock and the Making of Psycho

It's always a joy to observe a master creator at work, no matter what endeavor is being pursued. The passion for producing one's heartfelt desires is something to behold, not only for the one ensconced in the creative process, but also for anyone fortunate enough just to watch. But the experience is that much more exhilarating when we witness the creator taking bold chances in plying his or her craft, as is the case in the engaging biopic, "Hitchcock."

In 1959, legendary film director Alfred Hitchcock (1899-1980) (Anthony Hopkins) was at the top of his game. Having just released "North by Northwest," yet another in a string of successful pictures, he was riding high in Hollywood. Or was he? The master of suspense had earned a well-deserved reputation for making thrillers that captivated viewers and lit up box offices. But, despite his impressive track record, some began raising questions about the filmmaker and his work. He had made so many movies like his most recent release that some were wondering whether his creativity had peaked. Some also suggested that his recent foray into television with his enormously popular series *Alfred Hitchcock Presents* had "cheapened" his image as an artist. So was the auteur truly a man at the pinnacle of his career? Or was he perched atop the crest of a wave that was about to come crashing down?

As for the director himself, in spite of his advancing age and faltering health, he believed he still had some untapped creativity in the tank. Nevertheless, he also recognized that perhaps his work was becoming a little stale, that maybe he had taken his singular style of suspense as far as it could go, that he had to plumb new territory if he really wanted to push the creative envelope. To address this, he believed he needed to tackle material that was uniquely fresh and unreservedly audacious. But he also knew he'd meet with studio resistance in taking on such a risky project, mainly because any of his prior films that attempted to chart new ground, such as "Vertigo" (1958), generally (and inexplicably) bombed at the box office.

No matter how formidable these circumstances were, though, Hitchcock refused to be deterred, pushing ahead to find the right story that would meet his criteria, and he found it in, of all places, a chilling, grisly novel titled *Psycho*, by Robert Bloch. The book, loosely based on true events, chronicled the gruesome exploits of serial killer Norman Bates, and it told a horrific tale—one that Hitchcock *knew* would make a terrific picture.

Needless to say, given the movie's grotesque subject matter (which represented new territory in the film industry at the time), production on "Psycho" (1960) met with resistance at every turn. Members of the media were aghast at the picture's premise when Hitchcock introduced it at a press conference that was itself a rather macabre affair. Paramount Pictures President Barney Balaban (Richard Portnow) refused to bankroll it. Production Code Administrator Geoffrey Shurlock (Kurtwood Smith), who oversaw film industry censorship issues, threatened to withhold approval of the movie's release certificate. Even Hitchcock's wife and fiercely loyal collaborator, Alma Reville (Helen Mirren), was uncharacteristically hesitant about supporting the project, viewing it as a sensationalist, sadistic exercise that was beneath his considerable talent, sarcastically suggesting that maybe he should produce it as a musical starring Doris Day.

Hitchcock disagreed. Criticisms and impediments notwithstanding, he courageously forged ahead, even going so far as to mortgage his home to raise money and fund the movie as an independent production, with the studio serving only as distributor. He cast actress Janet Leigh (Scarlett Johansson) as his leading lady and relative newcomer Anthony Perkins (James D'Arcy) as the troubled protagonist, along with Hollywood staple Vera Miles (Jessica Biel) in a supporting role. "Psycho" was a *huge* gamble financially, artistically and professionally, but, in the end, it was one that paid off handsomely, becoming the most successful film of Hitchcock's career.

So much for the detractors.

Regardless of what one might think about the subject matter of Hitchcock's films, one can't deny that he truly was a master of his genre. "Psycho" in particular, as gruesome as it was, broke cinematic ground in many ways, featuring unprecedented depictions of violent and suggestive content never before seen on screen. It was even the first American picture to show the highly controversial image of a flushing toilet (horrors!). But, for better or worse, "Psycho" went on to attain considerable acclaim, including the distinction of being named the top celluloid thriller of all time according to the American Film Institute.

Hitchcock's tremendous accomplishments, both in "Psycho" and in virtually all of his films, stemmed from his conscious creation proficiency. He believed so passionately in his work that the elements of his creations came together with seemingly effortless precision, just as *any* materialization birthed by an ardent conscious creator operating from a position of fearless, unfettered intent would inevitably manifest. And, because Hitchcock intuitively understood this, success naturally followed. Like a maestro conducting a symphony, he took control of the creative process and milked it for all it was worth, even down to his expert, perfectly timed manipulation of audience responses (wait until you see the sequence portraying Hitchcock's reaction to viewers seeing the film for the first time!).

Even when faced with challenges to overcome, Hitchcock was masterful at being able to attract workable solutions. For instance, when he searched for someone to adapt Bloch's novel for the screen, he "fortuitously" stumbled upon Joseph Stefano (Ralph Macchio), an aspiring script writer with his own share of self-avowed neuroses (and who better to flesh out a character like Norman Bates?). Similarly, in casting Anthony Perkins as the tortured protagonist, Hitchcock found the perfect actor for the part, especially when Perkins confided to the director that there were elements of his character that he could relate to personally. Such synchronicities, as ghoulish as they might be, are nevertheless indicative of a law of attraction practitioner operating in top form. When one moves forward courageously, the means of manifestation make themselves apparent.

Of course, the director's success as a conscious creator arose in large part from him being true to himself and not really caring what others thought about it, a quality that typified both his personal and professional lives. For example, he made little attempt to conceal his passions for excess and the unconventional, be it in his work, his love of food and drink, and his infatuation with blonde femme fatales. He embraced such obsessions, attitudes and behaviors, no matter how crass, self-serving or unusual they may have been perceived, even by his beloved Alma.

Most importantly, Hitchcock didn't let fear stand in his way. He had no reservation examining subjects that no one else would touch. On some level, he had to have believed, as conscious creation maintains, that *all* probabilities are capable of being expressed, including those that arise from "the dark side," a quality that he sincerely believed we each possess. Some of us would probably like to deny our shadow's existence, but Hitchcock wasn't afraid to acknowledge it or even to explore it, as he did unhesitatingly (albeit "benignly") through his films. In that regard, we should all be so forthright.

When in need of insight, Hitchcock readily drew upon the resources available to him, too, again no matter how unconventional they were. For example, when he sought inspiration during the filming of "Psycho," he would try to envision what the killer would do, occasionally even appearing to tap into the consciousness of Ed Gein (Michael Wincott), the real-life individual on whom Norman's character was based. The "advice" of this gruesome muse would invariably help to show him the way. Likewise, when shooting the infamous shower scene in "Psycho," Hitchcock was not getting the reaction he wanted out of his leading lady; he believed Janet Leigh was coming across too timidly for the imminent terror her character was facing, and the actress's repeated failure to live up to his expectations angered him. He became so frustrated at this that he assumed the reins of Bates's character and lunged ferociously at Leigh, his rage fueled by the anger he was harboring toward those who he thought were sabotaging his project, such as Balaban and Shurlock. Needless to say, *that* impulsive gesture got him the reaction he was looking for.

But what was perhaps most significant about Hitchcock's work as a filmmaker (and his proficiency as a conscious creator) was his enduring desire to innovate. As noted above, he believed he still had untapped creativity within him at a time when some were suggesting that he should hang things up. He proved through his choice of "Psycho" as a project, his inventiveness in filming the picture, his inspired marketing campaign for the movie and even his novel means of financing it (atypical at the time) that he was courageously willing to try the untried, pushing the envelope not only for himself, but also for his art form and his industry. His eagerness to boldly take things in such new directions is one of the hallmarks of conscious creation, aptly reflecting the idea that we and our creations are all in a constant state of becoming.

"Hitchcock" is a thoroughly enjoyable movie, fun in virtually every respect. It's a terrifically campy romp through the Hollywood of 1960, a well-made period piece reminiscent of movies like "My

Week with Marilyn" (2011), meticulous in all of its historical details. It also features ample laughs and superb performances by Hopkins, Golden Globe Award nominee Mirren and a fine supporting cast. The film's portrayal of Hitchcock's private life (particularly the strain in his relationship with Alma) doesn't work quite as well as its depiction of his professional and creative sides, but it doesn't take away from the picture's overall quality either. In addition to Mirren's Globe nod, the picture also received an Oscar nomination for best makeup.

Alfred Hitchcock truly was an original, a one-of-a-kind whose likes and works may be imitated but never duplicated (as the forgettable 1998 remake of "Psycho" clearly illustrates). His contributions to cinema, no matter how one sees them, were undeniably innovative, opening doors that were previously closed, even unenvisioned, thereby paving the way for the many successors who would follow. To that end, he lived out his value fulfillment, masterfully and with distinction. "Hitchcock" is a fitting tribute to the man and his art and to what we can all achieve when we fearlessly allow ourselves to be the master creators we were all born to be.

Beating the Odds

"The Impossible"
Year of Release: 2012
Cast: Naomi Watts, Ewan McGregor, Tom Holland,
Samuel Joslin, Oaklee Pendergast, Marta Etura,
Sönke Möhring, Geraldine Chaplin, Ploy Jindachote,
Johan Sundberg, Jan Roland Sundberg, La-Orng Thongruang,
Tor Klathaley, Douglas Johansson, Emilio Riccardi, Nicola Harrison
Director: J.A. Bayona
Screenplay: Sergio G. Sánchez
Story: María Belón

Under trying conditions, reconciling oneself to seemingly obvious inevitabilities might look like the only option available. But is it really? What if another choice were possible? And what would it take to materialize it? Those are just some of the questions addressed in the affecting, fact-based drama, "The Impossible."

It's December 2004, and the Bennett family is anxiously looking forward to a Christmas vacation in Thailand. Parents Henry (Ewan McGregor) and Maria (Naomi Watts) and their three children, Lucas (Tom Holland), Thomas (Samuel Joslin) and Simon (Oaklee Pendergast), are excited about their upcoming stay at a luxurious beach resort in Khao Lak. They arrive on Christmas Eve and enjoy a festive time together, a suitable prelude to a merry yuletide celebration the next morning. But, on December 26, things change drastically, in ways no one ever could have predicted.

While swimming and sunning at the resort's pool, the Bennetts begin hearing, and then feeling, a deafening rumble, one that causes them and all of the other foreign tourists to stop dead in their tracks. Moments later, the source of that thunderous roar becomes apparent—an enormous and horrific tsunami crashing over the nearby shoreline, inundating the resort and washing away everything—and everyone—in its path.

In the wake of the huge wave, Maria and Lucas get swept away but miraculously manage to find one another. They take shelter in the branches of a tall tree along with Daniel (Johan Sundberg), a terrified young boy separated from his family. With debris swirling about beneath them, they await help in the relative safety of the sturdy boughs. And help truly is needed given Maria's condition; as a physician, she's well aware of the severity of her injuries and the consequences of what will happen to her without treatment.

While Maria and Lucas struggle to save themselves, Henry, Thomas and Simon somehow manage to survive the inundation by taking refuge at what's left of the resort. They anxiously await word of what might have happened to their loved ones, but, with such widespread devastation and virtually nonexistent communication, they're essentially helpless to do anything but wait. The trio later becomes separated intentionally when Henry sends his sons to an evacuation camp, opting to stay behind and search for his wife and son, a painful decision for the young father, compounding the flood of anguish that's already washed over him.

Meanwhile, Maria's and Lucas's prayers for a rescue are answered when two local residents (La-Orng Thongruang, Tor Klathaley) shepherd them to the safety of a nearby hospital. Maria's condition is grave, but she insists that Lucas go help others while she awaits treatment. He leaves her bedside reluctantly, but he's rewarded for his Samaritan efforts by helping to reunite a Swedish tourist (Douglas Johansson) and his injured son (Emilio Riccardi). Upon returning to his mother's hospital bed, however, he finds her gone with no word of her whereabouts or condition. Yet another separation for the family thus makes an already-trying time even more arduous.

Will the Bennetts reunite? Or will they be forever separated? And what of Maria's condition? Will she survive? These are the seemingly insurmountable challenges posed to an unsuspecting family that started out on its trip merely hoping for a pleasant vacation. Some might even say that the odds of such a reunion are "impossible." But then who's to say the odds are always right?

We all know that we draw to ourselves a reality that's in line with our beliefs and intents. But why, one might ask, would anyone draw to himself events as horrendous as this?

In conscious creation terms, incidents that occur on such a grand scale as this are called *mass events*, happenings that are co-created collectively by all of its "participants." While the event may be viewed as a single occurrence, it's actually made up of countless individual events that all unfold under the same umbrella, their larger stage providing a "suitable" backdrop for all of them to play out, no matter how distinct they may be from one another. The particular beliefs underlying such individual events generally have to do with whatever specific lessons their creators need to learn. And, in the case of this film's protagonists, there are numerous teachings that each of them is able to experience as a result of their involvement in the unfolding of this tragedy.

For instance, while on the plane on their way to Thailand, virtually all of the Bennett family members express trepidation about various fears that each of them is dealing with. In all of these instances, however, these fears pale in comparison to what they'll come to face during the course of their respective ordeals. The wave, as unquestionably devastating as it was physically and emotionally, nevertheless provides them with an opportunity for addressing lessons related to fear. To be sure, one would like to hope that resorting to means as drastic as this shouldn't be necessary for creating suitable learning opportunities, but sometimes we must attract such extreme circumstances to us in order to do so, especially if the issues in question have gone unaddressed for an unduly long time.

Likewise, the individual tragedies that unfold in the course of this mass event also provide prime learning opportunities for concepts like compassion, a lesson of particular importance for Lucas. While Lucas may be the least fearful of the family members, it's due largely to his strong survival instinct, a quality that doesn't always make allowances for considerations like helping others. The tsunami changes that, however. For instance, in the midst of the turmoil of trying to help his injured mother survive, Maria tells Lucas that they must try to help Daniel, even if it's the last thing they do. Lucas is initially reluctant, but Maria's insistence compels him to aid the lost young boy. These conditions prompt Lucas to rewrite his beliefs regarding altruism, ultimately providing a rewarding experience for him and those touched by his actions.

The act of rewriting one's beliefs can pay benefits in "unexpected" ways, too. For example, by saving Daniel, Lucas and Maria are themselves then saved by the local residents who rescue them from the tree. They get back what they put out, the outside world thus mirroring back to them tangibly what they intangibly believe on the inside. Their efforts are thus recognized by their divine collaborator in a way not unlike that depicted in the heartwarming film "Pay It Forward" (2000). Payback, it seems, can be a blessing.

Coming to understand that this is how the Universe operates helps to deepen our awareness of several other significant law of attraction concepts. First, it strengthens our belief in the notion that everything is inherently connected. It's truly amazing to see how one mass event can include all of the links integral to the manifestation of so many diverse individual scenarios. Even seemingly "unrelated" influences carry intrinsic connections. If you doubt that, consider where the earthquake occurred that caused the tsunami; who would have thought that an event transpiring hundreds of miles away could wreak havoc in such a distant locale? But the connectedness of the Universe binds all things, no matter how seemingly remote or disparate, which is why we should be cognizant of this notion in the beliefs we form and the existence we seek to create. The Bennetts come to see this for themselves, too, and in countless ways.

But, perhaps even more significantly, this film makes the case for having *faith*. No matter how utterly improbable things may seem, truly "miraculous" events can occur, even in the face of the unlikeliest of odds, provided that one *believes* they're possible. Even when things are at their darkest, the Bennetts never lose hope in finding one another. By fearlessly holding on to that belief and paying attention to the synchronicities that steer them in the right direction, a family separated by tragedy has an opportunity to come together once again, emerging from the ordeal stronger than ever.

Given the nature of a picture like this, it's not too difficult to predict the outcome, even from the very beginning. Thus the trick in making a story like this compelling is the means by which the filmmaker gets the audience to the conclusion. But, because of the movie's inspirational narrative, as well as its comparably uplifting trailer, I must admit to having had some reservations going in. I was concerned that the film might easily be sappy and overly sentimental, riddled with clichés and manipulative plot devices. I couldn't have been more wrong.

"The Impossible" is a truly heartfelt drama that *earns* the emotional reactions it evokes. In large part that's due to the fact that the filmmakers have not sugarcoated their depiction of the tsunami. While the picture never descends to the level of being gratuitous, it nevertheless does not hesitate to show the tragedy and its effects in a frank, candid manner. When viewers see what the characters are up against, the responses induced are indeed genuine. This is due in part to the incredible re-creation of events, as well as to the stellar performances of McGregor and Watts, who deservedly earned Oscar and Golden Globe nominations as best lead actress.

Adversity can be a great teacher in many ways, as this film clearly shows. However, perhaps the greatest lesson it can teach us is that all need not be lost, even in the face of seemingly insurmountable circumstances. Indeed, "the impossible" need only be so if we allow it to be, and, when faced with such an outcome, the alternative might well seem preferable—as long as we believe it so.

Finding One's Voice

"The King's Speech"
Year of Release: 2010
Cast: Colin Firth, Geoffrey Rush, Helena Bonham Carter,
Derek Jacobi, Guy Pearce, Michael Gambon,
Claire Bloom, Jennifer Ehle, Freya Wilson,
Ramona Marquez, Eve Best, Timothy Spall,
Anthony Andrews, Roger Parrott
Director: Tom Hooper
Screenplay: David Seidler

The journey to find ourselves nearly always involves the search for our own voice, usually figuratively, but sometimes quite literally. It can be a terribly painful process, one that requires tremendous courage, stamina and fortitude. But the payoff that comes from successfully locating that often-elusive expression of ourselves can be beyond words. Such is the case of a reluctant, stammering monarch who is unexpectedly thrust into leading his nation during wartime in the compelling biopic, "The King's Speech."

England's King George VI (1895-1952) (Colin Firth) might best be described, to paraphrase Rudyard Kipling, as "the man who *wouldn't* be king." In fact, he often eschewed the public eye due to a debilitating stutter that seriously hampered his public speaking abilities. However, when his older brother, King Edward VIII (1894-1972) (Guy Pearce), abdicated the throne to marry the love of his life, twice-divorced American socialite Wallis Simpson (Eve Best), George was next in line to ascend the kingship, a prospect that, because of his condition, terrified him. But, if that weren't enough, he assumed his reign not long before England entered World War II, a distressing time when his country looked to its sovereign, ironically enough, for a voice of confidence and reassurance.

In the years before he became king, "Bertie" (George's nickname in royal circles, a derivation of his given name, Albert) had undergone countless forms of treatment for his stammer but to no avail. After many futile attempts at overcoming his condition, Bertie was ready to give up. But, thanks to the patient, persistent support and clandestine resourcefulness of his wife, Queen Elizabeth (who in later years would affectionately come to be known as the

Queen Mum) (1900-2002) (Helena Bonham Carter), the future king would enter into treatment with an unconventional speech therapist, Lionel Logue (Geoffrey Rush), an Australian transplant who brilliantly worked his magic on the hesitant heir to the throne.

Unlike Bertie's prior speech therapists, who focused exclusively on attempting to alter the mechanics of his speaking voice, Logue quite astutely searched for the psychological and emotional reasons underlying his condition. This was a tall order, however; coaxing a stiff upper-lipped royal to open up about his personal life to a commoner was like trying to pry open a bank vault with a paper clip. What's more, Lionel's capabilities and qualifications were called into question, particularly by perfunctory, brown-nosing insiders like Archbishop Cosmo Lang (Derek Jacobi), who saw the upstart outsider as an opportunistic interloper unworthy of his appointment. But, given how much Bertie wanted to overcome his linguistic challenges, and because Logue insisted that George play by his rules, the hesitant patient went along with his therapist's unusual techniques. In doing so, Logue forced the future king to face the fears driving his stutter, many of which stemmed from the stringent demands placed on him by his late father, King George V (1865-1936) (Michael Gambon), and the mercilessly cruel teasing that he experienced at the hands of others, including royal family members. It was a painful process for Bertie to undergo, but the effort paid off at a time when he—and his entire nation—needed it most.

"The King's Speech" effectively explores the fear factor, particularly in terms of how to overcome it. Had Bertie not been willing to make such a bold move, one can only imagine how he would have handled himself as king, especially at a time when his country desperately needed a strong leader. But, as difficult as taking this step had to have been, it was positively essential, since facing fears is crucial to develop the courage to change one's circumstances and live heroically.

In depicting how the king faced his fears, audiences are given a glimpse of how our outer world reflects the inner realm of our thoughts and beliefs. This becomes especially apparent when Lionel presses Bertie on revealing the reasons behind his stammering. The fear-based beliefs that the king had allowed to become stubbornly internalized rise to the surface, thereby revealing the source of his stutter; their subsequent internal rewriting, in turn, helped enable the outward alleviation of his condition.

In a similar vein, viewers also witness how Lionel and Bertie serve as mirrors of one another. For instance, even though Logue had achieved a reasonable degree of success as a speech therapist and elocution expert, his real passion was to appear on stage as a Shakespearean actor, a dream that nearly always resulted in disappointment. This is illustrated, quite ironically, in a scene when Lionel unsuccessfully auditions for the lead role in *Richard III*, the tragedy about another English king who, like George, is afflicted with a disability. The mirrored circumstances in this are anything but coincidental.

As this intensely personal story unfolds, viewers also watch a larger story play out, with George and Lionel serving as metaphors for bigger issues. For example, each character clearly symbolizes his social status, and their sometimes-incendiary interactions unabashedly reveal the polite but palpable disdain that frequently existed between their respective classes. Similarly, the often-tense relationship between Logue, an Australian, and Bertie, a British native son, effectively illustrates the prevailing arm's-length association between the homeland and the colonies. In both of these contexts, a lack of familiarity with one another—brought about by the fearfulness of crossing previously unbreached boundaries—keeps them apart at first. Fortunately, the clashes gradually give way to a new degree of understanding on many levels. With the dissolution of the animosity and uncertainty related to engaging in such a previously untried relationship, an amicable bond is forged, both on the micro level of the protagonists' interactions and on the macro levels of class and nationality. The experience ultimately gives rise to what would prove to be a life-long friendship and a new relationship between the crown and its subjects.

"The King's Speech" is a flat-out winner on many fronts. The acting is superb, the writing is crisp and witty, and the production values are all top shelf. It takes a story whose premise might ordinarily be seen as dry and uninteresting and elevates it to the level of a real crowd-pleaser, full of humor, warmth and emotion. And, for its efforts, the film was lavished with all kinds of recognition. The picture received 12 Oscar nominations, capturing four awards for best picture, best director, best original screenplay and best actor (Firth). Likewise, the film earned seven Golden Globe nominations, including recognition as best dramatic picture, best supporting actor and actress, best screenplay, best director, best musical score and best actor (for which it won).

The inspiration "The King's Speech" evokes is enough to stir the emotions of even the stodgiest of moviegoers. It captures the trials and triumphs of a courageous, soul-searching hero to overcome his adversity. And, in the end, Bertie's valiant efforts just might move you to tears—or leave you speechless.

6

INTEGRITY

It should go without saying that our most satisfying creations result from those that arise from genuinely honest intents, those that are launched into being by beliefs firmly rooted in *integrity*. While it's true that *all* of our materializations faithfully reflect the metaphysical sources from which they spring, some of them may prove less than fulfilling if the beliefs and intents that birth them are tinged with provisos or conditions that qualify them or detract from their sincerity.

As most of us are probably aware, a fudged outcome is rarely as rewarding as one that emerges without "blemishes" of any kind, which is why it's so important to imbue our creative intents with the highest degree of integrity that we're capable of mustering. This requires us to be brutally honest with ourselves, and it forces us to get real about any ways in which we might try to color our personal truths to achieve a desired outcome. This is especially crucial when we intuitively know that a coveted but insincere result will not serve us as optimally as one that's innately grounded in untainted truthfulness.

Those who create their realities by employing this principle often serve as heroic role models for the rest of us, and the protagonists in this Chapter's pictures—many of which are based on factual accounts—reflect that notion with supreme clarity. Regardless of the context of expression, this thinking rules the day in the lives of the characters, who include a passionate gay rights activist, a talented athlete competing under extraordinary circumstances, a religious leader with a crisis of conscience, a government operative attempting to perform her duties under trumped-up duress and an unlikely ambassador faced with a difficult choice that carries unimaginable consequences.

Honesty has long been regarded as the best policy, and those skilled in conscious creation know that to be a fact. To do less is to miss the mark—and to risk outcomes that fail to live up to their heartfelt potential.

A Visionary Hero

"Milk"
Year of Release: 2008
Cast: Sean Penn, Emile Hirsch, Josh Brolin, Diego Luna,
James Franco, Alison Pill, Denis O'Hare,
Lucas Grabeel, Victor Garber, Zvi Howard Rosenman
Director: Gus Van Sant
Screenplay: Dustin Lance Black

Heroes arise from every conceivable milieu. Some may seem like obvious candidates, while others are the unlikeliest of champions. But, no matter what backgrounds these noble souls may hail from, once they come into their own, they're forces to be reckoned with. Those who promote humanitarian objectives can be especially formidable, for they nearly always operate with a strong sense of integrity. Their ability to reshape their worlds is impressive, as is seen in what is undeniably one of the best biopics of recent years, "Milk."

This outstanding film tells the life story of Harvey Milk (1930-1978) (Sean Penn), a mild-mannered, discreet, somewhat unfocused gay New Yorker who moves to San Francisco with his lover, Scott (James Franco), in the early '70s in search of doing something constructive with his life. Little did he realize what would come of it.

Not long after opening a camera shop in San Francisco's Castro district, a once-conservative neighborhood that was quickly becoming home to the city's emerging gay population, Milk grew increasingly dissatisfied with the prejudice and injustice heaped upon his peers by everyone from local business owners to the police. But, rather than become indignant and embittered about these patently

Chapter 6: Integrity

discriminatory practices, Milk channeled his energy into politics, organizing his constituents into a voting bloc ready to exercise its power. For his efforts, Milk was elected to the San Francisco City Council as the first openly gay politician to hold major public office in the country.

But Milk's vision extended beyond the Bay Area. He looked outward across the nation, hoping to use his experience and that of his community to influence activities elsewhere. He was particularly troubled by initiatives launched to overturn gay rights ordinances in communities across the country, a movement spearheaded by former beauty queen Anita Bryant. To squelch the campaign, Milk ultimately brought the fight to California, an effort through which he was successful in stemming the tide on both the local and state level. His efforts gave a significant boost to the emerging gay rights movement, helping it to spread across the country in the years since. And it all came to pass simply because he sincerely believed in the justness of his cause—and refused to compromise his principles about it.

Milk's success arose in large part because of his tenacity, which was a direct outgrowth of his ample personal integrity. His willingness to openly and genuinely express his sexual identity, and his efforts to fight for the civil rights of his peers at a time when acceptance of such lifestyles was considerably harder to come by, helped to further a cause that has come a long way over the past 40 years. And to think it all resulted simply from Harvey Milk being true to himself. But, then, being oneself generally yields the most satisfying and most productive outcomes, regardless of the context in which one seeks to express oneself.

In pursuing these goals, Milk faced down his share of fears, including death threats, which he defiantly brushed off as evidence that he must have been successful in getting his message across. In this regard, Milk was every bit the embodiment of the hero one needs to be to become a truly adept conscious creator. But, as important as this quality was to his success, Milk was proficient at an even more important law of attraction skill—the ability to envision outcomes. He clearly saw what he wanted to achieve and believed passionately in the possibility of its fulfillment. And, when he most needed for those results to come to fruition, they did, without qualification. In effectively promoting such humanitarian goals, Milk left a legacy that raised the bar for us all, gay and straight alike.

Despite his success and defiance, however, Milk made enemies along the way, too, most notably fellow Councilman Dan White (1946-1985) (Josh Brolin). Frustrated at his inability to achieve his own goals, White eventually resigned from the Council but later regretted his decision. When his reinstatement was denied by Mayor George Moscone (1929-1978) (Victor Garber), White took out his anger on those he believed were most responsible for thwarting his efforts, Moscone and Milk, shooting and killing them both in San Francisco City Hall.

But Milk's impact did not die with his death. In the wake of his murder, 30,000 San Francisco residents marched on City Hall to hold a candlelight vigil. He became a symbol of the gay rights movement, inspiring countless initiatives at the state and local level across the country. A number of accounts of his life were produced, too, including the Oscar-winning documentary "The Times of Harvey Milk" (1984), as well as this award-winning film.

"Milk" is a top-notch picture from beginning to end. Penn's performance in the lead role is outstanding, as are the portrayals by Brolin as Milk's troubled nemesis and by Emile Hirsch as Milk's protégé, Cleve Jones. Credit screenwriter Dustin Lance Black with giving an excellent script to the superb ensemble cast and director Gus Van Sant for pulling it all together into a riveting package. The film won two Oscars, for Penn's lead actor performance (for which he also received a Golden Globe nod) and for best original screenplay, on eight nominations, including best picture, best director and Brolin's performance as best supporting actor.

The inspiration this film delivers is palpable. On one level, there's the inspiration of a champion leading the charge in a humanitarian cause. On another, there's the inspiration of a conscious creator practicing his art in full flower. But, no matter which perspective we choose to view this picture from, we can't help but be awed by the protagonist's passion, commitment and integrity and the tremendous sense of empowerment these qualities engender. And that in itself is both heroic and visionary.

'Express' Intent

"The Express"
(originally titled "The Express: The Ernie Davis Story")
Year of Release: 2008
Cast: Rob Brown, Dennis Quaid, Darrin Dewitt Henson,
Omar Benson Miller, Nelsan Ellis, Charles S. Dutton,
Justin Martin, Justin Jones, Nicole Beharie,
Aunjanue Ellis, Elizabeth Shivers, Saul Rubinek,
Chelcie Ross, Chadwick Boseman
Director: Gary Fleder
Screenplay: Charles Leavitt
Book: Robert Gallagher,
Ernie Davis: The Elmira Express

Honestly showing the world who we are and what we can do is the best way to give expression to our true selves, no matter what aspect of creation may be involved. This notion is often well-depicted in sports movies, where the hero has an opportunity to showcase his or her talents, with the protagonist's sense of personal and professional integrity on display for all to see. That effect is heightened when the accomplishments are achieved under extenuating circumstances, as is the case in "The Express."

This well-crafted biopic tells the short but glorious life story of Ernie Davis (1939-1963) (Rob Brown), "the Elmira Express," a charismatic, lightning fast halfback from upstate New York who went on to tremendous success in the football program at Syracuse University. Davis played a pivotal role in leading his team to the 1960 national collegiate championship through an undefeated regular season and a post-season victory in the Cotton Bowl, a game in which he was named MVP. Two years later, Davis would go on to win the prestigious Heisman Trophy as the most valuable player in all of college football, the first African-American so honored.

But Davis's accomplishments extended beyond the playing field. At a time when the country was still rife with racial prejudice and blatant segregation, Davis earned respect for himself without stooping to the crass, confrontational ways of those who tried to hold him back. He let his accomplishments on the field speak for themselves, all the while keeping sight of who he truly was as an individual off the field, and never allowing himself, in either venue, to engage in the kind of hateful, petty, close-minded attitudes relied on by his detractors. In doing so, he set an example not only as an athlete but also as a humanitarian, embodying principles we should all seek to emulate.

En route to achieving these accomplishments, we see Davis's law of attraction skills at work (even if he wasn't consciously aware that he was employing them). Beginning as early as childhood, we see through flashbacks how a young Ernie (Justin Martin) drew upon the power of belief within himself to achieve such goals as overcoming stuttering and developing outstanding skills as a runner. Later, upon entering college, we see Davis envisioning the goals he wishes to achieve as a football player—winning a national championship for Syracuse (which had never been done before) and the Heisman (which no African-American had ever received), objectives that indeed would become realized. Such outcomes are directly attributable to Davis's sense of integrity. By remaining true to himself and employing that principle in his conscious creation efforts, he accomplished much of what he set out to do.

Davis's achievements also show us what's capable of being attained through collective, and not just individual, efforts. His spirit of teamwork aptly illustrates his understanding of the significance of the connectedness of all things and the role it plays in effective *co-creation*, the manifestation of materializations through joint efforts. But his teamwork undertakings weren't limited to the gridiron. Through the example he set as someone intent on seeking to quietly promote equality for everyone, he brought an enlightened, humanitarian message to those most in need of hearing it. When Ernie won, everybody did, and in ways other than on the scoreboard.

Davis had plenty of mentors along the way, too, and he never shied away from availing himself of their wisdom. First there was his kindly grandfather Pops (Charles S. Dutton), who played a huge role in shaping young Ernie's upbringing. Then there was Jim Brown (Darrin Dewitt Henson), the NFL great who preceded Davis at Syracuse and who helped recruit his protégé to play at SU. But perhaps one of the biggest influences was Davis's coach, Ben Schwartzwalder (1909-1993) (Dennis Quaid), who ultimately learned as much from Davis as Davis would learn from him. The mentor role was one that suited Davis well, too; in addition to the influence he had on his coach, he was later instrumental in mentoring his protégé, Syracuse and NFL great Floyd Little (Chadwick Boseman).

Sadly, Davis's football accomplishments ended when his collegiate career was over. He was drafted by the NFL's Cleveland Browns, where he looked forward to sharing the backfield with his idol, Jim Brown. However, Davis was stricken with leukemia and died at age 23. Nevertheless, despite that fact, Davis's many accomplishments were so respected by the professional team he never played for that the jersey number that was to be assigned to him was retired without him ever having taken a snap of the ball.

"The Express" is a wonderful film on many levels—inspiring, touching and entertaining, all without being trite or overly sentimental. It's a great period piece and features a dynamite performance by Quaid, some of the best work he's ever done. But one of the things I like most about the picture is that it's a film one can enjoy *without* necessarily being a football fan. It's about people, and humanity, and, if there's nothing else Ernie taught us, it's that people count, and that's a wonderful "Express" intent if I've ever seen one.

On a personal note, and in the interest of full disclosure, I must say that I'm probably a bit partial about this film, given that I am myself a Syracuse graduate. Davis's playing days were over long before I attended, so I never got to witness the magic he worked on the field. But, when the film was released, I was proud to see his story finally make it to the big screen, given that almost 50 years had elapsed since he achieved his enviable accomplishments. Davis has sometimes been referred to as one of the greatest football players no one has ever heard of, but this film helped to change that, earning him the recognition he deserves for his achievements both on and off the field.

Challenging Spiritual Assumptions

"We Have a Pope" ("*Habemus Papam*")
Year of Release: 2012
Cast: Michel Piccoli, Nanni Moretti,
Margherita Buy, Jerzy Stuhr, Gianluca Gobbi
Director: Nanni Moretti
Screenplay: Nanni Moretti, Francesco Piccolo
and Federica Pontremoli

Many of us probably like to think we have a pretty good handle on our spiritual beliefs. But do we? What if we were faced with circumstances that caused us to question the nature of those supposedly rock-solid truths? How would we respond? Would we be true to ourselves, or would we squelch such impulses to save face? Such is the challenge faced by the protagonist in the Italian comedy-drama, "We Have a Pope" ("*Habemus Papam*").

Upon the passing of the Pope, the College of Cardinals convenes a Vatican conclave to select the new worldwide leader of the Roman Catholic Church. It's a solemn occasion (the Holy Father has just died, after all), but it's also one that's seemingly full of hope and promise with the selection of a new shepherd at hand. In light of that, outside observers might be tempted to think that it's an auspicious occasion, especially for those candidates who are considered leading contenders to ascend to the papacy. But, in this instance, when viewers are let in on the internal musings of the Cardinals, one finds them full of dread, praying fervently *not* to be selected by their peers. As a group of mostly stodgy old men, they're generally content with the status they've attained and have little interest in being saddled with the formidable responsibilities of managing one of the globe's largest religious institutions during the waning years of their lives.

Through several rounds of voting, no candidate receives a mandate. Speculation abounds in the press and in the assembled crowds in St. Peter's Square about what's transpiring, but no news is forthcoming from this secret proceeding. According to protocol, the Cardinals must conduct their work in strict privacy and remain sequestered until a new Pope is selected and introduced to the public.

Chapter 6: Integrity

Finally, after several attempts at making a selection, the Cardinals choose a successor, and he's not one of the favorites. A reserved, little-known member of the College, Cardinal Melville (Michel Piccoli), is chosen as the new leader of the Church, an unexpected development that takes everyone—including the soft-spoken Cardinal—by surprise.

With the new Pope selected, the Cardinals prepare to introduce him to the public. But, just before the new Pontiff is about to make his first appearance on the balcony above St. Peter's Square, he flees in panic, claiming he cannot carry out his responsibilities. He aimlessly wanders about the Vatican, desperately trying to figure out what to do. Meanwhile, the Vatican's handlers, especially its chief spokesperson (Jerzy Stuhr), frantically go into damage control mode to save face, saying that the Pope has secluded himself in his apartment to pray for guidance. It's an unprecedented situation for an institution that's accustomed to everything proceeding with clockwork precision.

To help the new Pope cope with his circumstances, the Vatican calls upon an eminent psychiatrist (Nanni Moretti) to offer counsel. He's of little help, though, because he's not allowed to conduct his therapy sessions in private, and the Pontiff is reluctant to open up about himself when encircled by a band of inquisitive Cardinals hanging on his every word. It also doesn't help that the counselor is an atheist, his background not having been vetted by the Pope's handlers before being called upon to assist the Holy Father. What's more, even though the counseling sessions don't work out, the good doctor is told that, due to the confidential nature of his assignment, he must remain sequestered inside the Vatican with all of the Cardinals until the new Pope has been officially introduced to the world. Anxiety thus begins to set in for both the new Pontiff and the Vatican staff.

With the crisis dragging on for days, the Pope's handlers decide to try a more radical strategy. They plan to smuggle the Pontiff out of the Vatican to see another psychiatrist (Margherita Buy)—who just happens to be the estranged wife of the counselor who tried treating him initially—hoping that getting him away from everything will put him more at ease, allowing him to engage in meaningful therapy sessions. The staff tells no one of the plan, informing the press and the increasingly anxious Cardinals that the Pope remains secluded in his apartment, continuing to pray for guidance.

Everything initially seems to go according to plan—that is, until the Pope decides to flee his handlers, escaping into the streets of Rome. He wanders about in anonymity, attempting to sort out his thoughts. Along the way he meets with an assortment of people who help him unravel his anxiety. He seems especially taken with a troupe of actors, who ultimately help him uncover the source of his trepidation. But, even with this question answered, he must still decide whether he wants to go back to the Vatican to assume the mantle that awaits him there, raising the all-important question, will he do it?

Challenging assumptions related to our spiritual beliefs can be daunting, to be sure. We often consider such truths as unquestionable givens. Yet there are times when we think we know what we want when, in fact, we don't. And, when circumstances arise that put such issues to the test, we're often ill-equipped to handle them. When matters of head and heart, intellect and intuition, thought and feeling, don't match up in spiritual matters, the result is often a crisis of faith.

Under these circumstances, at the very least, we may feel disoriented, and, at worst, we can experience a full-fledged meltdown. In such instances, fear is nearly always the first reaction, but, once that initial fright passes, we're still left with the conundrum of what to do. In many cases, we usually gravitate to one of two options: (1) we stay locked in place, keeping our beliefs at bay, desperately trying to maintain appearances and denying our true selves, or (2) we move forward and evolve, allowing our inner feelings to come into alignment with our outer reality, a truly liberating experience if ever there were one. All of the principals in this film must come to grips with this choice, but the most important concern for each of them is, what will they do?

This is where the importance of integrity becomes apparent. By genuinely listening to and following our intuitive inner voice, the one that guides us to certain actions (even if difficult or seemingly implausible), we can find our way clear. In fact, it just may be the *salvation* we seek to get us through the crisis at hand. The new Pope would serve himself well to follow this advice. He's obviously unprepared for his new calling, aware of the inherent disconnect between how he feels on the inside and how he's *supposed* to feel for the mission he's expected to carry out. He's unable to reconcile the discrepancy and doesn't know what to do about it. His wandering through the streets of Rome aptly reflects his internal soul-searching and his pursuit of an answer that ever seems to elude him.

Of course, the Pope isn't the only one who's conflicted. The other Cardinals, for example, are clearly torn at the film's outset when they desperately pray to God not to be selected to serve the institution that they supposedly so ardently represent. The psychiatrist has his own quandary, too, as becomes apparent when he, as an avowed atheist, quotes from the Bible to justify his contentions to his religious detractors.

The Pope's breakthrough comes when he encounters the acting troupe. At one point, he confesses that he had wanted to be an actor when he was younger but that he failed at it because he wasn't talented enough. So is it any wonder, then, that he feels fundamentally incapable of taking on the responsibility of leading an institution so concerned with keeping up appearances? He suspects he can't do that, because he's simply not that good an actor. He clearly had the insight to follow his instincts and hold fast to his integrity when he made that earlier decision, but will he do the same again this time? Or will he succumb to pressure to live up to his "responsibility" for sustaining an image that he believes he may be ill-prepared to adequately convey?

Keeping up appearances is indeed important to the Church, something that impacts not only the papacy but also everyone and everything the institution touches. In fact, the Vatican handlers are so desperate to convey the impression that everything is under control that they enlist one of the Swiss guards (Gianluca Gobbi) to take up residence in the Pope's apartment to periodically give onlookers a vague, veiled impression that the Pontiff is indeed secluded inside. (It's enough to make viewers—and the faithful—wonder what other kinds of appearances the Church might be trying to keep up as well.)

The Cardinals come to question their circumstances, too, thanks to the assistance of their involuntarily sequestered psychiatric companion, who unwittingly assumes the role of an impromptu activities director. To alleviate the frustration of enforced seclusion, the good doctor plays cards with his religious cohorts and even organizes an ecclesiastical volleyball tournament. The once-rigid Cardinals, who probably never would have thought of engaging in such uninhibited secular activities, relish their newfound freedom, experiencing more genuine fun than they likely have had in years. With the shackles of their self-imposed limitations removed, they allow their joy of living to shine through, something that emerges in stark contrast to the highly regimented lives they've been living for ages.

Of course, liberation need not always be quite so dramatic or deliberate in nature. Sometimes simple acts, like walking away from an intractable situation, may be the most effective response to one's circumstances. It may also have the greatest impact, too, provided its significance is recognized for what it truly is. (Now *that's* integrity.)

"We Have a Pope," a *Palme d'Or* nominee at the Cannes Film Festival, is a surprisingly substantive film on many levels. Its treatment of the subject matter is deftly handled, subtly yet effectively depicting the parallels between the Pope's personal struggles and those of an institution increasingly wrestling with its own identity, and it does so without ever becoming crass or taking cheap shots. It also features a lot of good humor, providing an effective counterbalance to the picture's more dramatic material. Admittedly, some of the jokes go on a little too long, but most are genuinely inspired. The writing and acting are crisp, too, even if the pacing is a bit uneven at times, particularly in the film's first 30 minutes. Overall, however, this is a very entertaining, thought-provoking film that's well worth a look.

Taking time to take stock of our core beliefs (especially those of a spiritual nature) can be a worthwhile practice, particularly if we've allowed outmoded, inflexible assumptions to take hold of us. Even if we decide not to change anything after such an exercise, at least it affords us the opportunity to reaffirm what we *do* believe and to boost the joy of living that such beliefs give rise to. No matter what we do, however, we'd help ourselves most by listening to our hearts and proceeding with a sense of integrity, for that inner truthfulness is what will ultimately set us free.

Hungering for the Truth

"Fair Game"
Year of Release: 2010
Cast: Naomi Watts, Sean Penn, Noah Emmerich,
Michael Kelly, David Andrews, Bruce McGill,
Liraz Charhi, Khaled Nabawy, Adam LeFevre,
Sam Shepard, Polly Holliday
Director: Doug Liman
Screenplay: Jez Butterworth and John-Henry Butterworth
Source Books: Joseph Wilson, The Politics of Truth: Inside
the Lies that Led to War and Betrayed My Wife's
CIA Identity: A Diplomat's Memoir,
and Valerie Plame Wilson, Fair Game: My Life as a Spy,
My Betrayal by the White House

What is truth? That's a question that philosophers, theologians and scientists have pondered without resolution for centuries. When that question is examined in a conscious creation context, definitive answers become even more elusive, for, if we're each responsible for manifesting what we experience, one could argue that truth is a *relative* matter, not a *universal* one (even if that goes against what most of us would like to think). That being the case, then, what we ultimately see as "truth" is something that comes down to the beliefs we each hold. And, if we wish to be clear about what that "truth" is, we had better approach that question from the standpoint of integrity. That notion provides a significant metaphysical undercurrent in the storyline of the fact-based political thriller, "Fair Game."

"Fair Game" recounts the back story of "Plamegate," an incident that captured national headlines during the administration of President George W. Bush. The affair centered on Valerie Plame (Naomi Watts), a covert CIA operative whose identity was publicly revealed—by name—in newspaper reports stemming from what were believed to be intentional leaks by high-ranking (though never definitively identified) administration officials. Those leaks were allegedly initiated in retribution for the actions of Plame's husband, former ambassador Joe Wilson (Sean Penn), who blew the whistle on the administration's faulty pre-war assessments of Iraq's WMD arsenals shortly after the 2003 U.S.-led invasion began.

In the run-up to the Iraq War, the Bush administration attempted to use trumped-up "facts" about Iraqi President Saddam Hussein's weapons capabilities, including the alleged acquisition of huge stockpiles of yellowcake uranium from the African nation of Niger to be used in nuclear weapons production, to justify its preemptive military actions. Wilson, who had firsthand knowledge that the administration's contentions were grossly exaggerated, brought the misinformation to light in a *New York Times* op-ed piece, "What I Didn't Find in Africa," an act that allegedly led to the leaks about his wife shortly thereafter. As a consequence, Wilson's reputation and his new business ventures were seriously harmed. But, even worse, Plame's cover was compromised, leaving her exposed and endangering the lives of her contacts in the field, including some who were in the process of gathering sensitive intelligence information on the ground inside Iraq at the time.

In addition to recounting the events that made headlines, "Fair Game" also shows the incident's impact on the family's home life. The film thus takes a very public news event and brings it down to a personal level, showing the struggles that the couple experienced as a result of the administration's hardball tactics and the incessant, biased press coverage that followed (much of which painted the couple as unpatriotic, at best, and traitors, at worst). Death threats, phone harassment and constant media scrutiny ensued, making everyday life impossible. Eventually, however, the incident prompted a grand jury investigation and government hearings at which Plame testified, bringing the whole ugly affair to light. While no one in government was officially indicted for leaking Plame's name, the probe did result in an investigation, and subsequent conviction, of Vice-presidential Chief of Staff Scooter Libby (David Andrews) on felony charges related to the incident.

As viewers watch the narrative unfold on screen, it's quite intriguing to see the role that beliefs play in the film's storyline, both from a theoretical standpoint and in relation to the particulars of the plot. As in everyday life, we're posed with choices on what beliefs we choose to adopt and which ones we opt to ignore. And, to get optimum results, we fare best when we approach such assessments from a standpoint of personal integrity.

For example, on the one hand, we witness intelligence-gathering insiders (including Plame) diligently working at attempting to develop accurate assessments of what was going on inside Iraq, based on what they thought to be reasonably reliable field information. From that, they sincerely came to believe that Saddam Hussein's weapons capabilities were far less menacing than initially thought. In going about their work, they simply did their jobs of collecting data and assessing it to arrive at conclusions based on the impressions they received. They operated from a sense of integrity in developing the beliefs they employed in making official recommendations to higher-ups.

By contrast, we simultaneously witness an administration hell-bent on going to war, pursuing a course of action that it was willing to justify by virtually any means, including the manipulation of data to formulate "beliefs" that allegedly supported its objective. It then unhesitatingly sold these contentions to the public (even if the underlying information didn't support their viability) to build support for these "facts" and the policies they spawned. Anyone who didn't buy in to this "official" view was suddenly demonized, including the intelligence experts who were charged with gathering the information to be used in formulating official policy in the first place. Since Wilson's actions ran counter to the official beliefs that everyone was supposed to accept without question, he and anyone closely associated with him (such as his wife) were suddenly "fair game" for ridicule, retribution and unfair scrutiny. The negative public reaction to their allegedly disloyal actions, in turn, lent more support to the administration's official stance, further strengthening the beliefs that gave rise to it—that is, until the supposed sources of the leaks were themselves revealed.

In both sides of this incident, the power driving their associated beliefs was palpable. That's important to recognize, not only here, but also in *any* situation we encounter, for the impact that results from that kind of power can be significant, as both of the foregoing scenarios illustrate. (For more on Power, see Chapter 7.)

Regardless of how one views this incident, the Plamegate affair (and its depiction here) nevertheless help to illustrate a significant conscious creation principle: Considering the power of our beliefs and the fallout that can materialize from them, it's vital that we gather and assess the input of our intellect and intuition carefully, thoughtfully and with integrity to develop *informed* beliefs. This is especially important when the stakes are high, and, given the magnitude of the stakes involved in matters as critical as war and peace, personal and professional reputations, and even one's peace of mind, it's easy to see why.

So how accurate is this film in depicting the events that transpired? That's hard to say, since movies such as this always bill themselves as "based on actual events," a disclaimer that provides some convenient wiggle room for invoking dramatic license. That issue is further compounded by the fact that I (and probably most viewers) neither know the principals involved nor have direct personal knowledge of the story's particulars. And, even if I had been closely acquainted with the situation, who's to say that I would have been able to discern the "real" truth of things; I'd only be able to assess matters based on beliefs developed from my own sense of personal integrity. That might be easier said than done, however, given that many of the characters in this film are involved in the murky world of intelligence gathering, a process often rife with intentional deception and misdirection. This is aptly illustrated by Plame's own chameleon-like ability to easily adopt fictitious personas and to convincingly pass herself off as a mild-mannered suburban housewife while all the time engaging in highly secretive activities, circumstances sure to affect whatever beliefs I (or anyone else) might have held about all this.

In the end, the degree to which one assumes that a picture like this is presenting an accurate portrayal of "the truth" ultimately depends on the beliefs one holds going in and subsequently forms while watching the movie. From where I stand, I believe it presents an accurate depiction of events (and does so quite well). But then that's just my opinion.

The protagonists in this film are depicted as integrity personified, particularly Wilson. He was *insistent* about making the truth known, not only because of the repercussions for his and his wife's reputations, but also because the fate of American democracy itself was on the line. Even when the going got tough, Wilson and Plame saw the need to stand their ground. There was simply too much at stake for them to do otherwise. And, in the end, we've all benefitted from their courage, conviction and integrity. We can only hope that anyone else under comparable circumstances will have the strength to do the same.

"Fair Game" is a gripping political thriller, as well as an excellent examination of how a married couple holds up under pressure, an unusual fusion of narratives but one that works well. Its script is clear and concise, especially in its presentation of the complicated political and intelligence-gathering maneuverings. But its real strength rests with its performances. Watts's portrayal of Plame was *easily* the best female lead of 2010, but, sadly (and inexplicably), she was overlooked for any kind of awards consideration. And, except for a Cannes Film Festival *Palme d'Or* nomination, the same was true of the picture itself, an outcome that I find very strange, to say the least.

Truth is something that we all must ultimately decide for ourselves, and this picture shows just how important it is for us to get things right with regard to it. But, when we create our reality with integrity and steadfastly stick to our guns about it, we surely come out ahead in the long run, no matter what trials and tribulations we may have to endure along the way. If we fail at this, however, we may one day find ourselves to be our own fair game.

Living in Harmony

"Avatar"
Year of Release: 2009
Cast: Sam Worthington, Zoë Saldana, Sigourney Weaver, Stephen Lang, Michelle Rodriguez, Giovanni Ribisi, Joel David Moore, Dileep Rao, CCH Pounder, Wes Studi, Laz Alonso
Director: James Cameron
Screenplay: James Cameron

Given the many challenges our planet faces today, it's becoming increasingly apparent that the only way we'll resolve them is if we all cooperate to find workable, mutually acceptable, enlightened solutions. If those solutions one day call for us to go off-world to find the means to make their implementation possible, we had better learn that lesson first, for, if our journeys connect us with the indigenous beings of such far-off planets, then the need for sincerity, integrity and cooperation will multiply exponentially. But, even if such an eventuality never comes to pass, the lesson it offers us is one we should take to heart in fashioning the reality of our own world, an idea skillfully depicted in the sci-fi fantasy, "Avatar."

When paraplegic Marine Jake Sully (Sam Worthington) has a chance to begin his life anew, he grabs it. He's offered an opportunity to work off-world on the lushly forested moon Pandora, where a mining consortium seeks to acquire the mineral unobtanium, a substance that promises to solve Earth's energy crisis. But getting this precious commodity isn't easy, because its richest concentrations are located in the homelands of the Na'vi, the moon's 10-foot-tall, blue-skinned native inhabitants. Like many indigenous people, they have a strong tie to their land, communing with it as one, so they protect it fiercely against the advances of the human marauders, much to the mining company's growing consternation.

This is where Jake comes in. He's part of an operation known as "the avatar program" in which hybrid beings created from a combination of human and Na'vi DNA are sent into the forest to interact as liaisons with the natives. Each avatar is linked to the consciousness of a human "driver" (like Jake), thereby making it possible for the avatars to engage the Na'vi with no physical harm to the humans directing their actions. Guiding Jake in his efforts are program director Dr. Grace Augustine (Sigourney Weaver), fellow driver Norm Spellman (Joel David Moore), researcher Max Patel (Dileep Rao) and pilot Trudy Chacon (Michelle Rodriguez). Together they seek to engage harmoniously with the Na'vi, while simultaneously making it possible for the mining operation to move forward with its objectives. It's a well-intentioned, delicately balanced diplomatic and anthropological mission, one approached with sincerity and integrity, at least on the part of the avatar team members.

But, despite such good intentions, the avatar program's progress is too slow for the mining company's administrator, Parker Selfridge (Giovanni Ribisi), and his army of mercenaries, led by Colonel Miles Quaritch (Stephen Lang). So, to help speed things along, Quaritch secretly promises Jake that, if he provides him with intelligence on how to infiltrate the Na'vi, he'll arrange for Jake to get an expensive (but effective) surgery to restore the use of his legs. It's an offer Jake finds hard to refuse.

All of that changes, however, when Jake engages the Na'vi through his avatar. While on a reconnaissance mission with his teammates, he becomes separated from them and must learn to deal with the natives one-on-one. Through his contact with the warrior princess Neytiri (Zoë Saldana), Jake learns the ways of this enlightened people and suddenly finds himself torn—which master will he serve? He'll ultimately need to choose, though, for the fates of Pandora—and two species—depend on his decision.

Jake's integrity is put to the test when he communes with the Na'vi. He knows he must cooperate with Quaritch if he ever hopes to get his restorative surgery, a consideration clearly driven by self-interest. But, after spending time with Pandora's indigenous people, Jake also comes to see that their way of life, with its focus on serving *everyone*, speaks to a higher calling, a consideration that he realizes is, at heart, more in line with his truest intents and his personal well-being. Even with that realization, though, Jake struggles with which voice to follow; how he ultimately proceeds will obviously depend on which one he listens to.

Struggling with one's integrity thus plays a central role in how the narrative of "Avatar" unfolds. But the film is rich in other metaphysical themes as well, all of which are delivered rather matter-of-factly, skillfully avoiding the pitfall of heavy-handedly brow-beating viewers in imparting its messages. In doing so, it draws inspiration from pictures as diverse as clash-of-cultures movies like "Dances with Wolves" (1990) and "At Play in the Fields of the Lord" (1991) to profit-at-all-costs films like "Aliens" (1986) (one of director James Cameron's earlier offerings) to any number of movies with environmental messages and even the morality plays of the "Star Wars" series.

The film also has much to say about important conscious creation principles, such as the intrinsic connectedness of one another (a notion beautifully depicted in a scene when Jake is officially welcomed into the Na'vi community) and of all things in nature (a concept that the humans in this film, and that most of us in the industrialized world at large, have largely lost sight of). (For more on Connection, see Chapter 8.) But, perhaps most importantly, viewers are regularly shown through the experience of the Na'vi how the world around them originates *from within* through their thoughts, beliefs and intents, just the way the law of attraction works for all of us. Again, this is where the concepts of integrity and harmony come into play, for they form the basis of how the Na'vi live their lives with one another and how they create the world in which they dwell.

These principles not only serve the Na'vi well, but they would also benefit their human neighbors if only they would pay attention to such enlightened teachings. And, ultimately, that message is just as much for *us* as it is for the earthlings depicted on screen. As we struggle with reshaping our own world, we would be wise to follow such guidance. In fact, so potent was the impact of this message that it contributed to the birth of a phenomenon that became known as "the 'Avatar' effect."

Not long after the picture's release, CNN and other news agencies reported that some of the film's viewers became depressed, even suicidal. Their reason? After witnessing the pristine forested world of Pandora and the enlightened culture of the Na'vi, they longed to interact with such wonders firsthand, not just through a vicarious cinematic experience. Viewers' inability to fundamentally engage with these characters and settings left them despondent, especially when they compared the on-screen paradise with the world of their everyday lives. Such reactions even spawned comment board threads on Internet movie fan pages with subjects like "Ways to cope with the depression of the dream of Pandora being intangible," as on the web site "Avatar Forums" (www.avatar-forums.com).

The foregoing helps to illustrate the powerful impact of this picture. If viewers came away from it upset about the state of their world compared to that of Pandora, then perhaps the way of life depicted on screen may be just inspirational enough to get them to do something about their real-world reality. As I blogged about this at the time of the picture's initial release, I suggested that, instead of lamenting that the film's magical world cannot be experienced firsthand, perhaps viewers could channel their energy into imagining what it would be like to transform *this* world to become more like it. Even though it may not be possible to take viewers to Pandora, it just may be possible to bring Pandora to viewers through the power of conscious creation, provided we employ the process on a concerted basis with stringent integrity.

If the world of "Avatar" has been such an inspiration that audiences long to experience it directly, then perhaps it's time we take steps to make that happen for real. All we need do is believe that it's possible. And, after all, isn't that what conscious creation is all about?

Having said that, though, I must add that, despite the film's many laudable thematic qualities, the picture is not without its shortcomings. For instance, its narrative is rather predictable, its characters are often one-dimensional, and its dialogue is at times a little trite and uninspired. But, given the mythic quality of the tale and the value of its attendant themes, it's easier to overlook such weaknesses here than they would be in a lesser movie.

What "Avatar" may lack in plotline originality it more than makes up for in artistic inventiveness. The film is visually stunning, with brilliant performance capture CGI special effects. Its breathtaking scenery and surreal landscapes resemble animated versions of Roger Dean album covers from the 1970s, taking viewers to otherworldly venues of resplendent beauty. The picture received three Oscars on nine nominations (including nods for best picture and best director) and two Golden Globes (for best director and best dramatic picture) on four nominations.

Living in harmony is a goal that has always seemed to elude us as a species. The time has come now to set aside excuses about our failure to effectively pursue this objective, and "Avatar" provides a plethora of reasons for why we should do so. Whether we seek to achieve the goal in our interactions with off-world beings or simply amongst ourselves on planet Earth, may we all come away from watching this picture with the inspired integrity and the genuine resolve we need to get the job done.

7

POWER

To those of us accustomed to dealing with the physical nature of reality, it seems almost counterintuitive that something as intangible as an idea or a belief could possess incredible *power*. Yet this unseen force is amazingly potent, providing the impetus behind the conscious creation process. It's entirely capable of manifesting tremendous wonders.

What's even more astonishing is that we each possess such power, even if we're unaware of it or doubt this notion's very plausibility. Nevertheless, we have the innate ability to wield it to create the existence that surrounds us (preferably to our liking).

In light of this, it should be obvious that managing this capability properly is a tremendous concern. It's truly a force to be reckoned with, one that carries an inherent responsibility to use it wisely. However, in the process of becoming accustomed to doing so, we're bound to "make mistakes" along the way as part of our learning curve, either by way of abusing the power, misdirecting it or giving it away, practices that ultimately neither serve us nor benefit the welfare of others.

The films in this Chapter examine the issue of our power from a variety of angles. One clearly demonstrates what happens when we willingly hand it over to others to manage it for us. Another chronicles the fallout that results when our beliefs become wrapped up in power struggles driven by conflicting intents. Others show the dangers of letting our power control us or what can occur when we lose control over its management. But, for all these illustrations of potential pitfalls, there's also a fine example of how we can get our power back and use it to our advantage.

In many ways, power is like a tool, one that, in the right hands, can be used to forge magnificent creations. But it's also an implement that, in the wrong hands, can be employed for purposes ranging from the mischievous to the unspeakable. We can only hope that we all come to know which set of hands we should place it in.

Conceding One's Power

"Never Let Me Go"
Year of Release: 2010
Cast: Carey Mulligan, Andrew Garfield, Keira Knightley, Charlotte Rampling, Isobel Meikle-Small, Charlie Rowe, Ella Purnell, Sally Hawkins, Hannah Sharp, Andrea Riseborough, Domhnall Gleeson
Director: Mark Romanek
Screenplay: Alex Garland
Book: Kazuo Ishiguro, Never Let Me Go

One of the primary aims of practicing conscious creation is to be able to use it to feel one's sense of personal power. Fewer things are more fulfilling than the satisfaction that comes from successfully putting that power to use through one's thoughts, beliefs and intents to manifest the reality one wishes to experience. By contrast, fewer things more readily evoke despair than the act of giving away that power, a point made all too apparent in the haunting drama, "Never Let Me Go."

Life seems blissfully idyllic at Britain's Hailsham boarding school. The happy-faced, apple-cheeked youngsters live what appear to be perfectly satisfying lives, even if those lives are obediently spent entirely within the confines of the school grounds out of fear of what lies beyond in the outside world (a behavior response carefully cultivated, presumably by the staff, through rumors of gruesome fates that befell former students who dared ignore the rules). But such obedience, and the unquestioning dependency on the school staff that results therefrom, is crucial to the upbringing of these children, for they're all being prepared for a very special purpose—one that they're not told about, however, until their education is nearly complete.

The story primarily follows the lives of three Hailsham students, Kathy (Isobel Meikle-Small), Tommy (Charlie Rowe) and Ruth (Ella Purnell), a seemingly inseparable trio of friends. They grapple with the evolution of their relationships with one another, as well as with the usual coming-of-age issues that teens typically go through. Yet, because of their oppressively micromanaged existence, their lack of worldly experience and their often-docile personalities, they generally lack the maturity or coping skills for dealing with such issues, many times choosing to defer their handling of them, even as they grow into young adulthood. And these everyday challenges become ever more difficult to reconcile once their elder selves learn about the nature of the special purpose for which they've been groomed. Integrating a new set of complex, potentially overwhelming circumstances into the lives of those ill-prepared for handling even the most basic aspects of daily life is the ordeal that the grown-up versions of Kathy (Carey Mulligan), Tommy (Andrew Garfield) and Ruth (Keira Knightley) must address as they embark upon their unsettling destiny.

If this summary sounds a bit cryptic, you're right. That's because telling more would give away too much of the plot. The special purpose that Hailsham's students are prepared for is actually revealed quite early on in the film, but divulging that here would, in my opinion, constitute a spoiler, and I'm not one to disclose such critical information. Let it suffice to say, however, that the special purpose is one that most of us would probably not want to face.

So, if the Hailsham students' destiny is so seemingly abhorrent, why would they create a reality of that nature for themselves in the first place? In part, on a purely theoretical basis, one could chalk it up to the premise that *all* probabilities are equally viable of manifestation through the law of attraction. But that assessment, as valid as it is, arguably might seem a little too cold, clinical or glib in this context, especially among those looking for a more meaningful answer. Which brings me to the other reason why Kathy, Tommy, Ruth and their peers may have created the existence they've chosen to experience—to serve as a cautionary tale on what can happen when we concede our personal power.

By embracing beliefs in which we abrogate our personal power, we turn ourselves into sheep. It thrusts us into a life of victimhood, making us easy pickings for those who would seek to take advantage of us. We lose our "response-ability" to cope with the conditions that manifest around us, and we end up leading lives that are most likely anything but satisfying. In many ways, it's the antithesis of what the conscious creation process strives for.

Is that a life worth living? I suppose it might be if one has never experienced such an existence and feels compelled to go through it just for the sake of having it. But, if one has already had such an experience, why repeat it? The Hailsham students' odyssey provides us with a stern warning about something we may wish to avoid—and that we might effectively be able to do, provided we hold on to our power to begin with.

"Never Let Me Go" definitely won't appeal to everyone. It's one of the saddest movies I've ever seen, and it's probably not the kind of picture you'd want to watch unless you're in the right mood for it. With that said, however, it's a well-crafted film on most fronts, with stellar performances by the actors who portray the three principals as both youngsters and adults and by Charlotte Rampling as Hailsham's steely head mistress, Miss Emily. The pacing drags a bit in the middle, with writing that meanders somewhat, but the payoff viewers get from the story as it progresses toward its completion is well worth enduring whatever slowness may get in the way beforehand. Beautiful cinematography and an emotive musical score by Rachel Portman effectively enhance the story as it unfolds on screen.

Viewers might easily come away unnerved by this picture, but, if that's the case, then the movie has done its job. It effectively shows the results of disempowerment and of the abandonment of our inherent ability to act as conscious creators. It also illustrates the pain involved in attempting to deal with our innate sense of humanity in a context where that quality is all but absent. But, then, such circumstances often occur when we concede our power—a lesson that I'd like to hope we can all dispense with as quickly as possible.

The Power of Belief

"The Social Network"
Year of Release: 2010
Cast: Jesse Eisenberg, Andrew Garfield, Justin Timberlake,
Armie Hammer, Max Minghella, Joseph Mazzello,
Rooney Mara, Brenda Song, Douglas Urbanski, David Selby
Director: David Fincher
Screenplay: Aaron Sorkin
Book: Ben Mezrich, The Accidental Billionaires

As any conscious creator knows, beliefs are powerful things. Sometimes they're so powerful that they seemingly take on a life of their own, especially when infused with the input of the mass consciousness, thereby enabling their associated creations to proliferate. The growth of the Internet in general, and of social networking media in particular, is one such example of this, a scenario explored in the docudrama, "The Social Network."

The film tells the alleged back story behind the formation of the social networking web site Facebook, as outlined in the book *The Accidental Billionaires*. The story chronicles how Harvard undergrad Mark Zuckerberg (Jesse Eisenberg), a fast-talking *wunderkind* computer tech, developed a social networking site for the University's student body, a resource that unified the school's existing patchwork of loosely connected but largely uncoordinated web sites. Aided by his peers Dustin Moskovitz (Joseph Mazzello), who handled the programming, and Eduardo Saverin (Andrew Garfield), who managed the money, Zuckerberg built his brainchild into a cyber-phenomenon that initially expanded from Harvard to other universities and then to the Internet at large, achieving astounding success that quickly made Zuckerberg the world's youngest billionaire.

However, Zuckerberg's success came at a price when he became embroiled in two nasty lawsuits. (The pretrial/settlement discussion proceedings from these suits actually carry much of the film's narrative, introducing viewers to the particulars through flashbacks and thus showing how Zuckerberg and his opponents got to this point.) One of the suits involved a claim that Zuckerberg stole the idea for Facebook from a trio of well-heeled classmates, identical twins

Cameron and Tyler Winklevoss (Armie Hammer) and Divya Narendra (Max Minghella). The other proceeding centered on a claim brought by Saverin, who argued that he was unfairly railroaded into a seriously devalued stake in the company by a group of new investors/partners who Zuckerberg courted with the aid of Napster founder Sean Parker (Justin Timberlake). According to the film, the claims were ultimately resolved through large settlement payouts (but, then, what's a few million bucks to the world's youngest billionaire?).

If that all sounds a little cynical, you're right, but, then, that attitude would be very much in line with much of this film's tone. Admittedly, I don't know any of the story's principals personally, nor can I vouch for the accuracy of the narrative as it's presented here, so I can't speak authoritatively to the story's level of authenticity. But that doesn't change the fact that the characters, as they're depicted in the film, are largely cynical, self-serving schemers. And, knowing that, it makes me want to ask, "Why should viewers care about all this?" After viewing the picture, part of me wanted to say, "*So what?*"

When I ran this picture's story through the filter of conscious creation principles, however, I could see where it had its merits. For starters, given the phenomenal growth of Facebook, the movie clearly illustrates the impact of the power of belief and the role it plays in the manifestation of consciously created materializations. It's quite obvious that, despite some of the founders' motives (some of which they may not have been fully aware of themselves at the time), the protagonists (especially Zuckerberg) were very passionate about the beliefs underlying their creation, an attitude that no doubt played a huge role in its success. Their clarity of thought, unimpeded by the hindrances of fear, doubt or contradiction, allowed their passion to blossom. And, when that passion was augmented by the energized supporting beliefs of the mass consciousness, the power of the initiating beliefs was significantly amplified, ultimately contributing to the creation's explosive growth. (That's quite a probability.)

The film is also remarkably insightful about another important conscious creation concept. On several occasions, Zuckerberg observes that his creation will never be finished, that it will continue to evolve as an intrinsic part of its nature (as anyone who has had to cope with the ever-changing nature of Facebook default settings can attest). These observations are sublime reflections of the notion that we're all in a constant state of becoming. Such metaphysical thinking, whether or not it was consciously in the minds of the founders at the time they were setting up Facebook, clearly played a large role in the creation's growth and success.

However, as laudable as these depictions of conscious creation principles are, the film also illustrates another of the philosophy's significant concepts (and one about which the on-screen characters, arguably, have much to learn). With the use of law of attraction power comes the *responsibility* to manage it effectively. While many Facebook users would likely applaud the founders for their creation, there are those (such as the parties to the lawsuits depicted in the film) who would probably beg to differ, calling into question the founders' ability to responsibly manage the power that went into materializing their manifestation. By blindly disregarding the fallout from their actions, the characters veer dangerously close to engaging in *un*-conscious creation or creation by default. (And this doesn't even begin to take into account the responsibility of power issue as it relates to the myriad privacy concerns that have been raised by many real-world Facebook users, a consideration *not* addressed in the film but that's nevertheless part of this phenomenon's larger, off-screen story.) In this regard, then, the picture offers viewers a cautionary tale about the responsibility of managing one's conscious creation power, for the consequences that flow out from ill-considered beliefs can be quite considerable indeed.

While the film is effective at depicting the aforementioned concepts, given the picture's overall tone, I still can't help but think there are better cinematic examples that viewers could draw upon for inspiration. Achieving success needn't be a descent into cynicism, an exercise in potentially questionable practices or an engagement with dubious characters as long as the underlying beliefs are sound and honorable. Indeed, alternate probabilities are as close at hand as a simple change in one's beliefs.

With all that said, however, I must also admit that "The Social Network" is a well-made movie. Aaron Sorkin's writing is razor sharp, despite occasional lapses into legalese and tech-speak, and the performances are excellent across the board, especially Eisenberg (who earned Golden Globe and Oscar nominations for best lead actor), Garfield (who garnered a Golden Globe nod for best supporting actor) and Timberlake. I only wish I could say I enjoyed the picture's story as much as I enjoyed its technical, artistic and thematic attributes.

The film won three Academy Awards, including best adapted screenplay, on eight nominations, including best picture and best director. It also captured four Golden Globe Awards, including best dramatic picture, best director and best screenplay, on six nominations.

The power of belief is an amazing force, as this film demonstrates. May we all come away from it aware of that power and of the responsibility that comes from using it wisely.

When Beliefs Become Addictions

"The Hurt Locker"
Year of Release: 2009
Cast: Jeremy Renner, Anthony Mackie, Brian Geraghty,
Guy Pearce, Christian Camargo, Ralph Fiennes,
David Morse, Christopher Sayegh, Evangeline Lilly
Director: Kathryn Bigelow
Screenplay: Mark Boal

Beliefs can be stubborn things at times, as most conscious creators can probably attest. They settle in, make themselves comfortable and often switch to autopilot, persistently manifesting the familiar elements of our personal realities and faithfully creating—and continually re-creating—the existences to which we've grown accustomed. It's an arrangement we probably take for granted, but it's also one that can be exceedingly difficult to alter, even if the desire to do so is strong, because of the power our beliefs wield in materializing the reality we experience. It can be a hellish state of affairs to find oneself in, particularly when our reality is in dire need of change. Such is the lot faced by the characters in the gritty war drama, "The Hurt Locker."

Every day is a matter of life and death—literally—for members of Bravo Company, an elite military unit on duty in Iraq responsible for defusing car bombs, IEDs and other opportunistic weapons. So it is a shock—but one that nevertheless comes with the territory—when the team's leader, Sgt. Matt Thompson (Guy Pearce), is killed in action. Surviving unit members Sgt. J.T. Sanborn (Anthony Mackie) and Spec. Owen Eldridge (Brian Geraghty) are subsequently assigned a new leader, Staff Sgt. William James (Jeremy Renner), and they welcome their new comrade with open arms. But Sanborn and Eldridge quickly grow uneasy about their new superior when they witness him taking jaw-droppingly careless risks in doing his job, cavalier to the point of recklessness.

With their time in Iraq growing short, Sanborn and Eldridge are most concerned about doing whatever it takes to get out of the country alive. For James, however, the mission is something else entirely; he sees it as a just, heroic cause. But, all seemingly well-intentioned nobility aside, the renegade leader fails to understand that his beliefs have also engaged him in a dangerous, quixotic undertaking, one driven by undercurrents of unchecked power, vanity and obsession that regularly puts the lives of himself and his fellow soldiers at risk. So, as the unit's tour of duty winds down, the question that looms increasingly large is, "Will they make it out alive?"

"The Hurt Locker" is an excellent exploration into the persistence, power and pervasiveness of beliefs. For whatever reason, the characters in this film have materialized, through the law of attraction, the war in which they find themselves, whether they're aware of it or not. And it's a creation that's all around them, everywhere they go, whether they're defusing a grenade hidden in a sack of garbage or investigating the after-effects of a tanker truck explosion in Baghdad's Green Zone. But it doesn't stop there; the same beliefs responsible for manifesting the omnipresent combat conditions carry over into other, more personal aspects of their realities, mimicking the larger conflict on a smaller scale. When Sanborn and Eldridge become leery of James's actions, for example, a war of wills breaks out amongst them, leading to the same sort of animosity and mistrust of one another that these battlefield comrades have of the enemy they're fighting. In fact, so pervasive is this belief-driven sense of combativeness that it even spills over into the soldiers' off-hours, when they engage in drunken gut-punching as a leisure time pursuit. One can't help but wonder where it will all finally end.

But, then, knowing how persistent and pervasive beliefs of almost *any* nature can be, should it come as any surprise that things would play out any differently when it comes to the beliefs responsible for creating warfare and everything that goes with it? As was illustrated in the conscious creation primer "What the #$*! Do We (K)now!?" (2004) and discussed in such writings as Bruce Lipton's *The Biology of Belief*, beliefs can become so entrenched in one's consciousness that they consequently become just as imbedded in one's biology, spawning the development of addictive characteristics. This, in turn, can result in compulsions and behaviors that are next to impossible to shut off, no matter how blatantly unhealthy they might be and no matter how clearly they're in need of change. Even stateside leave with loved ones, for instance, is not enough to keep one unit member from searching for a way to get his much-needed combat fix.

In light of this, it's easy to see why habits are hard to change. The more intense the source of the addiction, the harder the addiction cycle is to break, all because of the power driving our beliefs. Learning how to temper that power by bringing perspective to the conscious creation process is crucial; if we fail at this, we run the risk of letting the power of our beliefs consume us.

"The Hurt Locker" is an intense, gripping picture that's definitely not for the squeamish, but it's an excellent example of depicting what happens when our beliefs get out of control (or, more precisely, when we *allow* them to overpower us). This is made possible in part by the film's largely apolitical nature; by focusing on the characters and the job they're assigned to do, rather than letting the story become bogged down in the politics of the conflict, the movie gives us an insightful look into the minds of the protagonists, the creations their beliefs materialize and the effects those manifestations have upon them. From the standpoint of effective storytelling mechanics, this was a wise choice, regardless of how one views the politics and rationale of the Iraq War.

Admittedly, the movie's pacing is a bit slow at times, and some plotlines don't play out to completion as satisfactorily as they probably could have, but overall it is a fine piece of filmmaking in all other respects. Credit director Kathryn Bigelow and the fine ensemble cast of Renner, Mackie and Geraghty for bringing this story to life. In awards circles, the film won six Oscars on nine nominations, including awards for best picture, best director and best original screenplay and a best actor nomination for Renner, as well as three Globe Globe nods (for best dramatic picture, best director and best screenplay) but no awards.

The next time you're tempted to make light of the power, persistence and pervasiveness of beliefs, think about this picture. You just might find that changing your mind, although always possible, is sometimes not as easy as you might think.

The Responsibility of Power

"Watchmen"
Year of Release: 2009
Cast: Malin Akerman, Billy Crudup, Matthew Goode,
Jackie Earle Haley, Jeffrey Dean Morgan, Patrick Wilson,
Carla Gugino, Matt Frewer, Stephen McHattie,
Laura Mennell, Rob LaBelle, Robert Wisden
Director: Zack Snyder
Screenplay: David Hayter and Alex Tse
Graphic Novel Source: Alan Moore (author)
and Dave Gibbons (illustrator), Watchmen

As author and consciousness explorer Jane Roberts wrote in one of her seminal works, *The Nature of Personal Reality*, our beliefs contain enough power to send a rocket to the moon, an impressive capability, to say the least. Consequently, there's a tremendous responsibility incumbent upon each of us to manage that power properly so that it's not abused. It's a consideration that should be integral to every creation we seek to manifest, no matter how seemingly great or small. And it's that very theme that's central to the cinematic fantasy, "Watchmen."

The storyline of this sweeping spectacle is far too complicated to detail here, but, in a nutshell, it follows the exploits of the Watchmen, a group of superheroes who have been forced underground for what are seen as renegade vigilante activities. Having been looked upon approvingly by the public for decades, with their ranks even spawning a second generation of selfless Samaritans, these now-discredited (and unemployed) champions of society are subjected to dealing with their forced retirement. They spend most of their time engaged in a variety of lackluster personal and professional pursuits, their lives mere shadows of their past glories. But that all changes one night when they're reunited, albeit somewhat reluctantly, by a common goal—investigating the murder of one of their own, a grisly crime that gives them pause to ponder their own safety and a new purpose—tracking down whoever is responsible for their colleague's death. In doing so, however, they wind up uncovering the plan of a secret initiative whose staggering global ramifications are almost incomprehensible.

Set against the backdrop of an alternate version of 1985, the film takes viewers into a violent and crime-ridden world somewhat reminiscent of that in the sci-fi classic "Blade Runner" (1982). It's a bleak existence where the Cold War rages on relentlessly and where Richard Nixon is still President (talk about scary). At the same time, forces are feverishly at work to resolve the planet's many troubles and to prevent World War III from breaking out. But will they achieve their goals in time? And at what cost? What's more, are the seeming altruists behind these efforts everything they appear to be? All of these factors (and more) figure into our heroes' quest to solve the mystery of their colleague's demise, taking them—and us—on a harrowing journey fraught with countless perils, ever-present danger and endless wonder.

What I found most engaging about this film is its exploration of the management of our conscious creation power. The subject is eloquently addressed by one of the Watchmen, Dr. Manhattan (Billy Crudup), a former scientist who, as a result of an experiment gone terribly awry, has become the embodiment of a quantum being, one who can manipulate matter on a whim and experience virtually any probable existence he wants in an instant. Despite the stupendous marvels such vast powers make possible, however, he struggles with them, for, at his core, he is attempting to manage these mind-boggling capabilities based on his much more limited experience as a human being with all of man's frailties and failings. Over time, though, he comes to terms with this metaphysical conundrum. He sees the potential for the abuse of such powers and tries to convey that message to his human counterparts, hoping that his words can spare them the anguish he's had to endure.

But will they listen? Or will they ignore his warning and use their power for self-serving ends, giving in to what he sees as man's inherent savagery? Based on many of the situations that unfold in the film, the good doctor would appear to have ample reason for being discouraged, especially when this question becomes an issue for his superhero peers. This is a potent message for a world seemingly gone mad, one that both characters—and viewers—would be wise to heed.

"Watchmen" is by no means a perfect movie. When it's on, it's brilliant. Its special effects are visually stunning, and its profound metaphysical insights are presented with remarkable clarity. It also has a superb soundtrack and loads of tongue-in-cheek humor. When it's off, however, the picture can be somewhat tedious. At a running time of 2:42, it could have benefitted from some judicious pruning of extraneous detail to make the film tighter all around. It's also gratuitously and grotesquely violent in a number of sequences, with some visuals that could make even the strong of stomach more than a little queasy at times (yours truly included). On the one hand, I question the need for the inclusion of such imagery. But, then, if you consider the premise postulated by Dr. Manhattan regarding man's inherent savagery, I suppose a case could be made for including such revolting displays to drive home his point (still, keep the barf bag handy if you're easily upset by such sights).

If you haven't already guessed, this is *not* a film for the kiddies! Even though this picture is based on comic book-style superhero characters, this movie is far different from this genre's comparatively tame counterparts. The film is rated R, though I must admit that I'm amazed it managed to evade the stronger NC-17 rating, due to its strong violence, pervasive adult language and frequent nudity (even if computer-generated in nature). Parents should strongly consider the suitability of this picture for younger viewers (no matter how much the little ones may beg, whimper or pout).

"Watchmen" packs a punch on many levels, but it does so most effectively when dealing with its central theme of managing our personal power responsibly. It's a message that's as relevant to our own outer world today as it is within the context of the film's alternate timeline. Indeed, this is one history lesson we'd all be well-served to learn from.

A Fable for Our Times

"Alice in Wonderland"
Year of Release: 2010
Cast: Mia Wasikowska, Johnny Depp, Helena Bonham Carter,
Anne Hathaway, Crispin Glover, Matt Lucas,
Stephen Fry (voice), Michael Sheen (voice), Alan Rickman (voice),
Barbara Windsor (voice), Paul Whitehouse (voice),
Timothy Spall (voice), Christopher Lee (voice),
Imelda Staunton (voice), Marton Csokas,
Lindsay Duncan, Mairi Ella Challen, Leo Bill,
Tim Pigott-Smith, Geraldine James, Jemma Powell,
John Hopkins, Frances de la Tour, Eleanor Gecks, Eleanor Tomlinson
Director: Tim Burton
Screenplay: Linda Woolverton
Source Books: Lewis Carroll, Alice's Adventures in Wonderland
and Through the Looking Glass

Remaking a cinematic classic is always a risky proposition, especially when it involves beloved characters who viewers feel they know like family. The ante gets upped further if that remake involves changing the characters or the story in unfamiliar ways, a move that can easily prompt audience alienation. So it's no small feat when a director is able to circumvent these potential pitfalls and pull things off successfully, as is the case with the latest edition of the time-honored favorite, "Alice in Wonderland."

Director Tim Burton's take on this epic childhood fantasy is every bit as captivating as the material on which the film is based, yet it plumbs territory of the title character's life never before explored. It also deals with themes that transcend the intended audience of its original source material.

As the movie opens, we briefly meet Alice as a child (Mairi Ella Challen), a bright young girl whose wildly imaginative dreams take her to a strange place with outlandish characters, including a talking rabbit in a waistcoat, a hookah-smoking blue caterpillar and a smiling cat with the ability to disappear. She's troubled by these vivid dreams, fearing her mind's "going 'round the bend." But Alice's adventurous, consoling father (Marton Csokas) assures her they're nothing to worry about, that they may even be a great source of unconventional inspiration—advice that proves valuable for what's to follow.

Flash ahead 13 years, when we meet Alice as a 20-year-old woman (Mia Wasikowska). She and her widowed mother (Lindsay Duncan) attend a high-brow garden party on a ritzy English estate, a social affair Alice approaches with an undefined but undeniable sense of uneasiness. Her fears are confirmed when she learns that the soirée is being thrown to announce her arranged betrothal—an agreement she knew nothing about—to an insipid young aristocrat (Leo Bill), a sheltered simp she can barely stand. Alice's impulse is to flee, and she gets that opportunity when she unexpectedly catches a glimpse of the dapper rabbit from her childhood dreams. She casts aside logic, social conventions and thoughts of hallucination and impulsively chases the fleet-footed creature through the garden to a hole at the base of a mighty tree, where she promptly falls in and descends to a magical land that's both peculiar yet eerily familiar.

Before long, Alice realizes where she is—the land of her long-ago sleepy time fantasies. Once reacquainted, she becomes immersed in an adventure with all her old companions, some of whom are nice, such as the rabbit (Michael Sheen), the caterpillar (Alan Rickman), the Cheshire Cat (Stephen Fry), the Tweedle twins (Matt Lucas), the Mad Hatter (Johnny Depp) and the White Queen (Anne Hathaway), and some of whom are positively vile, such as the Red Queen (Helena Bonham Carter), Stayne (Crispin Glover) and the Jabberwocky (Christopher Lee). Alice is ultimately called upon to save her friends from her foes, a task that requires her to rediscover her "muchness," her innate senses of feistiness, self-assuredness, independence, courage and personal power. These are qualities she once freely exhibited but has since apparently forgotten, attributes that will not only prove useful in helping her survive her Wonderland ordeals but also her aboveground real-world challenges.

The story's primary message—how to connect with our sense of inner strength, personal power and self-worth—is undoubtedly an important lesson for kids to learn. But, given that this version of the Alice saga involves our heroine *reconnecting* with those qualities, it's a lesson that's equally important for adults, especially those who feel they've lost their own "muchness" and want it back. Being able to draw upon our capacities for facing fears and courageously living our lives with personal integrity is essential not only for becoming proficient in conscious creation practices, but also for surviving everyday life, and this picture casts a brilliant light on these ideas for children and grown-ups alike. Tapping into such qualities is particularly critical when the odds are seemingly stacked against us, when our personal power and individual freedoms are on the line, as one might contend is very much the case in today's challenging social, political and economic climates (themes that are less than subtly portrayed in the film). So it's in all these myriad ways, then, that "Alice" truly is a rich, articulate fable for our times.

Seeing how our inner world is reflected outwardly—the basis of how conscious creation works—is another of the picture's strengths. The visual parallels between Alice's "real" life and her Wonderland existence are mirrored poetically, showing the many ways in which our internal thoughts and beliefs create the reality that surrounds us. We thus get to see what the looking glass *truly* reflects back to us, a concept depicted here with a great sense of fun, whimsy and playfulness, an approach we should all employ to get the most out of the law of attraction process.

I liked virtually everything about "Alice in Wonderland." It's technically brilliant in areas like art direction and special effects, and it features exceptional performances by many of the players, especially Bonham Carter, Depp and Hathaway, all of whom are perfectly cast. In fact, about the only thing I didn't like was the film's title, which may account for the dissatisfaction expressed by some viewers. Those expecting a faithful retelling of the original tale may be a little disappointed by the variations in the storyline, perhaps seeing the title as misleading. Calling the picture something like "The Further Adventures of Alice in Wonderland" may have been more accurate, but that shortcoming shouldn't deter audiences from thoroughly enjoying this story or this picture. The film earned two Oscars on three nominations and three Golden Globe nods, including best comedy picture and best comic lead actor (for Depp).

Parents of small children should exercise caution with this film if their tykes are on the sensitive side, as the picture can be rather intense at times (it is Tim Burton, after all). But, if nothing else, parents (and adults of all kinds) should see this movie *for themselves*, for this modern-day fable may be just the tonic needed to help them grow big and restore their own muchness, as well as to reconnect with the sense of magic that comes from everyday living in this Wonderland we call existence.

8

CONNECTION

When we look at a mosaic, do we typically see it as a collection of discrete, distinct tiles or as a uniform, complete whole? Chances are, most of us see a picture rather than its constituent parts, and we assume without hesitation that's how we're supposed to view it.

So why is it, then, that we often look upon our reality in the opposite manner, seeing it as a collection of individual components that just happen to be thrown together either seemingly at random or as intentionally manifested but nevertheless separate elements? Such outlooks are skewed, to say the least, for, if all of these elements occur within the same time and space, then they must have some kind of intrinsic commonality or *connection* applicable to them all.

Those who are well-schooled in metaphysical studies take it for granted that everything in the Universe is innately connected. Even those who are well-versed in science give tacit acknowledgment to this idea through their belief in the notion that everything is made up of the common elements we know as atoms.

Yet, despite such learned exceptions, many of us either lack a fundamental understanding of connection or possess a wavering awareness or appreciation of it. So, if we truly wish to get a better handle on how we create the reality we experience, it's incumbent upon us to realize that, when we practice conscious creation, we manifest the *totality* of our existence, not just parts of it and not just some of the time. In fact, those who fully understand the multidimensional nature of existence also realize that our beliefs and intents may well have linkages *across* the span of multiple dimensions and *across* the expanse of time, encompassing all probabilities, including those of which we may be presently unaware.

Now *that's* connection!

To illustrate these concepts, the movies in this Chapter skillfully depict connection in many ways. One shows how connections pervade the river of time. Others show how our connections bind all of us and all things on this beautiful little blue ball we call home. And others still offer helpful advice on how to recognize our connections and employ measures to make best use of them for the welfare of us all.

So, the next take you gaze upon a mosaic, think about how you're viewing it, and then take that skill and apply it to how you perceive the totality of your life. By doing so, you just might see it in a whole new light.

The Connectedness of All Things

"Cloud Atlas"
Year of Release: 2012
Cast: Tom Hanks, Halle Berry, Jim Broadbent,
Hugo Weaving, Susan Sarandon, Hugh Grant,
Jim Sturgess, James D'Arcy, Doona Bae,
Ben Whishaw, Xun Zhou, Keith David,
David Gyasi, Brody Nicholas Lee
Directors: Tom Tykwer, Andy Wachowski
and Lana Wachowski
Screenplay: Lana Wachowski, Tom Tykwer
and Andy Wachowski
Book: David Mitchell, Cloud Atlas

What do a 19th Century lawyer, a 20th Century composer, an investigative reporter, a frazzled book publishing executive, a genetically engineered human and a post-apocalyptic tribesman have in common? Surprisingly, plenty, their disparate realities full of unlikely and uncanny connections that link them to one another across the span of time. Those seemingly unrelated bonds are brought to life in the inspiring, innovatively engaging film, "Cloud Atlas."

"Cloud Atlas" is arguably one of the most unique and ambitious pictures to come out in a long time. It features six interwoven

CHAPTER 8: CONNECTION   159

plotlines, spanning several centuries, that, at first glance, come across like stories capable of standing on their own. Yet the incredible parallels that permeate them draw attention to a number of common threads, themes that connect the different narratives across time. These connections are further reinforced through the film's stellar writing, its deftly executed editing and the performances of its principal cast members, most of whom play multiple roles in the picture's various sequences, suggesting reincarnational, even karmic, links among the characters—and their eternal spirits—through the ages.

As the film opens, viewers are provided with setups for each of the following storylines:

* Adam Ewing (Jim Sturgess), a young lawyer working for his wealthy, slave-owning father-in-law (Hugo Weaving), seeks to curry favor with the old man by handling a business deal for him in the South Pacific's Chatham Islands in 1849. In doing so, Adam gets to see firsthand the deplorable treatment inflicted upon the slave population, a circumstance that quietly troubles him. Also, as one who's unaccustomed to the harsh conditions of this far-off land, he falls ill. He's placed under the care of Dr. Henry Goose (Tom Hanks), an ostensibly kind physician, but one whose treatments are questionable, to say the least. So, with his business concluded and his health failing, Adam sets sail for home. However, despite Dr. Goose's seemingly attentive care, Adam grows weaker with each passing day, and, before long, he finds himself on a journey that places his life and his fortunes at risk. His only aid comes from an unlikely source—Autua (David Gyasi), a stowaway slave for whom Adam secures freedom. But, given Adam's progressively dire condition, it's unclear whether he'll be able to survive the trip back to America. And, even if he does, his life is unlikely to be the same ever again.

* Robert Frobisher (Ben Whishaw) is one of the most talented—and most unknown—contemporary composers in 1930s England. His lack of notoriety is fueled, in part, by the "reputation" that dogs him; despite his efforts at maintaining discretion, word of Robert's sexual exploits with members of both genders has a way of leaking out. In fact, that reputation contributes to his decision to part company with the love of his

life, Rufus Sixsmith (James D'Arcy), an aspiring Cambridge physicist; he doesn't want to sully the good name of his companion, even if his own is tarnished. Besides, Robert has an opportunity to advance his career by relocating to Scotland to work as an amanuensis for a once-famous but aging composer, Vyvyan Ayrs (Jim Broadbent), who seeks to have his remaining pieces transcribed before his demise. Through his association with Ayrs, the young composer has a chance to birth his own material and to make new connections in the music world, as well as an opportunity to redeem himself. But will his senior associate allow that? And just how far is Robert willing to go to see his aspirations realized?

* Investigative reporter Luisa Rey (Halle Berry) is looking for *the* story that gives her that sought-after big break. Working as a journalist for a San Francisco alternative newspaper in 1973, she's assigned to report on a controversial nuclear power plant. She initially feels like she's being "handled" by the power company's spin masters, such as CEO Lloyd Hooks (Hugh Grant). However, through a series of seemingly improbable synchronicities, Luisa makes contact with several would-be whistleblowers—one of the plant's chief physicists, Rufus Sixsmith (remember him?), who has compiled potentially devastating information about the facility's reactor, and Dr. Isaac Sachs (Tom Hanks), one of Sixsmith's colleagues, who discreetly keeps his peer's findings secret. Will the damaging information be made public? Or will Luisa and her sources fall prey to the strong-arm silencing tactics of the power company's enforcer, Bill Smoke (Hugo Weaving)? The stakes are high for everyone involved—as well as the residents of the nearby Bay Area.

* Financially beleaguered publisher Timothy Cavendish (Jim Broadbent) unexpectedly becomes a hot commodity when one of his authors, gangster Dermot Hoggins (Tom Hanks), brutally kills an unflattering critic at a present-day high-profile book release party in London. Timothy is initially appalled by the tragic events, but he's quickly elated when the title becomes a surprise hit. Timothy's jubilation is short-lived, though, when Dermot's family puts the screws to him, demanding outlandishly

enormous royalty payments—in cash. Timothy seeks assistance from his wealthy older brother, Denholm (Hugh Grant), but he summarily dismisses his junior sibling's request due to his repeated failures to repay past debts. Denholm does offer his brother a place to go into hiding, however, a location where no one is likely to find him—ever.

* Life is very different in the high-tech, consumer-driven, totalitarian world of Korea's Neo Seoul in 2144. "Pure-blood" humans live lives of privilege, comfort and luxury, served dutifully by genetically engineered beings known as "fabricants." The cloned humans attend to the wants and needs of pure-bloods without question—most of the time. But, when one of the fabricants, Sonmi-451 (Doona Bae), gets out of line (assisted by underground resistance fighter Hae Joo Chang (Jim Sturgess), who knows the real reason behind the created beings' existence), life in Neo Seoul is disrupted, threatening the prevailing social order—and the future—of a world precariously hanging in the balance.

* One hundred winters after "The Fall," humanity has degenerated into an existence not unlike that found in the "Mad Max" movies. Even in a locale as supposedly idyllic as Hawaii, daily life is a challenge. Were it not for the occasional visits of "the Prescients," the world's last-remaining civilized beings, life would be even more difficult for the tribal people of this lush but now dangerous land. But the Prescients call on the locals for reasons other than providing humanitarian assistance; they're looking for something, and they need the natives' help in finding it. They get that chance when the local abbess (Susan Sarandon) is unable to treat the deathly ill niece of Zachry (Tom Hanks), one of the island's tribesmen. Meronym (Halle Berry), a Prescient healer, steps in to help, restoring the young woman's well-being. In exchange for Meronym's assistance, Zachry consents to his Prescient visitor's request: that he escort her to the top of a nearby mountain, the home of what the locals believe to be evil spirits—and the alleged location of what Meronym and her colleagues are looking for. One can't even begin to imagine what they'll find there.

Thus begins the amazing odyssey that is "Cloud Atlas." And what a journey it is, both for its story and the concepts it embodies.

It goes without saying that everything in our reality is interconnected, bound by the consciousness that links everything in the Universe. Indeed, if we recognize that we use our thoughts, beliefs and intents to manifest the world around us, then we must also realize that we do so to create the *totality* of that surrounding reality. But this applies not only to the immediate world around us; it also relates to the greater existence of which we, as multidimensional beings, are a part. Our materialization initiatives thus extend beyond our localized existence, reaching into other timelines, and even other dimensional planes, in which other portions of our greater selves dwell. Because of that, we must endeavor to be conscious of the choices we make and the responsibility inherent in that, for these considerations carry implications that may be *far* more wide-ranging than we realize.

"Cloud Atlas" illustrates these notions brilliantly and in myriad ways. It's apparent in the recurrent themes connecting the various storylines. It's present in the relationships and interactions among the characters (and their spirits) across time. It's even visible in the undeniable sense of familiarity that bonds souls to one another from era to era, a connection more profound than anything that can be afforded by mere mutual physical existence.

Given the intrinsic nature of connectedness, it can be applied to every aspect of existence, and, as conscious creators, we're free to explore it from any angle we choose. Covering all the bases in this regard in any one film, however, would be unwieldy and impractical, so "Cloud Atlas" wisely focuses on a select handful of representative examples, offering them up as illustrations of this larger principle. Throughout its various narratives, the picture explores multiple permutations of such ideas as freedom vs. captivity, kindness vs. brutality, benevolence vs. greed and compassion vs. callousness. We repeatedly witness how the choices we make in these areas resonate through time, how the scenarios we create offer us opportunities to learn valuable life lessons, and how we may ultimately draw upon these experiences to grow and develop as human beings and as greater souls.

All of this, of course, assumes that reincarnation (or, more precisely, the phenomenon of multiple existences) is a given and that we each get opportunities to live out different kinds of lives. Our spirits can don the costumes of both villain and hero, creator and destroyer, healer and killer, as well as the trappings of both genders and all ethnicities (all clearly borne out through the multiple character portrayals of the principal cast members). These assorted incarnations allow us to experience the full range of probabilities that the law of attraction makes possible and provide us with opportunities to work out our karma, in all cases for better or worse, enabling us to become the individuals—and the spirits—we're each truly capable of being and of *becoming*.

As important as the foregoing considerations are, however, the narrative of "Cloud Atlas" ultimately draws our attention to an even larger and more significant issue—the idea that *separation is an illusion*. Our stubborn belief in this myth is likely driven by what we perceive as the character of physical existence, one in which everything *seems* separate and apart from everything else, even when in close tangible proximity to one another. But, even though the quality of individuality helps to distinguish the character of the components of physicality, it does *not* sanction an innate separateness among them. The mere fact that all of its components are physical, for example, illustrates that they have this intrinsic quality in common. And, given that we, like all of the components of our reality, are physical in nature further reinforces the idea that no inherent separation exists among us. The better we come to understand this, the deeper our understanding becomes of the fundamental nature of existence, both in its "present" state and in all of its other permutations across time, dimensions or other lines of probability.

"Cloud Atlas" is an incredibly ambitious project, well-executed in virtually every respect. The performances are terrific across the board, an amazing feat considering the demanding multiple characterizations involved (wait until you see the full list of who played who in the closing credits!). It's also technically brilliant, breathtakingly beautiful in its cinematography and special effects and masterful in its sets, designs, costumes and makeup, all backed up by an ethereal, emotive, Golden Globe-nominated musical score. It draws inspiration from a wide range of films in a variety of genres, including everything from "The Bounty" (1984) to "The China Syndrome"

(1979) to "Blade Runner" (1982), successfully paying homage to them all but without ever becoming a blatant impersonator.

The film is, admittedly, a little slow in the first 30 minutes, but, given the setup work involved in getting six storylines off the ground, that's easily overlooked. Likewise, the movie has a tendency to wear its metaphysics on its sleeve at times, but, considering the subject matter involved, I'd rather the film overcompensate on this aspect than cryptically understate its intentions. Perhaps the only area in need of some serious tweaking would be in some of the dialogue of the post-apocalyptic Hawaiian sequence; it's a little too "Mad Max" for my taste, at times almost indiscernible and a tad pretentious.

Nevertheless, at the risk of overstatement, "Cloud Atlas" truly is epic filmmaking, one of the most impressive releases in recent years and easily my favorite film of 2012. I must confess that I had some reservations about this picture going in, given that it was the product of the makers of "The Matrix" series, a collection of films that I thought was highly overrated. But not so with this offering; it lives up to every bit of its billing. The picture is best enjoyed on the big screen (if you're fortunate enough to catch it in such a setting); you'll want to savor every grand, sweeping moment as it majestically unfolds before you. And, if it affects you as much as it did me, you'll emerge from the darkness walking on air. But, then, with a title like "Cloud Atlas," who would expect anything less?

Celebrating the Power, Beauty and Glory of Creation

"Samsara"
Year of Release: 2012
Director: Ron Fricke
Writers: Ron Fricke and Mark Magidson
Concept: Ron Fricke and Mark Magidson

Whenever events in my world start to bring me down, I turn my thoughts to the classic Louis Armstrong recording of *What a Wonderful World*. No matter how bad things may get, the sentiments of that song's lyrics always restore my hope and faith in the beauty, power and glory of this creation we call Earth, a response not unlike what's evoked by the cinematic sensation, "Samsara."

Chapter 8: Connection

While "Samsara" has been rather loosely characterized as a "documentary," that label doesn't do the film justice. It's more of a cinematic meditation, a visual tone poem on our world and what's gone into its creation in its present state. It consists of only images, music and occasional nature sounds, with no dialogue, narration or graphics. It features gorgeously photographed vistas of natural and manmade beauty, as well as visuals of nature and man run amok, from 25 countries around the globe. It's a project that took director Ron Fricke and producer Mark Magidson five years to create, and it's an effort that was well worth the wait.

In exploring its central premise, "Samsara" looks at creation as a force that's capable of expression in myriad forms. The picture's creators never judge the results for "better" or "worse," always recognizing the intrinsic validity of each and every manifestation, no matter what its nature. Those decisions are left up to the viewer, who is free to evaluate the imagery and see the outcomes as he or she chooses, be it positively, negatively or neutrally.

In that sense, the film epitomizes the core principle underlying the conscious creation process. The picture essentially says that the world we see before us depends on what we each manifest from within, with the end results materializing in completed form before our eyes. *All* options are thus on the table in this metaphysical scenario, again, be they those of a positive, negative or neutral nature, depending on one's particular perspective.

Given the infinite range of probability options available to us, however, it would behoove us to choose our creations carefully. We're capable of creating great beauty, as seen in the images of temples, churches, palaces and skyscrapers from around the world. At the same time, we're equally capable of manifesting ugliness beyond belief, as evidenced by the shots of slums, garbage dumps and polluted sites found throughout the globe. And what's perhaps even more unsettling is our capacity for indifference, our uncaring disregard for the environment, the creatures with whom we share the planet and even our own fellow human beings, as shown in scenes of such places as food processing plants, prisons and border crossings.

In conveying these ideas, the film also shows us the undeniable connectedness of all of the foregoing. As disparate as these images are, they're *all* part of our world and our reality. For better or worse, it's who we are and what we've created. Indeed, we've materialized a magnificent terrestrial home for ourselves, so we'd better be careful with what we do with it.

Of course, it's somewhat comforting to know that we get multiple chances to get things right. If we screw up, there are always additional opportunities to make amends. That's because, as the film contends, our existence is innately based on a system of repeating, connected, unending cycles. The picture's title even reflects this; the word "samsara" is Sanskrit for "the ever-turning wheel of life," an infinite, incessant progression of creation, destruction and re-creation that we all experience, even if we're not aware of it or any of its integral components. Metaphorically speaking, this is perhaps best depicted in the images of Tibetan Buddhists spinning their prayer wheels, physical reminders that serve to enlighten us of this metaphysical concept. It's also apparent in the monks' creation of sand paintings, intricate, meticulously detailed images that are wiped clean upon their completion to signify the inherent impermanence of all things. Those who might be shocked at the destruction of these beautiful images should take heed, however, that, no matter how many of them might be destroyed, there are *always* new ones to be created to take their place, a certainty that's assured as long as the prayer wheels continue their spinning.

Those looking for clues as to which creations might be "preferable" and/or longest lasting can take cues from the attributes they share. Creations that celebrate our spiritual nature and our connection to the divine collaborator who helps us make our manifestations possible are among those images that are most enduring. To the contrary, those that appeal to our more secular inclinations seem much more prone to decline and deterioration. That's particularly true for those tied to our baser instincts, especially those that glorify our lacks, fears, wants and worries, concerns that would seem to validate a belief that the Universe doesn't support us. But, if that were indeed true, surely we wouldn't have been blessed with such a grand and glorious home as we have, now would we? In this pursuit, as in any other of a conscious creation-related nature, we truly get back what we concentrate upon.

"Samsara" recalls many other films that director Fricke has worked on, including his prior works "Baraka" (1992) and "Chronos"

(1985), as well as the immensely popular "Koyaanisqatsi" (1982), for which he served as cinematographer. In some ways, "Samsara" is an extension of these other pictures, not so much as a narrative sequel but as a continuing kaleidoscopic treatment of subjects that are just as timeless now as they were 30 years ago (and that will likely be just as timely 30 or more years hence). The picture is stunningly photographed on 70-millimeter film (you *must* see this on the big screen) and beautifully scored by Michael Stearns, Lisa Gerrard and Marcello De Francisci. The editing of some sequences might have been handled better, especially in some of the picture's transitions, although this shortcoming doesn't detract significantly from the overall quality of this truly superb film.

Whenever natural or manmade disasters occur, I'll invariably encounter individuals who lament the state of the world, seeing it in a predominantly negative light and woefully decrying the inherently flawed nature of physical existence. Their impassioned arguments can, admittedly, be quite persuasive, too. But, at times like that, I look to shift my perspective. In particular, I like to recall a vacation that I took with my partner to Maine's Acadia National Park in 2011. While sitting atop the summit of Cadillac Mountain looking down upon the splendor of the New England seacoast and the charming seaport of Bar Harbor, I told him about the doom seekers, observing, "You know, no matter how bad things may get in this world, it's comforting to know that creations as beautiful as this still exist." Experiences like that little moment renew and reinforce my faith in the belief that the world can be just as magnificent as it can be horrendous. "Samsara" echoes that same notion, and it does so impeccably.

What a wonderful world indeed.

Unlocking the Mysteries of Existence
"Something Unknown Is Doing We Don't Know What"
Year of Release: 2009
Cast: Charles Tart, Dean Radin, Gary Schwartz,
Roger Nelson, Rupert Sheldrake, Hal Puthoff,
Larry Dossey, Edgar D. Mitchell, David Dosa,
Arielle Ford, Rebecca Good, Nancy Myer,
Catherine Yunt, Eric Pearl
Director: Renée Scheltema
Writer: Renée Scheltema

Overcoming our personal limitations is one of the primary aspirations of becoming an effective conscious creator. To achieve this, it helps immensely to learn how to stretch our manifestation capabilities, those that allow us to envision—and ultimately yield—better outcomes with our hoped-for materializations. This specifically involves abilities most of us have yet to tap, let alone master, such as our psychic faculties and related skills, as well as our capacity to sense the connectedness of all things in the Universe. That's why documentaries like "Something Unknown Is Doing We Don't Know What" are so valuable.

The study of psychic phenomena is rife with anecdotal evidence, but sources of quantified scientific data about the subject have long been scarce and scattered. Many researchers have stayed away from it for fear of ridicule by peers, and those who have courageously ventured into such "risky" territory have often had their findings relegated to the realm of obscurity. That's where this film comes in.

Director Renée Scheltema has compiled a wide range of information on various areas of parapsychology research, including in-depth examinations of abilities like telepathy, precognition, clairvoyance, psychokinesis and psychic healing, what Prof. Charles Tart, one of the film's many expert commentators, refers to as "the big five" topics of psychic investigation. Throughout the course of the film, Scheltema reports on a number of groundbreaking studies in these areas, backing up her findings with interviews by such experts as Gary Schwartz, Roger Nelson, Rupert Sheldrake, Hal Puthoff, Larry Dossey and Edgar D. Mitchell, among others.

In addition to reporting on these subjects, Scheltema takes viewers into the laboratory and into the field to show us the researchers at work. For instance, one sequence involving Institute of Noetic Sciences investigator Dean Radin illustrates his efforts to quantify whether we're capable of evoking waking state physical reactions to events yet to occur, thereby giving us potentially tangible markers of precognitive abilities. Through studies like this, what was once thought of as paranormal suddenly seems considerably more ordinary.

Subsequent sequences examine such phenomena as matter manipulation through spoon bending experiments, remote viewing as a tool for identifying physical objects or probable events across the spans of distance and time, random number generation as a predictive indicator of stirrings in the collective unconscious, and the rejuvenating power of various Chinese medicine practices and the Reconnective Healing® technique of Dr. Eric Pearl. Collectively, these segments paint a very different picture of the nature of reality than most of us have traditionally been accustomed to—a new, paradigm-shifting view that's backed up by evidence to substantiate it.

As diverse as these phenomena may seem superficially, there's a strong suggestion here that they're all related to one another, that they all speak to a connection to something greater than that with which we're most familiar—a link to the divine and to the consciousness that binds and manifests all things in the Universe. Even though some of us may be more adept at one particular parapsychological skill than another, it's suggested that we may all have the potential to tap into any number of these capabilities, that they're all somehow part of a network of innate, largely unexplored natural talents that we're just now beginning to discover and understand. But imagine what might be possible when such abilities are more widely recognized and better understood? That's a prospect this film addresses quite eloquently.

Another theme that runs throughout the film is an examination of the remarkably uncanny parallels between science and spirituality. Many of the commentators discuss how these two disciplines are essentially opposite sides of the same coin. After addressing how scientific methodologies can be used to validate various parapsychological phenomena, many of the experts go on to explain how the manifested effects of these phenomena have traditionally been invoked through ancient mystical, spiritual and religious practices. While these effects may have been described more poetically than scientifically in these age-old traditions, the results in both instances are frequently comparable, lending credence to the notion that these often-quarrelsome disciplines truly are not as far apart as we've generally been led to believe. This is especially true in the area of healing, where miracles are not only possible but inherently matter-of-fact—provided that would-be recipients allow them.

Those who engage in conscious creation will no doubt find this material mesmerizing. Besides providing examples of the existence of these phenomena, "Something Unknown" also enlightens us on how we might employ these abilities in our everyday lives. And, when considered in the context of consciously manifesting the reality we experience, we can see that we have a host of powerful tools at our disposal for materializing the existence we desire.

Despite a somewhat choppy opening sequence that could have been better organized and more effectively edited, the bulk of the film's material is presented cogently and succinctly. Those looking for an authoritative and engaging overview of this subject matter will find a superb offering in this work.

Things unknown need not remain a mystery, especially when they can be put to use in creating a more fulfilling life. That's the message of this film, and it's one we can all avail ourselves of to manifest a better world. And, given the many challenges we face today, goodness knows, we're likely to benefit from any guidance we can get. It may be just what we need to restore the noticeably absent connections in our lives, especially those linking us to the greater scheme of things of which we're a part.

What's Right and Wrong with the World

"I Am"

Year of Release: 2010
Cast: Tom Shadyac, Ray Anderson, Marc Ian Barasch,
Coleman Barks, Noam Chomsky, John Francis,
Elisabet Sahtouris, Dacher Keltner, Rollin McCraty,
Chris Jordan, Lynne McTaggart, Daniel Quinn,
Dean Radin, Thom Hartmann, Marilyn Schlitz,
Richard Shadyac, David Suzuki, Desmond Tutu, Howard Zinn
Director: Tom Shadyac
Writer: Tom Shadyac

Examining what's right and wrong with the world is a tall order in almost any context, but doing so within the body of a documentary (without an unreasonably long running time) is, arguably, a seemingly insurmountable challenge. However, director Tom Shadyac has done an excellent job in tackling that very task, effectively and succinctly encapsulating his take on these grand notions in his highly personal and thought-provoking film, "I Am."

"I Am" is both a philosophical and a personal journey. Shadyac, who directed huge hit comedies like "Ace Ventura: Pet Detective" (1994), "Patch Adams" (1998) and "Bruce Almighty" (2003), had attained a high level of what society defines as success. But, in spite of these accomplishments, he felt a certain unrelenting emptiness. Those feelings were exacerbated not long thereafter when he suffered severe injuries in a biking accident that left him with lingering psychological issues, launching him into a profound, seemingly incessant depression. It wasn't until he began looking at alternative medical solutions and unconventional spiritual practices that the fog began to lift, after which he felt a compelling need to document his experience (and the concepts that he explored) through the medium with which he was most familiar—cinema.

Beginning with the simple question, "What's wrong with the world?", Shadyac came to a startling conclusion: The answer to his question was "I am." He realized that his experience exemplified the underlying problem—that the excesses of his success were fundamentally out of balance with the world and that the resources he was consuming were disproportionate to his individual needs, given their availability. He also surmised that this problem is made worse when other individuals—or even entire nation states—operate from this same premise. And, given that everything in our world is intrinsically connected, the effects are felt by everyone and everything across the spectrum of our existence.

In determining the reasoning behind this, Shadyac discovered that this disparity is primarily driven, ironically enough, by a collective mindset that's based on the notion of *competition* rather than *cooperation* among humans—*even though*, as he points out, researchers have conclusively shown that cooperation promotes, rather than hinders, survival in the wild, a notion that applies to animals *and* humans alike. The director contends that this false assumption of ours is based on a flawed interpretation (and subsequent perpetuation) of the theory of evolution, one that even its author, Charles Darwin (1809-1882), eventually came to downplay. However, because this belief has become a foundation of Western thought, it not only persists, but it also has caused us to lose a vital sense of our natural selves. We thus tend to see ourselves as entities that are separate and distinct rather than connected and unified, perpetuating the illusion of separation.

Unraveling this quandary, Shadyac maintains, is crucial to our species' and our planet's future survival. Through the film's various segments, he shows how we're actually hardwired for cooperation, even though we've lost sight of it and have bought into the concept of competition. These circumstances thus present us with a fundamental choice—and challenge—regarding which option we'll select for ourselves going forward. We're clearly capable of both, but which one will we opt for? Will we continue to fall prey to the idea that "I am the source of the problem," or will we change our minds to believe that "I am the source of the solution"?

The very notion of cooperation implies a sense of connection among us and everything in our world, that we were indeed all *meant* to work together. What's more, every problem we create suggests that there's an inherent solution embedded somewhere within it, just waiting to be uncovered. Our challenge at the moment, then, is *awakening* to these realizations, to see the interconnectedness in the elements of our existence and the implications that come from such an elevated awareness. "I Am" provides us with valuable clues on how to tackle that very task.

In backing up these contentions, Shadyac features interviews with experts in a variety of fields, such as scientists Dean Radin, Elisabet Sahtouris, Marilyn Schlitz, Rollin McCraty and David Suzuki; spiritualists Coleman Barks and Desmond Tutu; authors Lynne McTaggart, Daniel Quinn and Marc Ian Barasch; activists Noam Chomsky, Howard Zinn, Thom Hartmann and John Francis; educator Dacher Keltner; businessman Ray Anderson; and photographer Chris Jordan. Shadyac also includes an interview with his late father, Richard, co-founder of St. Jude's Research Hospital, showing what we're capable of as human beings (if we allow ourselves to do so) and ultimately providing us with an example of what's *right* with the world.

While "I Am" may not answer its core questions completely, it nevertheless provides an excellent blueprint that we can use as a starting point (and one that we shouldn't waste any time in getting to). And, unlike many other films of this genre, it benefits from the hand of a truly skilled filmmaker, presenting its material in a very polished, professional and entertaining manner. Shadyac truly has raised the bar for movies that delve into these topics, a development that, one would hope, will rub off on other filmmakers seeking to create pictures based on themes like these.

Given the many challenges in the world today, it's increasingly crucial that we make effective choices as we move into the future. "I Am" offers some very constructive suggestions that we'd be wise to heed if we all wish to do what's right for the world.

Looking for the Links

"Babel"
Year of Release: 2006
Cast: Brad Pitt, Cate Blanchett, Adriana Barraza,
Rinko Kikuchi, Gael García Bernal,
Kôji Yakusho, Satoshi Nikaido,
Boubker Ait El Caid, Said Tarchani, Mustapha Rachidi,
Abdelkader Bara, Driss Roukhe, Peter Wight,
Mohamed Akhzam, Elle Fanning, Nathan Gamble,
Michael Peña, Clifton Collins Jr.,
Robert "Bernie" Esquivel, Cynthia Montaño,
Wahiba Sahmi, Sfia Ait Benboullah
Director: Alejandro González Iñárritu
Screenplay: Guillermo Arriaga
Story: Guillermo Arriaga and Alejandro González Iñárritu

It's amazing how easily we can feel both intrinsically connected *and* disconnected at the same time. The benefits of being aware of our connectedness should be obvious, as should be the drawbacks that come with losing our sense of it. Unfortunately, we often assume that *disconnection is the norm*, a belief rife with disturbing consequences. What's more, it may be difficult to get back what we've lost, something that becomes painfully apparent in the interwoven storylines of a drama with truly global reach, "Babel."

What do Moroccan shepherds, American tourists, a Mexican wedding party and a deaf-mute Japanese teenager have in common?

More than you might think. Despite being seemingly a world apart, all of them are linked, just like all of us. Their bonds may not be apparent at first glance, but, in the true spirit of the connectedness of all creation, they're inherently tied to one another, and their interactions—no matter how seemingly disparate their individual actions might appear—provide a valuable lesson into this integral aspect of conscious creation.

The narrative of "Babel" features the following storylines:

* When Hassan Ibrahim (Abdelkader Bara), a Moroccan shepherd and hunting guide, offers to sell a high-powered rifle to his neighbor, Abdullah (Mustapha Rachidi), his fellow goat herder jumps at the chance to buy it. Not long after Abdullah makes the purchase, his sons, Yussef (Boubker Ait El Caid) and Ahmed (Said Tarchani), try their hand at the new weapon. They hope to use the gun to take out the jackals that frequently attack the family's flock. To prepare for that, they engage in some impromptu target practice, aiming mostly at rocks. But, when they naïvely take aim at a passing tour bus, they get more than they bargained for.

* The once-happy union between Richard and Susan Jones (Brad Pitt, Cate Blanchett) seems destined for dissolution. After suffering a family tragedy, the San Diego couple has drifted apart, their marriage verging on divorce. So, in an effort to save the relationship, Richard takes his wife on vacation to a destination that holds about as much interest for her as her marriage does these days. She reluctantly goes along but mopes much of the time, unable to see the point of making the journey—or the effort. That all changes, however, when the couple goes on a sightseeing expedition that takes them to a very important appointment with destiny.

* Amelia (Adriana Barraza), a nanny who lovingly cares for the two small children (Elle Fanning, Nathan Gamble) of a California couple, is thrilled to be attending the wedding of her son (Robert "Bernie" Esquivel) over the border in her native Mexico. But, right before leaving, Amelia's plans go awry. With the children's parents out of town and the scheduled caretakers cancelling at the last minute, Amelia has no one to watch the kids. She ultimately

decides to take them with her, although she has some reservations about her decision. The children don't seem eager to go, and she's making the trip with her nephew, Santiago (Gael García Bernal), who's something of a loose cannon. As anxious as she is to take part in the celebration, she also crosses her fingers that everything works out. For her sake, and that of everyone else involved, she had better keep those digits tightly clasped.

* The world is a lonely place for Chieko Wataya (Rinko Kikuchi). The deaf-mute Tokyo teenager longs to connect with others, for a variety of reasons. The unrelenting silence that characterizes her disability, for example, sets her apart from much of a world that takes hearing for granted and that often treats those with her condition awkwardly at best. But her sense of isolation involves more than being cut off from the world of sound. She misses her mother, who committed suicide not long ago. And her businessman father, Yasujiro (Kôji Yakusho), is often absent, taking trips and going on hunting expeditions to exotic locales. She sincerely believes that she can vanquish her loneliness by losing her virginity, something that most of her peers have already done. She works at this goal with a vengeance, convinced it will bring her the feeling of connection she so desperately seeks. But will it?

If the foregoing summaries seem a bit vague, that's deliberate to avoid giving away too much of the film and the ties that bind the different stories. However, a close reading *will* provide hints about how these apparently unrelated plotlines are linked, cluing in viewers about the connectedness theme that permeates this picture's narrative and illustrating how everything in our reality is bound together, no matter how seemingly discrete its individual elements may appear.

But "Babel" does more than just point out the existence of this rather obvious notion. It also explores *why* our sense of separation exists and what we might do to overcome it. This is important for those of us who seek to become more proficient in our law of attraction practices, because it helps us identify some core beliefs that may hinder us and that could benefit from some judicious rewriting.

For instance, given the nature of physical existence, with all its distinct individual elements, many of us have come to think of our reality as a collection of "parts." We view all of the components in it as separate and unrelated to one another, unless we do something to intentionally combine them for a specific purpose, as if we were mixing the ingredients of a recipe. Even those of us who are fully aware that we create each of those elements with our beliefs may lose sight of the overarching fact that we manifest all of them through the same materialization process using the same basic building blocks. These elements of commonality help to make clear the connectedness that links all of the parts together, whether combined or not.

So, considering the prevalence of such thinking, is it any surprise that many of us, like the characters in this film, have come to accept separateness as a defining quality of reality? And, the more we buy into the idea, the more reinforced and entrenched the beliefs supporting it thus become. Indeed, it's a wonder any of us is able to successfully interact with one another at all.

The beliefs supporting this contention, in turn, tend to influence how we respond to the manifested conditions of our reality. Because we often view existence as a collection of individual components, we tend to take no issue with those elements that seem to be related to one another. We generally would not react with dismay, for example, at a living room setup that includes a sofa and an end table, because those "parts" seem to go together. But, if something "foreign" were to intrude upon that same space, such as a bathtub, we'd react defensively. We'd wonder about that wholly unrelated element with suspicion ("What's it doing here?") or even disdain ("We have to get this thing out of here!"). It probably would never occur to most of us that there was some kind of connection that linked the seemingly out-of-place object to all of its accompanying items. Yet, if we looked beneath the surface, there's bound to be some reason behind the "anomalous" manifestation's presence.

Taken to an extreme, the defensive beliefs driving such thinking could easily yield reactions based on suspicion and hostility, perhaps even resulting in us taking preemptive strikes against the "aberrations." There are "casualties" associated with such thinking, however, such as our capacities for understanding or even basic communication (as the film's title alludes to). That's unfortunate, because we may end up *compounding* whatever difficulties already exist. This occurs repeatedly in the film, making matters worse for all involved, and all because the characters simply can't see the connections that bind them.

Ironically, the difficulties that arise under such conditions are also the events that usually help us to overcome our lack of awareness. Those who find themselves in peril, for example, often obtain help from unexpected sources. For instance, a selfless tour guide (Mohamed Akhzam) and his medicine woman grandmother (Sfia Ait Benboullah) unhesitatingly come to the aid of Richard and Susan when the need arises. Likewise, a compassionate detective (Satoshi Nikaido) helps Chieko in a moment of crisis. These unlikely guardian angels not only restore their beneficiaries' faith in humanity, but they also rekindle their awareness of the fact that we're all connected, *that we're all one*. Their acts further remind us that workable solutions are available, that kindness and mercy do much more to bolster our sense of unity than anything thoughtless brutality or casual indifference could ever do.

In many ways, "Babel" does for the globe what "Crash" (2005) did for Los Angeles. It effectively shatters the notion that we're separate and apart from one another, that such thinking is an illusion that stems from "misdirected" beliefs. One could argue that experiencing such a state of being firsthand is necessary to overcome it and to move into a new state of understanding, and that contention would indeed have merit. We can only hope that we get the point of that lesson as quickly as we can.

The picture paints a spectacular mural of our world and its inherently rich, though always-connected, diversity. To that end, many of the images are incorporated for their own sake to show off the sheer beauty of this planet and those who inhabit it. That can make for some slow pacing at times, but that shortcoming is effectively offset by all of the film's other fine attributes, most notably its terrific performances by Barraza and Kikuchi (both of whom were Oscar and Golden Globe nominees), as well as Pitt (a Golden Globe nominee), who turns in one of his best on-screen portrayals.

"Babel" was highly decorated in awards ceremonies. It received one Academy Award on seven nominations, including best picture, best director, best original screenplay and two nods for best supporting actress. It also took home the Golden Globe for best dramatic picture, as well as nominations for best director, best screenplay, best supporting actor and two nods for best supporting actress. In addition, the film captured three wins at the Cannes Film Festival, including best director, on four total nominations, including a *Palme d'Or* nod.

It's often been asked why it takes a tragedy to bring us together. Perhaps it's because it takes something drastic to get our attention, to shake us out of our complacency and into a new state of awareness. It's as if our subconscious is giving us a metaphysical slap in the face to get us to wake up, much like what happens when we have nightmares to grasp dream messages that have gone ignored when delivered more gently. One would like to hope we shouldn't have to resort to such measures to get the lessons we need to learn, but, if that's what it takes, we can only hope that we move through the experiences as quickly as possible.

Or, to expedite the process, just watch "Babel."

9

CHANGE

With an infinite range of probabilities available for manifestation at any given time, is it truly realistic to expect that the circumstances of our reality will always stay the same? The mere fact that there are existence options beyond whatever we're currently experiencing suggests that the potential for our reality morphing into something new is always with us. But, even though *change* can be immensely positive, many of us fear it, viewing it as troubling or intimidating. So the question for us thus becomes, should we implement it? Or would we be better off leaving things as they are? Indeed, if they ain't broke, why should we tinker with them?

Perhaps the biggest concern about change is that it represents the unknown. But, then, did we truly know what the reality we're now in would be like *before* we manifested it? Any aspect of existence that comes into being, whether it's something new or the perpetuation of our current circumstances, is born in exactly the same way—through the power of our beliefs combined with the energy of our divine collaborator to materialize the world around us. When a change to our reality is viewed in this light, it suddenly seems considerably less scary, because we're able to see that it arises from the same fundamental process as the existence with which we're already familiar.

Given that conscious creation maintains we're all in a constant state of becoming, there's an inherent suggestion in that notion that change is an integral part of our existence, no matter how we might feel about it. When conditions become frustrating, for example, that in itself suggests our prevailing reality (and the beliefs that inspire it) are no longer serving us, that the Universe is prompting us to move on to something new (and, preferably, better). How easily those new circumstances come into being, however, depends entirely on how readily we embrace change. If we indeed hope for things to go smoothly, we'd be wise to do all we can to make friends with change for, as noted above, it's a fundamental attribute of our metaphysical birthright.

Change comes in many forms, and that's evident in the films in this Chapter. Whether it's expressed through the emergence of a new social movement, the birthing of a new line of probability for an existing mythology, adjustments to family and partnership relationships, or the living arrangements we create for our sunset years, change makes its presence felt in all of these scenarios. The ease with which it's ushered in, of course, ultimately rests with what the principal players in these narratives do with their beliefs to birth their new circumstances.

For anyone who goes through change (and who among us hasn't?), we often dread the process more than the outcome. In fact, many of us frequently say after the fact that we wished we'd made the decision to alter our realities sooner than we did. Knowing that, then, we shouldn't be afraid to make use of this powerful conscious creation tool. After all, it certainly beats the burden of regret we could end up carrying for *not* availing ourselves of it while we had the chance.

Like Ants Making Thunder

"Taking Woodstock"
Year of Release: 2009
Cast: Demetri Martin, Imelda Staunton,
Henry Goodman, Emile Hirsch, Eugene Levy,
Dan Fogler, Jonathan Groff, Mamie Gummer,
Skylar Astin, Daniel Eric Gold, Adam Pally,
Darren Pettie, Liev Schreiber,
Paul Dano, Kelli Garner
Director: Ang Lee
Screenplay: James Schamus
Book: Elliot Tiber and Tom Monte,
Taking Woodstock: A True Story of a Riot,
a Concert and a Life

CHAPTER 9: CHANGE

Every so often, a milestone event occurs that comes to distinguish an era. It may not be the most significant happening of its time, but it's often the most symbolic, given its size, scope or impact, particularly in terms of the changes it helps usher in. For those who came of age in the late '60s, such an event took place at a music festival in a sleepy hamlet in the Catskills, a gathering whose name would come to define a generation and the radically new social values it embodied. That legendary event is chronicled in the whimsical nostalgic comedy, "Taking Woodstock."

Based on the back story of the 1969 Woodstock Music Festival, the film focuses on how the event came together, thanks in part to the efforts of an unlikely young entrepreneur, Elliot Teichberg (Demetri Martin). Elliot secured the festival's hosting rights for the town of White Lake, NY, after the nearby community of Wallkill passed up the chance to hold the three-day concert, partly out of logistical concerns and partly out of fears it would be overrun by unruly hippies. He saw this as an opportunity to help promote his community and to boost business at the rundown "resort" he ran with his eccentric, miserly parents (Imelda Staunton, Henry Goodman). Little did he know he was helping to birth the phenomenon that would characterize "the Woodstock generation."

The film's first half details how Elliot worked with the concert's promoters (Jonathan Groff, Skylar Astin, Daniel Eric Gold, Adam Pally) to secure the venue for the festival, the dairy farm of Max Yasgur (Eugene Levy). Along the way, viewers are also introduced to the cavalcade of colorful characters who accompanied Elliot on his improbable journey, including a Vietnam veteran living on the edge of reality (Emile Hirsch), a cross-dressing security guard (Liev Schreiber), a hunky contractor who ignites Elliot's emerging gay sensibility (Darren Pettie) and a talent-starved acting troupe more interested in getting naked than in performing.

The picture's second half examines the festival once it's in full swing. The film doesn't focus on the concert *per se* (see the excellent documentary "Woodstock" (1970) for that) but, instead, recounts Elliot's firsthand Woodstock experience. Viewers also witness how this event impacted the national culture, specifically how it celebrated the values of those who brought it into being, as well as how it helped change the hearts and minds of those who initially opposed the festival and what it stood for, an accomplishment that was perhaps the most significant legacy of the event and the era of which it was a part.

It's quite remarkable how something so seemingly unremarkable as a concert could have such tremendous influence. But Woodstock helped galvanize the mindset and worldview of a new generation, one that preached love, peace, individuality and social justice, values sometimes scarce in prior generations. The event drew attention to these ideals, helping to prompt changes in society's attitudes toward them in subsequent years. And all it took was everyone who attended contributing a little of their own energy and consciousness to the creative mix. Such modest offerings, from ordinary, everyday folks, might not have amounted to much individually, but, collectively, they combined to produce a powerful, synergistic groundswell, the effect of which, as one concertgoer (Paul Dano) put it, was "like ants making thunder." It was a massive co-creation, illustrating conscious creation writ large. What a marvel it was!

The event also proved that life could be lived in other than traditional ways. Such unconventional thinking was crucial for a generation seeking to change the planet and to discover itself in the process. This is illustrated most clearly through Elliott, a young man coming into his own in ways he may have never thought possible—or even dreamed of.

"Taking Woodstock" is an enjoyable, entertaining film, though the picture's first half is definitely stronger than the second, which tends to meander at times. I also found the movie's occasional split screen filming technique—an homage to the innovative cinematic style of the aforementioned documentary—somewhat annoying, primarily because it adds little to the narrative while making the action needlessly difficult to follow. Nevertheless, the fine performances and generally solid writing more than compensate for these shortcomings. The picture was a *Palme d'Or* nominee at the Cannes Film Festival.

While Woodstock may not have single-handedly changed the world, it characterized a decade of effort with that goal in mind, promoting changes that worked their way into the culture and that have persisted to this day. And, even though the work of Woodstock might not be complete, it's further along than it would have been if the event hadn't happened, and this film reminds us of that.

Think about that the next time you feel like one of those ants.

To Boldly Go Where We've Been Before

"Star Trek"
Year of Release: 2009
*Cast: Chris Pine, Zachary Quinto, Leonard Nimoy,
Eric Bana, Bruce Greenwood, Karl Urban,
Zoë Saldana, Simon Pegg, Anton Yelchin, John Cho,
Ben Cross, Winona Ryder, Chris Hemsworth,
Jennifer Morrison, Faran Tahir, Tyler Perry
Director: J.J. Abrams
Screenplay: Roberto Orci and Alex Kurtzman
TV Series Source Material: Gene Roddenberry, Star Trek*

Rebooting a long-standing beloved entertainment franchise carries considerable risk. Scrutinous critics often wait in the wings, itching to pounce on the slightest of transgressions, especially where continuity issues are concerned. And then there are the diehard fans, traditionalists who don't hesitate to trot out their displeasure through inevitable comparisons to predecessor offerings. One way to successfully defuse all this, however, is to boldly and intentionally infuse change into the mix, particularly when done so skillfully that it effectively silences the objections of naysayers. Such was the case in 2009 with the release of the first installment of the revamped "Star Trek" movie franchise.

The film is essentially a prequel, telling the back story of how the crew of the *Starship Enterprise* from the original TV series (1966-1969) came together. It does so by featuring younger versions of the characters from that series, when they were still brash young recruits fresh out of their Starfleet Academy training. Viewers are thus treated to the inside scoop on the early days of long-running characters Capt. James T. Kirk (Chris Pine), First Officer Spock (Zachary Quinto), Chief Medical Officer Dr. Leonard "Bones" McCoy (Karl Urban), Communications Officer Lt. Nyota Uhura (Zoë Saldana), Chief Engineer Montgomery Scott (Simon Pegg), Helmsman Hikaru Sulu (John Cho) and Navigator Pavel Chekov (Anton Yelchin). Together with Capt. Christopher Pike (Bruce Greenwood), the starship's original skipper, the neophyte crew members do battle with the evil Nero (Eric Bana), a renegade spaceship commander from the Romulan Empire who threatens to destroy all the worlds of the United Federation of Planets, the galactic alliance that the *Enterprise* is sworn to protect. It's a tall order for all involved, especially the new kids.

However, those who think they know these characters may be surprised at what they see as this story unfolds, and that's where the element of change comes into play. Thanks to a seminal event at the film's outset in which an elder version of Spock (Leonard Nimoy) travels back into the past from the far distant future, the time line is changed, altering the line of probability in which the "Star Trek" mythology materializes. Because of that, everything fans *thought* they knew about the *Enterprise* crew is up for grabs going forward. With that new line of probability established, *anything* is possible, and the filmmakers capitalize on this without hesitation—and with an iron-clad justification for their (and their characters') "uncharacteristic" actions.

While there certainly are *familiar* elements involved in the narrative of this picture, not everything is identical to what came before in previous "Star Trek" iterations. What's more, such altered circumstances are applicable not only to the events of this particular release but also to any sequels that arise, as was the case in the series' most recent offering, "Star Trek Into Darkness" (2013). These conditions thus unquestionably validate the power of change and its attendant beliefs in shaping—and reshaping—reality.

As conscious creators well know, multiple probabilities are available to each of us at any given moment, and viewers can see how this applies to the lives of the *Enterprise* crew, as well as to the unfurling of events across the vast expanses of probable time and space. Given the deployment of the changed time line (*i.e.*, this altered line of probability) as a plot device, a whole range of new questions is raised: What will the characters do with the "new" options available to them? How will the choices they make—even those of a seemingly inconsequential nature—affect the evolution of events over time? And what impact will changes in circumstances have on them, their lives and the fate of the future? These are all profound law of attraction questions, and they're all addressed through the narrative in intriguingly captivating ways.

The flexibility afforded by the probability shift also affected how the filmmakers birthed this picture (and whatever progeny might arise subsequently). They thus have allowed themselves the same freedom to shape new destinies for their cinematic creations in the "real" world as their characters have available to them in their fictional reality. (And who says art doesn't imitate life (and vice versa)?)

Perhaps the biggest challenge for the creative forces behind this reboot involved decisions about which elements to retain, tweak or change from the original TV series, including everything from character traits to personal histories to starship technology. This required the filmmakers to take some risks, particularly where the issue of fan reaction was concerned. But the creators' well-calculated gambles paid off handsomely, with viewers being shown sides of beloved characters that they never knew existed, including some elements that seemingly run counter to what had been the prevailing wisdom. The characters' true multidimensional natures were thus allowed to shine through.

Change, it seems, can be good.

Admittedly, I was more than a bit skeptical before the picture's release. As a longtime "Trek" fan, I wondered whether this offering could live up to the high standards established by the franchise through its previous 10 theatrical films and five TV series. Questions abounded: What would the new movie be like? Would it have to rely on special effects and action to carry the story, or would it be character-driven as so many of its predecessors were? Could it effectively re-create (or, in some cases, reinvent) characters that viewers have come to know and love for over four decades? Or would it end up committing one of filmmaking's cardinal sins—that of failing to properly do justice to a classic? Fortunately, the film succeeds convincingly in all of the right ways, and it does so thanks to conscious creation, not only in terms of how it's reflected in the picture's storyline but also in terms of what it has done for the franchise, both in this offering and going forward.

Those who are unfamiliar with "Star Trek" needn't worry about knowing the history or characters of the original TV series to understand what is going on in this film; everything is adequately explained without belaboring anything. And those who are acquainted with the long-running mythology no doubt will enjoy the way this movie seamlessly and subtly weaves together a host of elements from, and references to, the original TV series, the theatrical films and even *The Next Generation* TV series. Effectively meeting the needs of both new and veteran viewers in this way is quite a feat indeed. For its efforts, the picture received one Oscar on four nominations, the first to be awarded in the history of this storied film franchise.

The cast and creators of "Star Trek" boldly went where we've gone before—and succeeded triumphantly in doing so. May the mission continue ....

Catalysts for Change

"The Kids Are All Right"
Year of Release: 2010
Cast: Annette Bening, Julianne Moore,
Mark Ruffalo, Mia Wasikowska,
Josh Hutcherson, Yaya Dacosta, Kunal Sharma,
Eddie Hassell, Zosia Mamet, Joaquín Garrido
Director: Lisa Cholodenko
Screenplay: Lisa Cholodenko and Stuart Blumberg

When we find ourselves leading lives that are less than satisfactory, it's time for a change. That's a prospect some may find unnerving, but the ability to make adjustments when things aren't acceptable is one of our basic conscious creation birthrights. All we need do is shift our beliefs. But what if we block out our awareness of the source of our discomfort, the driving force behind the manifestation of the unsatisfactory circumstances? In such situations, we may blind ourselves to the beliefs that are causing the problems or how we can effectively rewrite them. When that happens, it's time for a catalyst to get the change process rolling. Initially, we might not be aware of the catalyst's presence or the beliefs that drew it to us, but, once it makes its presence felt, its impact is undeniable. Such is the case in the heart-tugging comedy-drama, "The Kids Are All Right."

Nic (Annette Bening) and Jules (Julianne Moore) have been partnered for years. They've built a life together, including becoming the parents of two children, Joni (Mia Wasikowska) and Laser (Josh Hutcherson), by artificial insemination. Life generally seems good, though it has become very settled. What's more, a few tensions simmer beneath the surface of the couple's apparent domestic bliss. These issues threaten to come to a boil, especially now that the kids are teenagers. With Nic and Jules fast approaching their own version of the empty nest, the question that looms large is, will they be ready for it?

Since Nic and Jules seem largely unwilling to address these issues or to make any necessary changes, the kids unwittingly step up to the plate to manifest a much-needed catalyst to help the process along. They decide that they'd like to meet their sperm donor, a prospect made possible by Joni turning 18 and attaining legal adult status. And so, before long, Joni and Laser schedule a meeting with Paul (Mark Ruffalo), the man who helped make their lives possible.

After some initial trepidation, Paul and the kids hit it off well. In fact, it quickly becomes apparent that all three of them would like to continue their involvement with one another. But their interaction is more than just a passing diversion or idle curiosity; the kids like Paul, and vice versa, a development that shakes things up at home. And, once Paul meets Nic and Jules, things get shook up even further—and in highly unexpected ways.

Of course, the impact of all this affects not only Nic, Jules and the kids; it also has a profound influence on Paul. As a confirmed bachelor and free spirit, Paul has lived his life on his own terms. But, with the onset of middle age, the prospect of being a father and having a family holds much more appeal than it once did, especially now that he's had a taste of it for himself, even if only vicariously. So now he must ask himself, "What am I going to do about it? Am I willing to implement the changes I need to make to bring all of this about?" The catalyst thus gets turned back on itself.

As noted above, change can be a scary prospect for many of us. Upsetting the established order takes us out of our comfort zone and places us squarely in uncharted territory. But, ultimately, which prospect is preferable—staying stuck in less-than-satisfying circumstances or moving on to something more desirable? That's where the power of change comes into play, and, as one of the more powerful items available to us in our conscious creation toolbox, it's one that we shouldn't hesitate to draw upon when the need arises. Sometimes we may find that the changes we need to make are major; in other instances, the alterations may be minor, requiring only modest tweaking. But we'll never know, of course, unless we allow ourselves the opportunity to assess what's at hand and what might be.

"The Kids Are All Right" is likable in virtually every respect, providing viewers with considerable food for thought, as well as a thoroughly entertaining story. Smart writing and fine performances by all the major players make for good viewing fun. The movie was nominated for four Oscars, including best picture, best lead actress (Bening), best supporting actor (Ruffalo) and best original screenplay. It also fared well at the Golden Globe Awards, taking home two statues (for best comedy picture and Bening's best comedy actress performance) on four total nominations, including a second best comedy actress nod for Moore, as well as a nomination for best screenplay.

Thanks to the law of attraction, we always have a limitless range of options open to us to achieve satisfaction in the realities we materialize. Films like this help to show us the alternatives, both overtly and by implication, thereby reinforcing the inherent importance of this notion. All we need do is be willing to explore the possibilities—and change them when need be.

Fresh Starts

"The Best Exotic Marigold Hotel"
Year of Release: 2012
Cast: Judi Dench, Maggie Smith,
Tom Wilkinson, Bill Nighy, Penelope Wilton,
Ronald Pickup, Celia Imrie, Dev Patel,
Tena Desae, Seema Azmi, Diana Hardcastle,
Rajendra Gupta, Neena Kulkarni,
Lillette Dubey, Vishnu Sharma,
Sid Makkar, Bhuvnesh Shetty
Director: John Madden
Screenplay: Ol Parker
Book: Deborah Moggach, These Foolish Things

Facing the autumn of one's life can be challenging in many ways. Coming to terms with the realities of having fewer, rather than more, years ahead, as well as the increasingly debilitating effects of age, are daunting enough. But what if the means to live out those

Chapter 9: Change

remaining days in comfort are in peril, too? This combination of elements might seem deflating or overwhelming to some, but, with one's independence, dignity and survival at stake, the more adventurous and innovative among us may elect to make some extraordinary, uncharacteristic or even drastic changes to make the most of those circumstances, as seen in the delightful comedy, "The Best Exotic Marigold Hotel."

With retirement looming, seven British seniors weigh their options for what lies ahead:

* For Evelyn Greenslade (Judi Dench), the golden years look a lot bleaker than she had once anticipated. The lifelong, recently widowed housewife is forced into selling her residence to pay a backlog of debts left by her deceased husband, saddling her with a very uncertain future.

* Retired housekeeper Muriel Donnelly (Maggie Smith) needs hip replacement surgery but faces a six-month wait unless she's willing to try something a little more radical—not an easy decision for someone very set in her ways and her outlooks.

* Bored with his career and his life, Judge Graham Dashwood (Tom Wilkinson) can no longer continue with an existence that leaves him unsatisfied and longing for something more fulfilling. His search for genuine happiness clearly requires more than what his current routine can provide.

* Career civil servants Jean and Douglas Ainslie (Penelope Wilton, Bill Nighy) approach retirement community living with mixed feelings. Jean believes she deserves something better than what's on offer and doesn't hesitate to make her dissatisfaction known. Douglas, meanwhile, tries to assuage her, agreeing to pursue other options if doing so will help keep the peace in their increasingly precarious relationship.

* Spunky skirt-chaser Norman Cousins (Ronald Pickup) feels like a spry forty-something, even if his chronological odometer indicates otherwise. Nevertheless, how he feels, and how others react to his advances, such as the actual forty-somethings he tries to court, are two entirely different matters. Maybe it's time for Norman to turn his attention elsewhere.

* Madge Hardcastle (Celia Imrie) loves her family, but she tires of the demands they regularly place on her time, such as frequent requests for babysitting her young grandchildren. As someone who wants to enjoy life more in her remaining years, she yearns to take off and be a free spirit while she can—something she just might do, too.

Given their prevailing circumstances, the retirees each decide they need to pursue alternate paths. In doing so, they all stumble upon advertising for what seems to be the perfect solution to their respective situations—the Best Exotic Marigold Hotel for the Elderly and Beautiful. The ads for this luxurious but affordable facility promise its guests grand accommodations in a classic setting in the lively, colorful Indian city of Jaipur.

Everyone jumps at the opportunity, making reservations to move into this elegant pleasure palace. But there's just one catch: the hotel is nothing like what's in its promotional materials. In fact, the decrepit structure is not far from collapsing, its walls propped up by assorted forms of jerry-rigging and the infectious, if sometimes-unrealistic enthusiasm of hotelier Sonny Kapoor (Dev Patel).

Sonny struggles incessantly to keep his faltering business afloat. He does all he can to appease his disgruntled guests (many of whom are ready to turn back upon arrival) and his overbearing mother (Lillette Dubey), who constantly criticizes Sonny, forever flaunting his brothers' success in his face. He also strives to please his girlfriend, Sunaina (Tena Desae), an educated, upwardly mobile young woman whom he worries will leave him for someone more financially stable. It's quite a full plate for the wily young entrepreneur.

But, thanks to a hefty dose of Sonny's charm and the newfound friendships that spring up among the recent arrivals, the guests decide to stay. They thus embark on new journeys of personal discovery, some on their own and some by way of interactions with the hotel staff, the locals or each other. Their individual odysseys end up offering them possibilities for meaningful change, fresh starts unlike anything they could have possibly imagined before they left England.

At some point in our lives, fresh starts are welcome developments in the wake of unrelenting sameness, though embracing

Chapter 9: Change

such changes can become increasingly difficult for many of us as we age. As we allow the beliefs that shape our realities to settle in and become comfortable, we're more likely to look askance at possible upheavals in our routines, summarily rejecting them even before examining what they have to offer. We might even try justifying our resistance with arguments like "we're too old for that sort of thing." But are fresh starts only meant to be the provenance of the young?

The emergence of the mere *potential* of such manifestations indicates that there's some part of us deep down inside that wants to usher change into our lives, no matter how old or young we are. However, the more we resist those impulses, the more imposing, even threatening, they're likely to appear. Sometimes it may even seem as if change is being foisted upon us, with unwanted consequences and overwrought drama coming along for the ride.

Is this *really* how we want change to take hold in our lives? Must we become so dissatisfied with our situations that we allow ourselves to become ill, jaded or burned out before we'll even consider making alterations to our existence? Indeed, do we truly want change crammed down our throats?

In many ways, this is where the guests of the Marigold Hotel find themselves at the film's outset. They've put off making changes for so long that they now find themselves with their backs up against the proverbial wall. Their inner selves are telling them that change is *imperative* and that the only real decision they need to make is *how* to react to the impending circumstances.

Many of us have come to fear change, that the disappearance of the familiar will leave us sad, disoriented or less well off than we've grown accustomed to being. But it need not be that way at all. Change just means doing something *differently*, and it doesn't automatically equate to things being worse than they typically have been; it could indeed be the start of something far better than we could have possibly imagined but that we have not previously permitted to materialize. Allowing change of an especially positive nature can be truly life affirming, especially for those nearing the ends of their corporeal journeys. The residents of the Marigold Hotel come to see this for themselves once they're willing to embrace the beliefs that let it happen.

Our lives, like those of the Marigold Hotel guests, truly are journeys, explorations of self-discovery and constantly becoming who we were meant to be. To make the most of that experience, we would be wise to leave ourselves open to change to maximize the scope of our personal adventures, especially in the waning days of those expeditions. Let us hope that we all have the wisdom to make that possible for ourselves, to discover the joy that Evelyn, Muriel, Graham, Douglas, Jean, Norman and Madge find for themselves in their respective adventures.

"The Best Exotic Marigold Hotel" is a charming film, full of life, vibrancy and gentle humor. Its exquisite cinematography and mesmerizing soundtrack combine to paint a lush portrait of an exotic land in all its beauty and all its challenges. The excellent ensemble cast blends well together (especially Wilkinson, Nighy, Smith and Dench), though the writing sometimes fails them when it comes to the degree of interaction the principals have with one another (even though they're each following their own paths, it would have been nice to see those paths cross one another a little more than they do). The script also falls prey to a certain degree of predictability, but then that's compensated for by an equal measure of surprise, offsetting that minor shortcoming. The film received two Golden Globe nominations for best comedy picture and Dench's performance as best comedy actress.

This picture serves as a valuable reminder that time passes in this life far faster than most of us often realize and that we'd better make the most of it while we can, especially when the hourglass is running out. In life, as in the movies, I've found that some of the most rewarding moments come toward the end of the picture, a time that often undergoes some of the most significant plotline changes we'll experience. And, to get the most out of those moments, it's up to us to savor those times before the credits roll.

The Power of Love

"Amour" ("Love")
Year of Release: 2012
Cast: Jean-Louis Trintignant, Emmanuelle Riva,
Isabelle Huppert, William Shimell, Alexandre Tharaud
Director: Michael Haneke
Screenplay: Michael Haneke

Love is one of those sublime intangibles that artists of all callings, from Shakespeare to the Beatles, have sought to define, revere and embrace through their creations. Yet it encompasses such a vast array of qualities that it's difficult to properly pay homage to all that it makes possible, especially during trying times of change. Nevertheless, the daunting nature of that task has not deterred those seeking to pay tribute to the subject and what it makes possible, as is amply evidenced in director Michael Haneke's emotive drama, *"Amour"* ("Love").

Former music teachers Georges and Anne Laurent (Jean-Louis Trintignant, Emmanuelle Riva) enjoy a comfortable retirement. The middle class octogenarian couple lives a rich, rewarding life in Paris filled with evenings at the arts, visits from Eva, their daughter (Isabelle Huppert), and Alexandre, a now-famous former student (Alexandre Tharaud), and, above all, the loving company of one another. Indeed, despite the passage of many years, it's obvious that Georges and Anne are still *very* much in love with one another. Which is why it's so utterly heartbreaking when Anne's health takes a turn for the worse. She suffers a series of strokes, and each episode leads to progressively greater debilitation and steadily greater demands on Georges' ability to care for her.

With Anne's continual descent into incapacitation, the couple is forced to adapt to their new circumstances. While they struggle to preserve things as they always have been, they must increasingly face the reality of a future of things never being the same ever again. Perhaps the only constant in their lives is the love they share for one another, a bond that's persistently challenged as they move forward, its strength and resilience repeatedly tested. But is that love enough to see them through the onslaught of ever-changing circumstances?

Or will a breaking point be reached? And, if so, what then? Such are the challenging conditions the couple must address.

As we all know, there's tremendous power in our beliefs to shape our reality, especially when our thoughts turn to love. The power associated with beliefs behind this emotion is so formidable that it's sometimes difficult to fathom. But what wonders it can work! For instance, the power to create an intimate, committed relationship spanning decades, such as that enjoyed by Georges and Anne, is just one such example of what it can do. The power that it provides each of them to successfully maintain their bond for so long, especially in the face of ever-growing challenges and unceasing changes, is truly awe-inspiring, to say the least.

But love's ability to nurture and uphold a partnership over the long term represents only a portion of its capabilities. It's a power that enables its adherents to cope with beliefs related to other creations, particularly those that involve significant changes in circumstances, such as life and death, and the emotions associated with them, like those related to letting go and acceptance, not to mention the frustration that frequently accompanies such ordeals. While love may not be a panacea for such conditions, it can at least provide a cushioning buffer to ameliorate their impact, making them more manageable to deal with. The love two individuals share under these circumstances can even grow deeper, richer and more eloquent, changing for the better, even as things otherwise fall apart. Indeed, were it not for the belief in love that Georges and Anne have for one another, their journey together in their waning days would be far different—and considerably more difficult.

Beliefs also play a significant role in defining the world that Georges and Anne experience. As time goes by and circumstances begin to close in on them, their changing world becomes progressively—and noticeably—"smaller." Limitation significantly begins to characterize their existence. Moreover, "outside" influences, like the role of family and friends, play an increasingly irrelevant part in the protagonists' daily lives. So, as Georges and Anne approach the end of their time together, they use their beliefs to manifest a reality that centers almost exclusively on just the two of them. They spend virtually all of their time only with one another and only within the confines of their apartment. It's a feeling that audiences might find uncomfortably claustrophobic (especially given the way it's filmed), but it's also something that Georges and Anne willingly embrace, something they're unlikely to share with others; they're simply creating an existence that suits *their* needs and wants at the time, one that's designed to get them through this transition and that allows them to get as much out of their devotion for one another with whatever time they have left. Some might take issue with some of their choices, but, when we examine what's driving them, it's easy to see the characters' motivation—the love that they share—*despite* the prevailing conditions.

Now that's *amour*.

Director Michael Haneke has produced an excellent picture here, even if it's one that's painful to watch at times. Riva and Trintignant both turn in superb performances, evoking genuine, heartfelt (some would say heartbreaking) emotions throughout, so keep those handkerchiefs handy. And please *do* keep an open mind to what this film is saying; it's not merely a heart-tugging tearjerker but a thoughtful meditation on the power and beauty of the emotion that comprises the movie's title. I recommend it highly.

"*Amour*" came up a *big* surprise at the Academy Awards, capturing five nominations, including best picture, best actress (for Riva, who *truly* deserved to win), best director, best original screenplay and best foreign language film, which it won. The picture also won the *Palme d'Or* at the Cannes Film Festival and a Golden Globe Award for best foreign language film. It should be noted that foreign language movies seldom do so well in mainstream awards competitions, so the number of accolades it received speaks volumes about the picture's quality.

The power to love (and to be loved) has to be one of the greatest conceptions that we, as law of attraction practitioners, could have come up with in our exploration of reality creation. When we see what it makes possible, especially in the face of whatever change and adversity may accompany it, we can draw inspiration from this potent force to help us adapt. "*Amour*" sheds light on this notion and does so brilliantly, allowing us to see how each of us can make use of it to withstand whatever changes may come our way.

10

MISFIRES

In the course of perfecting our conscious creation skills, we each have lessons to learn. Given the trial-and-error nature of this process, we're all bound to make "missteps" along the paths of our respective learning curves. While it may be frustrating for us when things don't turn out as hoped for, we can also take comfort in the idea that such "failures" provide us with opportunities to learn from our "mistakes," to find the "flaws" in our beliefs so that, one hopes, we don't repeat them.

This concept is applicable to any aspect of our lives, be it career, romance, finances, creativity, spirituality, or even building a snowman or baking a soufflé. It's also relevant for filmmakers. Even the most talented directors have had their share of clunkers during their careers, but these *misfires* often help set them right for future projects, making them aware of their creative shortcomings and what areas of their art are in need of improvement.

While I generally avoid writing about films I dislike these days (see this book's Introduction), I nonetheless don't hesitate to do so when necessary, particularly when it comes to films that attempt to explore metaphysically oriented themes and fail in doing so. My reason for this is to caution those in the target audiences for these pictures, forewarning them about the time and money they can save themselves by eschewing pictures that miss the mark. In some instances, these films have major backing behind them and are plugged with intensive marketing campaigns to actively seek this specialty audience. But, in my opinion, if such films *truly* want to appeal to this segment of moviegoers, their creators had better have their cinematic acts together when it comes to the finished products.

Some might contend that I hold these pictures to a higher standard than I would other releases, and they're probably right. But, given that these movies aspire to a higher calling in terms of their content and message, I believe that they had better deliver the goods, too. Their viewers demand and deserve it; if such films fail to live up to their potential (and their promotional hype), I have no hesitation to call them on it.

Cinematic misfires have their place, though, in that they help filmmakers perfect their craft, as well as refine the beliefs that underlie the manifestation of their projects, a skill that should help them in *any* of their movie endeavors, regardless of message or content. That still doesn't equate to my endorsement of such pictures, but it does show how even those in the movie industry can learn by doing when it comes to honing their law of attraction skills.

Most of the misfires profiled in this Chapter were highly anticipated prior to their release, and they cover a wide range of metaphysically oriented subjects, including ancient Earth prophecies, the dream landscape, one woman's spiritual journey, the healing power of quantum physics and defining our relationship with God. And it would have indeed been wonderful if these offerings had lived up to their hype. But, as this Chapter's reviews reveal, they all missed the mark to one degree or another, sometimes in small ways and sometimes in epic proportions.

Thankfully, conscious creation offers all of us—even filmmakers—all the "do overs" we need to get things right. Let's just hope we don't have to belabor things to get that message.

An Unmitigated Disaster

"2012"
Year of Release: 2009
Cast: John Cusack, Amanda Peet, Chiwetel Ejiofor,
Thandie Newton, Danny Glover, Oliver Platt,
Woody Harrelson, Tom McCarthy, Liam James,
Morgan Lily, Zlatko Buric, Beatrice Rosen, Alexandre Haussmann,
Philippe Haussmann, Johann Urb, John Billingsley,
Chin Han, Osric Chau, Tseng Chang, Lisa Lu,
Blu Mankuma, George Segal, Stephen McHattie, Jimi Mistry, Henry O
Director: Roland Emmerich
Screenplay: Roland Emmerich and Harald Kloser

With the approach of the end of the Mayan calendar on December 21, 2012, considerable attention was devoted to this enigmatic event. Some saw it positively, a time for a new beginning; others viewed it as Armageddon come to life. It also prompted the creation of countless books, TV specials and films, chief among them being the much-anticipated disaster epic, "2012."

At the time of this picture's release, I had hoped, perhaps somewhat naïvely, that it might help to shed at least a little light on this potentially significant temporal (and spiritual) phenomenon. Sadly, however, it proved to be an unmitigated disaster—both in its story and as a finished product.

Given the film's premise, there's really not very much going on here. Essentially, the Earth is falling apart, and mankind is racing against time to save something of itself before the special effects budget runs out. Sequence after sequence depicts the obliteration of familiar landmarks and global capitals as a result of earthquakes, volcanoes and tsunamis. It's like watching every Irwin Allen movie ever made, all rolled up into one big, episodically linked, computer-generated package of madness, mayhem and destruction.

People are needed to carry the narrative, of course, so the film wisely incorporates some *bona fide* humans to accomplish this. Viewers thus get to watch Armageddon play out from various perspectives, including those of a down-and-out writer (John Cusack), his estranged wife (Amana Peet) and her new love interest (Tom McCarthy), all of whom always happen to be in the right place at the right time (they've obviously mastered the art of synchronicity, if nothing else); a team of intrepid scientists (Chiwetel Ejiofor, John Billingsley, Jimi Mistry) desperately struggling against impossible odds to use their expertise to save the planet (maybe now they'd wished they'd paid more attention in metaphysics class); a U.S. President (Danny Glover) attempting to hold things together in trying times, all the while badgered by a hyper-ambitious, self-serving political advisor (Oliver Platt) (some things never change, even with Judgment Day looming); and a gonzo alternative journalist (Woody Harrelson) who broadcasts from his ramshackle RV and comes across like a fusion of Robin Williams and radio host Art Bell.

Since the special effects are the real star of this story, however, the actors knew enough not to upstage their CGI counterparts, and so they accommodate their electronic co-stars by turning in performances so subdued that they might as well have phoned them in. But even the high-gloss special effects have issues, often portraying scenes in cartoonish, laughably implausible ways. It's amazing, for example, how a capsizing aircraft carrier can ride the crest of a massive tsunami for hundreds of miles with its planes still on deck and apparently intact (who says Americans can't build things the way they used to?).

Given the current calendar chronology, some would argue (and rightfully so) that this film is now irretrievably irrelevant. But, considering that it's still available for viewing, it also remains fair game for critical scrutiny. And there's *a lot* to take to task, too.

Most significantly, it's sad to see how shabbily this film treats the subject of the 2012 Mayan calendar prophecy, the supposed impetus behind the picture. While some viewed the ending of the Mayan calendar as a harbinger of planetary doom and destruction, many others saw it as the dawning of a new era characterized by fortuitous change and ample promise, a perspective that's completely ignored here. In fact, the calendar itself is barely mentioned, its existence essentially reduced to passing references that amount to little more than "Oh, and by the way, the Mayans predicted all this" (which, as most Mayans and Mayan scholars contended, was largely inaccurate, too). It's as if this temporal benchmark was used as nothing more than a convenient coat hook on which to hang this buffoonish tale of apocalyptic abomination.

Considering the metaphysical attributes that many associated with the Mayan calendar's ending, one would think that at least *something* of it would have been incorporated into the film. Conscious creators in particular looked to the time frame in question with much anticipation, anxiously wondering what we would end up manifesting, a concern that gave many practitioners pause to carefully assess what beliefs they held, given their role in shaping what existence would ultimately materialize. But such considerations, like all other philosophical and spiritual notions tied to 2012, are completely ignored in this picture, a disappointing result and a glaring oversight in light of the high level of interest placed in these issues prior to the event's arrival and at the time of the movie's release.

It's unfortunate so many film and television producers took such a dim view of the 2012 phenomenon in the run-up to the event. They painted a bleak picture that many viewers willingly bought into, unduly raising the anxiety level for the gullible and drawing attention away from the hope that many believed the calendar's ending was meant to signify. Indeed, when this picture was released, I couldn't help but wonder why *anyone* would want to model our future based on probabilities like those depicted in the movie. Even if we believe in the need to "cleanse" our planet of its many ills, as many thought at the time, must we really destroy Tokyo, Rio and Paducah to accomplish this? I'm relieved that we considered other options and chose our beliefs wisely before unleashing a firestorm of natural disasters and social collapse at calendar's end, especially since, as conscious creators are well aware, mass event co-creations can manifest as potent materializations (for better or worse) when energized by the power of the human collective.

As I noted in this book's Introduction and this Chapter's opening summary, I rarely write negative reviews of the films I watch. But, unless you're someone who really enjoys watching things blow up for 2½ hours (destroying the world takes time apparently), there's not much to recommend here. It's a shame that those behind this picture chose to tell a story about 2012 in this way. The filmmakers missed out on a chance to enlighten us on what could have been the inauguration of a miraculous time in the history of humanity and the planet. And such a missed opportunity, regrettably, is an even bigger disaster than any of the calamities depicted on screen.

A Missed Opportunity

"Inception"
Year of Release: 2010
Cast: Leonardo DiCaprio, Ellen Page, Joseph Gordon-Levitt,
Marion Cotillard, Tom Berenger, Michael Caine,
Tom Hardy, Ken Watanabe, Dileep Rao,
Cillian Murphy, Pete Postlethwaite
Director: Christopher Nolan
Screenplay: Christopher Nolan

In my opinion, the most critical factor in a film's success, from both a purely cinematic standpoint and in any of its associated metaphysical content, is the strength of its story. If a movie fails on this point, it lacks a suitable foundation upon which to build, regardless of its other attributes. This is especially true when a picture aspires to a sense of greatness, either in a strictly entertainment-related context or as a medium for imparting significant knowledge. And that's why it's so disappointing that one of the most ambitious and most anticipated sci-fi releases of recent years, "Inception," comes up short.

Dom Cobb (Leonardo DiCaprio) is an expert at extraction—not the kind that dentists perform but the kind that corporate saboteurs engage in. He works in the dream state to "extract" (*i.e.*, steal) secrets from the minds of high-profile executives for the strategic benefit of their rivals (his clients). Having developed a reputation as the best at what he does, Cobb is hired to perform a task for Mr. Saito (Ken Watanabe), head of a major multinational who wants to rid himself of his only significant competitor. But this assignment is a little different; instead of extracting information, Cobb is charged with *implanting* an idea in the mind of his target and to do so convincingly enough that the target believes the idea is his own, an act of "inception." Succeeding at inception is anything but guaranteed, however; few have tried it, and failure inevitably followed. But, being the expert that he is, Cobb has performed the procedure successfully and is thus tasked to do the job.

Cobb's target is Robert Fischer (Cillian Murphy), heir to the immense corporate empire built by his dying father, Maurice (Pete Postlethwaite). He's assigned to implant an idea in Fischer's mind that he should dissolve his father's empire upon his inheritance (thereby eliminating Saito's competition). As compensation for his efforts, Cobb is set to receive what he desires most—a cleared criminal record that will allow him to freely reenter the U.S. As a fugitive wanted for the alleged murder of his wife, Mal (Marion Cotillard), Cobb perpetually circles the globe to do jobs and to stay ahead of the law. But the one thing he most wants—the opportunity to return home—has eluded him, at least until now.

With such a powerful incentive looming, Cobb undertakes his assigned task. He assembles a team to assist him, including Arthur, his trusted associate (Joseph Gordon-Levitt); Ariadne, a gifted young architect charged with designing the structure of the dreamscape in which the mission is to be carried out (Ellen Page); Eames, a con artist par excellence who's capable of materializing effective deceptions on demand (Tom Hardy); and Yusuf, a chemist whose potent concoctions keep everyone sufficiently sedated long enough to complete the task (Dileep Rao). The big question for the team, of course, is, will they succeed in a netherworld as ethereal as the dream state?

While the foregoing summary probably makes the film sound like an otherworldly crime caper, its emphasis on exploring the character of the dream state provides the main focus of the movie's narrative, an aspect of the picture that, arguably, would seem to elevate its intentions to something more substantial. If a movie aspires to something that profound, though, the story and script have to deliver the goods, and this is where "Inception" misses the mark in several significant ways.

Alternate realities (like the dream state) provide venues for trying out new ideas and exploring uncharted scenarios, environments where essentially anything is possible. However, this film's depiction of the dream state is riddled with rules, regulations and limitations that undermine that basic premise. Granted, nearly all of these alleged restrictions are based on Cobb's own beliefs, convictions that he has allowed to color his views of all things dream-related and that he consequently draws upon (either consciously or unconsciously) to orchestrate how things play out in the dream world (or at least how *he* believes they play out in this alternate reality). But the problem with this is that these notions are generally presented as universal metaphysical absolutes, thereby seriously mischaracterizing the nature of the dream state (and all because their inclusion is necessary to make the storyline work). Not only does this make for an often-confusing plot, but it also does a disservice to viewers by presenting a skewed depiction of this material. (Missed Opportunity No. 1.)

In a similar vein, there are a number of discussions among characters regarding what's "real" and what isn't. Such discussions are painfully frustrating to sit through; again, as conscious creation practitioners know, just because a reality like the dream state operates according to a different set of rules doesn't mean that it's any less "real" than the waking consciousness state with which we're most familiar. *All* realities, including the dream state, are real and equally valid, regardless of the basis on which they function, a notion frequently disregarded by this film, thus doing viewers a major metaphysical disservice. (Missed Opportunity No. 2.)

Finally, I find it somewhat hard to accept that someone like Cobb, who's proficient at working in the dream state, would choose to apply his considerable expertise for the purposes that he ultimately does. Given his extensive experience in this area (told through flashbacks), we're shown a character who has come face to face with this reality's power—and the inherent *responsibility* and *respect* that come from working with it. In view of his subsequent choices, then, one can't help but wonder whether he learned anything from his own experiences, especially since he's elected to apply his skills for such singularly self-serving aims (and ones that purposely inflict significant harm on others, no less). It would seem that someone with his level of awareness would be more amenable to using his capabilities for something more worthwhile than engaging in acts of corporate espionage. What's more, the trials and tribulations he experiences while participating in such exploits leave me with little empathy for him when the going gets tough, despite the film's attempts at generating sympathy for him. Perhaps this reflects a personal prejudice on my part, but employing characters to demonstrate the potential of the dream state through the kinds of acts depicted on screen seems like yet another viewer disservice. (Missed Opportunity No. 3.)

To be sure, all possibilities are equally valid according to law of attraction principles, and the storyline presented here is no exception. However, for a film that seeks to aspire to something enlightening and instructive, this picture's story falls short of that mark. Some might contend I'm holding the movie to an unattainably high standard, but I'd argue that, considering what the film appears to be aiming for, I don't believe I'm being unfair. I'm pleased that it has raised public awareness of this subject; I just wish it had done a better job at it.

In light of this failing, then, I'd recommend that anyone who seriously wants to learn more about the nature of the dream state would be better served by reading one of the many excellent books on the subject. A few that I'd recommend are Robert Waggoner's *Lucid Dreaming: Gateway to the Inner Self* or any of the writings of author and dream researcher Robert Moss.

Nevertheless, with all that said, "Inception" does have its strong points. Its special effects are dazzling, and the performances are all quite engaging. It also effectively presents some valuable information about the nature of the dream state, such as showing how dreams often occur in levels and how they can be used for beneficial purposes like healing. Moreover, the picture poses some intriguing ambiguities, a quality often characteristic of the dream state; in fact, this is an aspect of the film that, if developed further, could have made the story more compelling (but that may have been difficult to implement in view of all the self-imposed storyline restrictions noted earlier). These attributes, as good as they are, however, aren't enough to rescue the film from all of its other inherent pitfalls.

In spite of its shortcomings, the picture had its share of fans, and that became apparent in major awards competitions. The movie took home four Oscars, all in technical categories, on eight total nominations, including best picture and best original screenplay. In addition, the film earned four Golden Globe nominations, including nods for best dramatic picture, best director and best screenplay, but no awards.

While "Inception" may have lived up to its hype, it's unfortunate that it didn't live up to its potential. Director Christopher Nolan has made some terrific films over the years, but he may have tried reaching too far (or perhaps not far enough?) with this offering. The picture may have provided an opportunity to entertain, but it certainly missed one to enlighten.

Travelogue Spirituality

"Eat Pray Love"
Year of Release: 2010
Cast: Julia Roberts, Javier Bardem, Richard Jenkins,
Viola Davis, Billy Crudup, James Franco, Hadi Subiyanto,
Mike O'Malley, Tuva Novotny, Luca Argentero,
Giuseppe Gandini, Sophie Thompson,
Rushita Singh, Christine Hakim
Director: Ryan Murphy
Screenplay: Ryan Murphy and Jennifer Salt
Book: Elizabeth Gilbert,
Eat Pray Love: One Woman's Search for Everything
Across Italy, India and Indonesia

The search for oneself, one's purpose in life and one's connection to the greater scheme of things is a common theme in stories of all kinds, from classic mythology to contemporary literature and even present-day cinema. That time-honored theme also took center stage in one of 2010's most anticipated theatrical releases, "Eat Pray Love."

Based on the best-selling memoir of the same name by writer Elizabeth (Liz) Gilbert, "Eat Pray Love" chronicles the year-long globe-trekking odyssey of the author (portrayed here by Julia Roberts) in her quest to find herself—and God. The story opens in New York not long before Liz's divorce from her husband, Stephen (Billy Crudup), a likable but ultimately lost soul. Rather than stay stuck in an unsatisfying marriage, Liz decides to end it and move on. But to what?

Liz initially takes up with David (James Franco), an aspiring young actor who bears a strikingly uncanny resemblance to her ex-husband, only in a younger version. But, upon realizing that she's on the road to repeating the same mistake, Liz decides she needs to pursue a more radical course. Having always had a strong sense of wanderlust, she decides to travel the world in search of herself and a new spiritual compass. Her itinerary takes her to Italy, then to an ashram in India, and finally to the Indonesian island of Bali.

Throughout the course of her journey, Liz learns various lessons about life. A colorful assortment of guides helps her along the way, too, including a transplanted Swede living in Rome (Tuva Novotny), an uprooted Texan looking to find himself in India (Richard Jenkins), a Balinese holy man (Hadi Subiyanto), a miracle-working medicine woman (Christine Hakim) and a sexy, sensitive Brazilian living in paradise (Javier Bardem). As a result of her experiences and interactions, Liz finds a new way of looking at herself, her existence and her relationship with the divine—or at least that's what viewers are told they're supposed to believe, which is where, in my opinion, this film fails to deliver.

While I'd like to believe that the creators of this movie had the best of intentions, sadly, those aspirations are not reflected in the finished product. That's because the picture focuses more on the surface trappings of Gilbert's story rather than on the inner, heartfelt insights she was supposed to have gleaned from her journey, ultimately emphasizing shallow style over meaningful substance. In doing so, the movie comes across as more travelogue than revelation. It showcases its worldly destinations beautifully, serving up a banquet of gorgeous location shots, but, when it comes to its spiritual and metaphysical aspects, it offers only the occasional morsel—and in carefully controlled portions at that.

In the course of Liz's odyssey, we learn that she is something of a quiet, but nevertheless self-avowed, control freak. To overcome this, what she really needs to do is let go and live life, and the filmmakers try very hard to convince us that that's precisely what she's done by story's end. Unfortunately, that's a stretch, given that the film itself is frequently flat, devoid of the passionate zest for living—in all its permutations—that makes such an accomplishment possible. In fact, the picture is so lacking in this regard that viewers practically have to take the filmmakers' word for it.

The movie's overarching spiritual message deals with learning how to embrace both the outer, secular world (as told through Liz's trip to Italy) and the inner, divine world (as told through her trip to India) and then how to successfully integrate the two (as explored in her Bali experience). And that's certainly a worthwhile ambition, not unlike some of the ideas embodied in conscious creation principles. However, given the message's presentation here, the relevance often gets lost in the depiction of local culture and attractions. Liz's Italian experience, for example, with its spotlight on the secular, features so many eating sequences that it's like watching programming from the Food Network. Similarly, the Indian sequence focuses more on religious ritual than it does on spiritual practice, frequently muddying the water when it comes to distinguishing the two and underemphasizing the significance of the latter. The Bali sequence, easily the film's strongest, comes across best in making its point, but even that is often diluted by the incorporation of sidebar stories that, as nice as they are, divert viewers from the main path, taking them down unnecessary secondary roads.

The foregoing issues aside, "Eat Pray Love" is not without its strengths. As noted above, it's beautiful to look at, and its performances effectively flesh out the characters (especially those of the guides), making the narrative appear stronger than it actually is. But, in the end, even these assets can't save a picture that's lost and in search of a point to make.

Viewers looking for films about seekers in search of themselves and their connection to the Universe have a long list of better selections to choose from, and they'd be wise to give those pictures a look before spending time on this underwhelming offering. Those searching for movies that address this topic from a woman's perspective in particular should check out such choices as "Under the Tuscan Sun" (2003), "Shirley Valentine" (1989), "An Unmarried Woman" (1978) or "Bread and Tulips" (2000), to name a few.

While I certainly see the value of addressing the kinds of ideas this film attempts to explore, I also believe these notions need to be given their just due when displayed on the silver screen. Revelatory insights merit more attention than passing notation like oh so many items on a travel guide's list of must-see attractions for a particular destination. Viewers truly deserve better when it comes to issues as important as this.

Tearjerker Metaphysics

"Rabbit Hole"
Year of Release: 2010
Cast: Nicole Kidman, Aaron Eckhart, Dianne Wiest,
Miles Teller, Tammy Blanchard, Sandra Oh,
Giancarlo Esposito, Jon Tenney, Stephen Mailer
Director: John Cameron Mitchell
Screenplay: David Lindsay-Abaire
Play: David Lindsay-Abaire, Rabbit Hole

Part of the process of coming to know ourselves involves learning to recognize (and honor) the multidimensional nature of our greater being. This requires us to acknowledge the aspects of our selves that we like and know, as well as those that we don't. While many of us readily embrace the "good" parts, we frequently avoid the "bad" ones and ignore or overlook the "unknown" elements. But, since all of these aspects are part of our innate greater being, sooner or later we must come to terms with all of them, for better or worse. Exploring the qualities we'd rather shun or that we don't know about might seem like a daunting, overwhelming prospect, but, if we leave ourselves open to experiencing them genuinely and with the same fervor we give to the aspects we cherish, we just might find that they spawn curious transformations in us, a premise probed in the drama, "Rabbit Hole."

In the wake of their young son's tragic death, an upscale Yonkers couple, Becca (Nicole Kidman) and Howie (Aaron Eckhart), struggles to understand their loss and their responses to it. They flail about emotionally, looking for answers that aren't to be found in life's little handbook. Should they feel sad? Angry? Guilty? Indifferent? And who's at fault for the accident that claimed their son's life—the teenage driver who struck and killed the child as he chased the dog he so adored into the street? The mother who left her child unattended momentarily to answer a ringing phone? The father who gave the child a dog to playfully pursue in the first place? Or, since we create our own realities, one could even argue that the responsibility lies with the child himself, cold as that may sound. Indeed, when it comes to questions like this, there are no clear, easy or consoling answers.

Seeking the comfort and counsel of others doesn't help much, either, as attempts at consolation often deteriorate into discussions that reopen old wounds or raise frustrating new challenges. Becca's conversations with her mother, Nat (Dianne Wiest), for instance, frequently recall the death of the drug-addicted adult son she lost years earlier, a tragedy Becca is willing to acknowledge but unwilling to compare to her own loss. Attending support group meetings for grieving parents is another option, but, even though Howie takes some comfort from these gatherings, they try Becca's patience, especially when the sessions evoke discussions involving religion, a particularly sore subject for her. And, if all that weren't enough, Becca and Howie must now wrestle with the revelation by Becca's sister, Izzy (Tammy Blanchard), that she's pregnant, news that serves as a constant reminder of their departed child's palpable absence.

With their world falling apart and the couple growing ever more distant from one another, Becca and Howie pursue different avenues to relieve their unrelenting sadness. Howie continues with the support group on his own, developing a close friendship with fellow group member Gaby (Sandra Oh), a long-term attendee of the sessions whose husband recently left her. Becca, meanwhile, develops a bond with Jason (Miles Teller), the driver of the ill-fated vehicle that killed her son. He's an aspiring graphic novel artist who's created a work called *The Rabbit Hole* in which the protagonist explores the infinite probabilities made possible by quantum theory (and conscious creation) to resolve the dilemmas in his life, an adventure through which the story's hero meets other versions of himself. Becca finds the budding author's ideas intriguing, because they speak to her in ways that other, more conventional sources of solace can't. But, as promising as these coping measures are, the question remains, will they be enough to help Becca and Howie resolve their feelings and heal their hearts?

Followers of conscious creation principles (and their related quantum physics concepts) know that we're each more than just the "localized" or "indigenous" selves with whom we're most familiar. They're well aware of our intrinsic multidimensionality, with different aspects (or "fragments") of our greater being busily exploring different (or parallel) probabilities of existence, some of which we might be able to envision (and draw inspiration from) and some of which are wholly unfathomable unless or until we interact with them directly. Some of those probable existences are pleasant, while others are not, and others still lie somewhere in between, thereby spanning the whole spectrum of reality capable of being experienced. And what's the ultimate mission of these widely dispersed selves? To engage in different expressions of reality, doing "field work" about various aspects of existence and reporting their findings back to the greater being of which each is a part.

For those who are new to these concepts, it's often hard to imagine that anyone would willingly want to experience probable existences that plumb the darker sides of life. The idea that anyone would freely sign up for a battery of unpleasantness seems implausible and counterintuitive. But, given that our greater selves ultimately seek to experience *all* that life has to offer, sooner or later we must also probe the negative sides of existence. Obviously that can be quite painful to endure, as Becca and Howie discover, but, in the end, it's all part of the aforementioned metaphysical education process.

Ironically enough, such unpleasantness may play a significant role in helping us better understand the full scope of probable existences. Difficult conditions frequently prompt us to observe, "There must be a better way," a notion that itself is often enough to open our minds to envision other, more palatable lines of reality. An awareness of such parallel paths of existence may suddenly seem much less far-fetched—perhaps even *attainable*.

Becca discovers this for herself in the film through readings of *The Rabbit Hole* and the book that inspired it, *Parallel Universes*, by author and quantum physicist Fred Alan Wolf. (Interestingly, the title of Jason's graphic novel is reflected in the subtitle—"Down the Rabbit Hole"—of the DVD release of "What the #$*! Do We (K)now!?" (2004), the groundbreaking cinematic treatise on quantum physics and conscious creation in which Wolf serves as one of the featured experts.) These books open doors for Becca that she hadn't previously considered, ultimately making it easier for her to cope with her circumstances, a lesson we could all learn from.

Exploring the notion of probable existences might seem like an odd element in the narrative of a film like this. Who would have thought that such an arguably esoteric concept could legitimately occupy a place in a story of personal tragedy? However, that may just be the point behind its inclusion, for it helps to show the way out of seemingly overwhelming conditions when other means of coping don't. In fact, if we were to apply this idea to the trials and tribulations of our own everyday experiences, we just might find that life can be considerably more manageable and fulfilling than we thought possible.

Admittedly, including a theme like this in the narrative of a story like this definitely took some courage, and I certainly applaud the nobility of this attempt at shedding light on an inventive approach to solving problems that seem to defy resolution. Unfortunately, the treatment this tactic receives in the screenplay is also the picture's undoing, keeping an otherwise-promising movie from fully living up to its potential.

From this summary, it would appear that this theme occupies a dominant place in the film, but that's not the case. To keep such an unconventional element from overpowering a narrative that's essentially a story of personal tragedy (and a rather formulaic one at that), the writing downplays the metaphysical material, timidly working it into the script. By giving this aspect of the story such kid gloves treatment, its presentation almost seems like an intrusion or afterthought, and that's unfortunate, given the crucial role it plays in helping Becca resolve her challenges. Instead, the screenplay focuses more on the conventional aspects of the story, turning the film into an often-predictable tearjerker. It loosely links a collection of "moments," many of them clichéd, yielding an uneven mixture of pathos, comic relief and pregnant pauses, with smatterings of alternative philosophy thrown in along the way, often awkwardly or offhandedly.

The film's acting is uneven, too. Despite her Golden Globe and Oscar nominations for best actress, Kidman turns in a mixed performance that includes a number of scenes where she positively nails the material, along with others where she clearly knows she's in front of the camera. Meanwhile, Teller's portrayal of the guilt-ridden teen is so understated that he looks like he's sleepwalking his way through it. Thankfully, Wiest, Blanchard, Oh and, most notably, Eckhart turn in some of the finest work of their careers, making the most out of their material (and often making it look better than it actually is).

Regrettably, "Rabbit Hole" comes up short of what it could have been. By mishandling the metaphysical subject matter as they did, the film's creators missed a prime opportunity to both entertain and enlighten. One can only hope that there's another version of this picture out there somewhere, down the rabbit hole of one of those other lines of probability, that makes up for its all-too-many shortcomings.

Trimming the Branches

"The Tree of Life"
Year of Release: 2011
Cast: Brad Pitt, Sean Penn, Jessica Chastain,
Hunter McCracken, Laramie Eppler,
Tye Sheridan, Fiona Shaw
Director: Terrence Malick
Screenplay: Terrence Malick

What's our place in the Universe? Is there a God? And, if so, what is He/She/It like? Does that supposed Supreme Being love us, or is It a capricious, unknowable entity that treats us like playthings for Its own amusement? These are profound questions that have wracked the brains, tried the patience and perplexed the minds of scholars and ordinary folks alike for eons—and nearly always without satisfactory resolution. Which is why it's so amazing that a movie would attempt to take on the ambitious challenge of addressing those very issues, as is the case with one of the most highly anticipated metaphysical releases of recent years, director Terrence Malick's enigmatic opus, "The Tree of Life."

"The Tree of Life" is a difficult film to categorize. In many respects, it's more a meditation than a narrative, exploring life's cosmic questions in cinematically poetic fashion. In fact, in that regard, many have astutely likened this picture to Stanley Kubrick's "2001: A Space Odyssey" (1968), continuing many of its predecessor's themes but with a focus that's more spiritual than cerebral. And, regardless of how one might view such an artistic venture, either as a concept or as a finished product, the attempt to fulfill the lofty goals to which "The Tree of Life" aspires definitely represents an audacious undertaking. However, in my view, the result is a mix of both brilliance and tedium, succeeding tremendously in some ways and disappointing greatly in others.

As in Kubrick's masterpiece, the story here is incidental when compared to the themes the picture seeks to explore. In a nutshell, disillusioned middle-aged architect Jack O'Brien (Sean Penn) looks back on his childhood in 1950s Texas, attempting to come to terms with his conflicted relationships with his parents (Brad Pitt, Jessica Chastain) and the unexpected loss of a brother at a young age. In doing so, Jack relives his youth through the memories of his younger self (Hunter McCracken), particularly his struggle to find his way in a world seemingly full of mixed messages, many of which come from parents who often appear to contradict themselves and each other. But there's much more going on here than just a coming-of-age story in which both the elder and younger Jack try to understand the tangible trappings of their respective worlds; they also seek to grasp the meaning behind it all—if there indeed *is* any meaning to be had.

Through the characters' experiences, many profound notions are raised and explored. One of the more prominent themes, which substantially frames the prevailing tenor of the film, is expressed in a voice-over by Jack's mother near the outset. In her narration, she speaks of the distinction between the state of grace and the state of nature; those who have faith in the former and accept whatever comes their way, for better or worse, will be rewarded with a blessed existence, while those who abide by the latter and attempt to force their existence into being will be met with disappointment, no matter how seemingly genuine their intentions. As Jack grows up, he grapples with understanding these ideas, a challenge made especially difficult by the actions and teachings of parents who embody each viewpoint, seemingly contradicting one another yet nearly always attaining results commensurate with their respective outlooks. The challenge in this for both the younger and the elder Jack is to decide which viewpoint to embrace.

The depiction of Jack's parents as symbolic representations of these two viewpoints illuminates another of the film's significant themes (and one near and dear to the hearts of conscious creation practitioners)—that of the physical and nonphysical worlds being reflections of one another. Jack's mother, for example, is a flesh-and-blood materialization of the concept of living in a state of grace, one who cooperatively collaborates with the spirit of the divine by allowing it to flow through her to shape the reality she experiences. Jack's father, by contrast, is clearly an embodiment of the state of nature, one who seeks to control his existence primarily through his own sheer will. Despite their differences in their approach to life, they both nevertheless exemplify ethereal concepts made flesh. In this way, they both also eloquently reflect the metaphysical corollary of "As above, so below" (or, more precisely, "As inside, so outside"), the core operating principle in philosophical doctrines like alchemy and, of course, conscious creation.

In a similar vein, Jack's parents also personify the universal concepts of the divine masculine and divine feminine, particularly how each has been portrayed in conventional spiritual and religious contexts. Jack's father, for example, alternates between being both a loving soul and a hardened authoritarian figure, much the way God *the father* has been portrayed in many of the world's established faith systems, such as traditional Christianity. His mother, by contrast, is often relegated to a secondary role, called upon to provide compassion when needed but seldom being allowed to offer substantively meaningful input on how the children are reared, a circumstance mirroring the woefully limited role that women have typically been allowed to play in most mainstream religious circles, both materially and theologically. However, the recent—and necessary—resurgence of the divine feminine in our outer and inner spiritual lives is depicted here, too, illustrating how things have, thankfully, begun to change in today's world.

Underlying all of these notions is yet another theme that characterizes much of the film's inherent nature—that we are just the latest manifestation in an ongoing series of materializations expressing an array of universal principles, such as those discussed above, in physical form. This is sublimely depicted through a lush montage of evolutionary images illustrating the continuity intrinsic to the physical expression of these concepts. Divinely inspired acts of compassion, for instance, are seen as timeless gestures that have been passed down through the Earth's ages; be they expressed by dinosaurs or by humans, these principles have, and always have had, a place in a world where a divine hand is at work in the act of conscious co-creation. This evolutionary aspect of existence also further evidences the concept that "we"—no matter what physical form "we" might take—are always in a constant state of becoming, materially evincing the nonphysical motivations that drive physical manifestation, regardless of what specific external appearances we may assume in the process.

Clearly, there's a lot going on here, but the film has drawn decidedly mixed reactions, and understandably so. Its poetic, image-based, nonlinear approach, for example, may be confounding to those accustomed to more conventional styles of filmmaking and storytelling. Its inclusion of beautiful imagery for its own sake, incorporated more for nuance than narrative significance, might test some viewers' patience. And its mixture of ethereal and secular imagery could be seen as downright inscrutable, even to the most sophisticated audiences.

Critics' reactions generally followed suit; many praised the film as revelatory, while others panned it as pretentious nonsense, and still others said it incorporates some of both elements. As for me, I would align myself with that third group. When this film is "on," it leaves us awestruck; when it's not, it leaves us wanting to hit the concession stand for a popcorn refill. Still, the picture does have its champions, as evidenced by its success in awards circles, such as the Cannes Film Festival, where it won the *Palme d'Or*. The film also received three Academy Award nominations, including best picture and best director.

The picture's biggest problem, from my perspective, is a need for some very judicious editing. This "tree" has too many branches, some of which need to be pruned to let the healthy growth flourish. Instead, we're given too many unnecessary, and often-redundant, images that would have been far better off left on the cutting room floor. A truly masterful director knows when to stop, but that's not the case here. As *St. Paul Pioneer Press* film critic Chris Hewitt aptly put it, "what we're left with is a scrapbook of stunning images"—and one that has a few too many pages in it.

Flaws aside, the film has a number of strengths. The Oscar-nominated cinematography—the real star of this show—truly is beautiful, and the picture's stunning special effects and engrossing soundtrack provide excellent enhancement for the exquisite on-screen imagery. The performances by Pitt, Chastain and, particularly, McCracken are all quite capable, too, though Penn's considerable talent goes largely untapped thanks to a script that doesn't call upon him to do much other than walk around and emote, a role that virtually anyone could have played. In the end, it's unfortunate that the film's other attributes don't live up to the quality of its strengths; if they had, this easily could have been a milestone picture in the annals of filmmaking.

As ascendant beings who ultimately seek the source from which we came, not unlike the trees that so patiently yet determinedly reach for the life-sustaining sunlight of the sky, we're innately committed to the search for meaningful guidance that will assist us in our terrestrial journey. "The Tree of Life" offers us much in that regard, but its overlong, sometimes needlessly cryptic treatment of its subject matter clouds issues as much as it clarifies them, especially when it tests the patience of viewers, who may regrettably but understandably begin tuning out the picture just as it's on the verge of offering its most beneficial counsel. It's at times like that when a metaphysical chainsaw would come in handy. And, based on the finished product, it's apparent the filmmakers could have used one.

11

REDEMPTION

OK, so you screwed up, and you know it. Now what?

When we experience some kind of setback, we may be tempted to retreat into our respective shells to lick our wounds, and that's fine to get over our pain and disappointment. But, as helpful as that practice can be in the short term, we must be careful *not* to take up permanent residence there, either, because "failure" does not automatically seal our fate nor condemn us to a life of unending despair.

Indeed, as noted throughout this book, one of the real beauties of conscious creation is that we always have infinite probabilities available to us at any given moment. Consequently, this means that we always have the capacities for choice and change available to us at any given moment as well. And, by extension, this also means that we always have the capacity for *redemption* at our disposal—that is, as long as we're willing to avail ourselves of it.

At its heart, redemption is a form of supremely positive change, brought about as a result of personal choice. In that regard, then, it's essentially an application of the law of attraction but one that's instituted in a profound way, one that, for all practical purposes, results in a complete turnaround in one's circumstances. It uplifts us, delivering us from a personally devastating experience and offering us a new beginning. It fills us with hope and demonstrates with unquestioned clarity how the past need not dictate our future.

As this Chapter's entries illustrate, no matter how bleak things may seem, we truly *can* change our destiny when we allow it. Whether we're recoiling from a serious lapse in personal judgment, the loss of a loved one, a miscarriage of justice, a devastating addiction or the pain of past transgressions, it's possible to recover from them, all through consciously created acts of redemption.

When life's unpleasantries befall us, it's easy to lose faith, both in ourselves and our future, especially when we're forced into facing up to the fact that we created these disappointments, too. But one of the disguised blessings in such setbacks is their ability to make us aware of our ability to rebound, something we may easily overlook due to the presence of the challenging conditions. And, in the end, this revelation might prove essential for some of us to become more proficient conscious creators by making us aware of the miracles we're each capable of manifesting.

Talk about redeeming qualities!

Redeeming One's Reality

"People v. The State of Illusion"
Year of Release: 2012
Cast, Fictional Segment: J.B. Tuttle,
Michael McCormick, Kevin McDonald,
Melanie Lindahl, Tad Jones, Amy Baklini;
Expert Commentators: Austin Vickers (narrator),
Thomas Moore, Candace Pert, Debbie Ford,
Joe Dispenza, Robert Jahn, Brenda Dunne,
Peter Senge, Michael Vandermark
Director: Scott Cervine
Screenplay: Austin Vickers

We all know how reality works, right? Or do we? Many of us like to think of our existence as an easily definable, quantifiable experience governed by readily identified laws that apply across the board. It's often seen as a fixed, unchanging experience, one in which we're reconciled to our fate. But is it really that simple, or is there something more subjective at work? What's more, can we change our circumstances, especially when we commit transgressions that make us feel like we'll be saddled with guilt and regret in perpetuity? Indeed, can we genuinely alter our destiny and achieve redemption? Those are some of the considerations addressed in the enlightening documentary, "People v. The State of Illusion."

Aaron Rogers (no relation to the Green Bay Packers quarterback) (J.B. Tuttle) is having a difficult time in life. Separated from his wife and potentially facing a layoff from his job, he struggles to get by. But that's all *before* things go downhill.

One evening, after attending a school play featuring his daughter, Hope (Melanie Lindahl), Aaron runs a red light while driving her home, causing a tragic car accident in which the driver of the other vehicle, a mother of two young children, is killed. But, if that weren't bad enough, he's also found to be legally drunk. Having attended happy hour before meeting Hope, he had enough alcohol in his system at the time of the accident to be charged with DUI—as well as manslaughter.

Not long thereafter, Aaron is tried, found guilty and sentenced to six years in prison. With his life falling apart, he sees no future for himself. He views his existence as a living hell, one that was bad on the outside before the accident but that has now been made that much worse inside his cell walls. Little does he know, however, that this self-assessment of his life will ultimately provide him with a fitting metaphor for defining the essence of the existence he's created—one that will also be the key in helping him understand how to turn things around.

While in jail, Aaron crosses paths with two people who play significant roles in helping him sort out his life, a prison guard (Kevin McDonald) and a janitor (Michael McCormick). Through his conversations with them, Aaron comes to realize that his circumstances, both before and after incarceration, are clearly the product of his own creation, physical manifestations of his prevailing beliefs and worldview. And, as a result of that newfound awareness, he subsequently comes to recognize that *changing* his fate going forward is *also* just as much a product of his beliefs and worldview—provided that he *allows* change to occur. Aaron's redemption is thus in his own hands, just as it is for *any* of us seeking to make amends for the actions of our past. The future is not necessarily dictated by what preceded it; rather, it's shaped by what we do *now* to fashion it in the form we choose for the future. Indeed, the point of power truly *is* in the present moment.

The storyline of this fictional narrative thus takes viewers through the process of personal awakening and self-discovery that

Aaron experiences. Each of the realizations that he comes upon as part of that process are commented on by a panel of experts in the fields of medicine, physiology, psychology and metaphysics. They explain the intrinsic connections between these various disciplines (and how those connections apply to each of us), illustrating how Aaron's circumstances, for better or worse, are, in fact, the result of his own making. The panelists show how those connections lead to the thoughts that become the things that make up Aaron's life—and that can help him redeem it as he moves ahead.

In reaching these conclusions, the experts essentially take the notion of conscious creation as a given, a fundamental starting point for understanding how reality works. They then walk viewers through the steps of how one's tangible existence arises from one's intangible beliefs. However, the experts hasten to add that the beliefs we draw upon to create the reality we experience represent only an infinitesimal part of the total range of belief options available to us. We could just as easily choose a different set of beliefs from the ones we adhere to, but, until we do, the reality we manifest will persist in materializing an existence in line with whatever beliefs prevail. For redemption to take hold, we must adopt beliefs in line with *that* possibility, intentions that will allow its manifestation in our existence.

In that sense, then, the reality we experience is essentially an "illusion," one of *many* subjective, customized possibilities we're each capable of materializing, not an intrinsically objective universal truth applicable to everyone. Learning how to liberate ourselves from such limited thinking, this constricting form of self-imposed imprisonment (a fitting analogy given Aaron's example), is the key to creating a life of greater fulfillment. Of course, becoming aware that we have other options at our disposal in the first place is crucial if we ever hope to escape the sense of confinement that we tend to view as unalterable. In doing so, we must also be willing to accept *responsibility* for what we manifest, because failure in this regard amounts to nothing more than a fundamental abrogation of our role in the process of creating the reality we experience. However, by witnessing Aaron's odyssey, combined with the insights of the expert commentators, we're provided with clues as to how we can do the same for ourselves as the protagonist does for himself.

Those familiar with the enormously popular documentaries "What the #$*! Do We (K)now!?" (2004) and "The Secret" (2006) will undoubtedly recognize the parallels between those films and this production in terms of approach, format and content. However, as commendable as both of those films are, I believe that "People v. The State of Illusion" represents a significant step up from those pictures, providing viewers with clearly defined, highly practical, easily understood information on the reality of reality. Its concise, no-nonsense approach makes its arguments impeccably clear and to the point, and even those who are new to these ideas are likely to come away from this film with an indisputable understanding of the concepts it covers.

The presentation of the picture's central themes in the context of a "trial" is an inspired approach, one that undoubtedly came naturally to screenwriter and narrator Austin Vickers, himself a former litigator. While the narrative doesn't follow a trial format *per se*, the protagonist's actions are clearly on trial in the view of the "people" (*i.e.*, the audience), his contentions countered by the prosecutorial arguments of his prison peers, the narrator and the expert witnesses. And, in the end, after hearing the cases made by each side, we're left to render a verdict on the process outlined in the film, not only as it applies to Aaron but also to *ourselves*.

Birthing an existence that suits us can be an exciting yet tricky process, especially if we intentionally don blinders that keep us from seeing all of the possibilities open to us, including those of a redemptive nature. But, if we're willing to consider the range of options available and pursue the desired outcomes, we can reap tremendous rewards for ourselves. And that's no illusion.

Getting Off the Couch

"Shrink"

Year of Release: 2009
Cast: Kevin Spacey, Mark Webber, Keke Palmer,
Saffron Burrows, Jack Huston, Pell James, Dallas Roberts,
Jesse Plemons, Robert Loggia, Joel Gretsch, Laura Ramsey,
Robin Williams, Gore Vidal
Director: Jonas Pate
Screenplay: Thomas Moffett
Story: Henry Reardon

When we feel like life has let us down, it's easy to become withdrawn and despondent. At times like this, we often want to seclude ourselves, hiding from what we see as a cruel, unfair world. But, under such conditions, we can serve ourselves best by searching for something to pull us out of our depression, manifesting something to give our lives meaning and making us feel renewed. The search for just such a spark provides the basis for one man's quest to redeem himself in the offbeat comedy-drama, "Shrink."

Dr. Henry Carter (Kevin Spacey) is Hollywood's preeminent psychiatrist to the stars and a best-selling author of feel-good self-help books. He's also on the verge of losing it all, precariously tottering on the edge of his own psychological abyss. Having slipped into a deep depression driven by a personal tragedy, Henry slides through life. He's perpetually adrift in the stupor of his self-medication program, which consists primarily of imbibing in different forms of designer pot supplied by his trusty dealer, Jesus (Jesse Plemons). He's living out a lost weekend that's threatening to become permanent.

Somehow, though, Henry manages to make it to work each day, where he half-heartedly listens to the troubles of his self-absorbed clients, including Patrick, a high-powered, highly paranoid talent agent (Dallas Roberts); Shamus, a rising star who's having trouble coping with the ways of the Hollywood system (Jack Huston); Kate, a beautiful but aging actress who's quietly watching her career and relationship slip away (Saffron Burrows); and Holden, a high-profile actor struggling to remain faithful to his wife in the face of sexually compulsive tendencies (Robin Williams). Henry also informally counsels his wife's godson, Jeremy, a creative screenwriter wrangling with issues of frustration, anger management and cash flow troubles (Mark Webber). With clients like that, it's no wonder Henry wants to stay stoned; in light of all he's facing, he's clearly in need of something to give his life and work renewed purpose.

That need gets fulfilled one day, and it arrives in a most unexpected form—a teenage pro bono patient named Jemma (Keke Palmer) recommended by Henry's father and fellow therapist, Robert (Robert Loggia). At first, Henry is highly reluctant to take on the challenges of a "real" patient, but he quickly relents, especially when he realizes that Jemma's troubles are far worse than any of the others he deals with every day (including his own). As time passes, he sees that treating the problems of this young patient are exactly what he needs to re-engage in his vocation—and to redeem his own life.

I was intrigued by this film in many ways, especially in terms of how it shows that our outer realities truly are reflections of our inner states of mind. In Henry's case, everyone in his world reflects his diverse array of beliefs and feelings, almost as if they were walking archetypes, a menagerie of his innermost emotions made flesh. Through his interaction with them, Henry has an opportunity to see what beliefs they each represent, enabling him to make sense of the web of feelings he's woven for himself and to seek clarity on how to begin his life anew.

Jemma, for example, is in many ways Henry's mirror, while Robert symbolizes his conscience/higher self, sternly but lovingly encouraging him to seek resolution to his troubles. But, to heed the messages of these two symbolic envoys, he must first get past the fear that Patrick represents, the sense of denial that Jesus persuasively peddles, the lost feeling that Shamus embodies and the compulsion to wallow in unhealthy behavior that Holden typifies. He must also learn to embrace for himself the sense of compassion and self-love that Kate, in spite of her challenges, so graciously personifies. But, perhaps most importantly, like Jeremy, Henry must creatively channel the anger and frustration he feels into a new pursuit so that he can write a new script for his life. That's crucial if he ever hopes to redeem himself.

Some have said that conscious creation exercises are much like the process one goes through when engaged in therapy, for both require getting in touch with the beliefs and feelings driving one's life. This film would seem to confirm that, for Henry needs to figure out what his beliefs are to create a new life for himself as a conscious creator in the same way that his patients need to sort out their feelings to find suitable therapeutic solutions to their problems. And, in both of these instances, it's essential that open minds are part of the equation, for they're integral to the development of viable outcomes. As famed scientist Albert Einstein wrote, "we can't solve problems by using the same kind of thinking we used when we created them," and the same is true here, too.

"Shrink" has a lot going for it besides its smart script and storyline. It features a fine ensemble cast, with excellent performances all around, particularly by Palmer, Spacey, Plemons, Burrows and Roberts. The film's original score by Ken Andrews and Brian Reitzell has a haunting beauty about it, and the stylish cinematography of Lukas Ettlin and Isaac Phillips is often gorgeous and mesmerizing.

Life's challenges sometimes leave us overwhelmed, but their presence also makes much possible, such as personal growth and development. This can be especially important when we wish to move past our past, to shed the self-imposed shackles that keep us from moving forward and prevent us from redeeming ourselves. In Henry's case, it's particularly ironic that it takes a patient to cure a psychiatrist of his psychological ills, but, as long as the outcome is what we hope to achieve, does it really matter *how* we realize that result? Whatever it takes to help us find new meaning is what ultimately matters most, and, when we find it, we should avail ourselves of it if we ever hope to get up off the couch.

Trial by Belief

"Conviction"
Year of Release: 2010
Cast: Hilary Swank, Sam Rockwell, Minnie Driver,
Melissa Leo, Juliette Lewis, Loren Dean,
Peter Gallagher, Clea DuVall, Karen Young,
Ari Graynor, Conor Donovan, Owen Campbell,
Bailee Madison, Tobias Campbell, Michele Messmer
Director: Tony Goldwyn
Screenplay: Pamela Gray

Popular fiction has taught us that the wrongly accused are always vindicated (and usually swiftly). But, given the many post-conviction exonerations we seem to hear about on the nightly news (often after long incarcerations), it's obvious that idealized assumption doesn't always hold true. How someone can end up mired in such difficult circumstances may puzzle some of us, but, as with all acts of conscious creation, we can be sure that it occurs as a result of beliefs. All need not be lost, however; redeeming oneself is possible, as evidenced in the legal drama, "Conviction."

Based on actual events, "Conviction" tells the story of former inmate Kenny Waters (Sam Rockwell) and his younger sister, Betty

Anne (Hilary Swank). The brother and sister are about as close as two siblings can be, and they've been that way all of their lives, which hasn't always been easy. And, as the film aptly illustrates, preserving that bond over time becomes even more challenging than either of them ever could have imagined.

Having grown up under the unpredictable, intermittent care of an unreliable mother (Karen Young) in rural Ayer, Massachusetts, young Kenny (Tobias Campbell) and young Betty Anne (Bailee Madison) were in and out of foster homes repeatedly. With a lack of consistent supervision, they frequently got into trouble, and, while the siblings' transgressions were minor in nature (trespassing, shoplifting, etc.), they nevertheless came under heavy scrutiny by local authorities. They became branded as known troublemakers early on. Kenny in particular was often cited for his rambunctious, confrontational behavior. But his outbursts usually arose in the defense of others, most notably his sister, who wouldn't hesitate to return the favor when needed. In fact, there was little that the Waters kids wouldn't do for one another when circumstances threatened.

As Betty Anne grew into adulthood, she settled down somewhat, although she never finished high school. And, despite becoming the loving, protective father of a young daughter, Kenny stayed feisty, routinely getting caught up in minor skirmishes, like bar fights. Consequently, he remained under the ever-watchful eye of the local police, particularly Nancy Taylor (Melissa Leo), an ambitious officer who, as the only woman on the force, perpetually sought to make a name for herself. As a seemingly perennial suspect, Kenny was scrutinized by authorities whenever trouble broke out in the area. Fortunately, Betty Anne always had her brother's back, and that support proved indispensable, especially in 1980, when the siblings faced their biggest crisis of all.

When local resident Katharina Brow (Michele Messmer) was brutally murdered during a home invasion, the police immediately suspected Kenny. Two years later, he was summarily convicted in a trial involving circumstantial evidence and testimony by questionable witnesses (Clea DuVall, Juliette Lewis). He was subsequently sentenced to life in prison without parole.

In Kenny's defense, Betty Anne *knew* that her brother was incapable of such an unspeakable act, and she was determined to prove his innocence. To that end, she made a bold decision: She decided to go to law school to get her degree and become his attorney. Of course, she knew she would have to get her GED and earn an undergraduate degree before she could even *consider* enrolling in law school, but, where justice and her love for Kenny were concerned, there was no stopping her.

The story picks up with Betty Anne pursuing her law degree and her brother's exoneration. She faces many challenges in the course of her quest, like divorce from her husband, Rick (Loren Dean), working her way through school, and supporting two sons (Conor Donovan, Owen Campbell) as a single mother. But she's not without help, either, such as the invaluable assistance she receives from fellow law student Abra Rice (Minnie Driver) and from civil liberties attorney Barry Scheck (Peter Gallagher) of the Innocence Project, an organization committed to clearing the names of wrongly convicted inmates through the admission of new vindicating evidence (in Kenny's case, DNA proof of his innocence—technology that didn't exist at the time of his conviction). Yet, even with such compelling new evidence, justice isn't always as easy to come by as one might assume, as Betty Anne, Kenny and their peers all find out.

Given the nature of this story (and the fact that it's based on actual events), it's not difficult to predict how the movie ends. Nevertheless, it's quite an intriguing tale in terms of the conscious creation concepts it explores, particularly those with regard to the theme of this Chapter.

Considering the behavior of their youth, Kenny and Betty Anne would no doubt be deemed mischievous, at the very least, by most outside observers. As depicted in the film, they engaged in acts that certainly warranted monitoring, perhaps even reprimanding at times. But should the rascally acts of a couple of children from a broken home necessarily make them targets for more intense, ramification-laden scrutiny years later?

From the perspective of local law enforcement officials, the answer obviously would be "yes," their beliefs clearly reflective of their opinions of the Waters kids (especially Kenny). But is such prejudiced labeling fair, even *accurate*? And is such a tainted view enough in itself to pursue and obtain a conviction without more substantial supporting evidence?

To be sure, Kenny and Betty Anne had some atoning to do for their childhood pranks, but little did they realize how extensive their pursuit of redemption would one day need to be. The "penance" they were expected to pay was grossly disproportionate to their transgressions, *especially* since the most serious accusations leveled against Kenny were inherently false. Thankfully, conscious creation *always* makes redemption possible, even under the most arduous circumstances, as long as we believe in its potential for manifestation. It's something that Kenny and Betty Anne would have to believe in quite fervently—with *conviction*—to see their dream realized.

Kenny and Betty Anne faced an uphill battle in their quest for redemption, so maintaining their beliefs in it became paramount. For starters, to put herself in a position to be able to help her brother, Betty Anne first needed to complete all of the preliminary steps required to even *apply* to law school. If she succeeded in making it that far, she would then need to graduate and pass the bar exam, something that proved exceedingly difficult in light of her many other obligations. After graduation, she would then need to mount a workable strategy to appeal Kenny's conviction, a difficult task considering the judicial system's reluctance to admit error. Manifesting any one of those steps would prove challenging enough in itself, let alone succeeding at all of them. But Betty Anne's belief in her brother's innocence was so secure, and Kenny's faith in his sister's abilities was so strong, that it enabled them to materialize whatever they each needed to carry on their fight.

For instance, Kenny survived his ordeal by simply managing to stay alive, not always the easiest feat for someone in prison. He also aided his cause by securing a conviction (false though it was) that *didn't* carry the death penalty, a punishment not on the books in Massachusetts, despite its prevalence elsewhere (had he been convicted of a comparable offense in another state, he likely would have been executed before his sister even finished law school).

Betty Anne, meanwhile, furthered her cause by creating the backing she needed to get her through her successive challenges. She first drew to herself the loyal, dedicated support of Abra and Barry. Then she got unsolicited help from her sons, who volunteered to move in with their father to help ease her burden. But her biggest break came with the development of the new DNA identification technology that could conclusively prove Kenny's guilt or innocence. Were it not for the materialization of all of these forms of assistance, Betty Anne and Kenny may have faced a very different outcome. But then none of these tools of redemption would have manifested were it not for the beliefs that made their existence—and purpose—possible.

Most importantly, Betty Anne's ability to carry on was rooted in her faith in her brother's innocence, an obvious product of her beliefs. The formation of those beliefs was made possible through a successful and astute integration of her perceptions, intellect and intuition. Having known Kenny all of her life, she had an opportunity to observe his behavior, and those observations gave her a clear indication of what actions he was—and *wasn't*—capable of. But the sense of *inner knowing* she developed about her brother fed her intuition, strengthening her conviction about Kenny's erroneous imprisonment, another driving factor in the quest to fulfill her goal.

Still, no matter what successes they may have achieved, one probably can't help but wonder *why* Kenny and Betty Anne created these circumstances in the first place. Was there something bigger at work here than just clearing Kenny's name?

Indeed, as important as Betty Anne's work on Kenny's case was, it proved to be a catalyst for something even greater. Having seen the injustice inflicted upon her brother, Betty Anne was inspired to see the innocent set free elsewhere, too. Even though she initially insisted she had no desire to practice law, that her sole purpose in becoming an attorney was to exonerate Kenny, Betty Anne nevertheless couldn't let her talents go unused after achieving her goal. She continues to champion the cause of others who are falsely accused, working to overturn erroneous convictions and seeking the release of those wrongly incarcerated.

Betty Anne's involvement in her brother's case and with the Innocence Project ended up revealing her value fulfillment, her reason for being for the betterment of herself and those around her. In many ways, her legal activism allowed her to see her purpose in life. But, on a personal level, it also enabled her to invoke *her own* form of redemption, a means to make up for whatever "transgressions" she may have engaged in during her misspent youth. Indeed, as Betty Anne's experience shows, sometimes our creations serve purposes far greater than what we're aware of when we're in the midst of pursuing them, and the results we realize can be some of the most redeeming actions we could ever undertake.

"Conviction" is one of those movies that sneaks up on you and stirs your emotions without resorting to blatant manipulation or cheap plot devices. Admittedly, the narrative is rather formulaic, and the fact-based nature of the story never leaves the outcome in doubt, but *how* the filmmakers get viewers to the conclusion is what makes the picture work. The smartly written script effectively incorporates flashbacks into the main storyline, showing how the protagonists got to where they are and why they have to contend with what they now face. The performances are solid, too, especially by Swank, Lewis (some of her best work in years) and Rockwell, who had been considered a possible awards contender at one time but, regrettably, failed to nab any formal accolades. To be sure, this isn't groundbreaking cinema, but it's an inspiring story that's well told and makes its point without becoming preachy, smug or self-righteous.

We all like to think that justice is something that just occurs naturally, but experience doesn't always bear that out. Sometimes we encounter circumstances that appear patently unfair, and it may be difficult for some of us to accept those conditions, including our involvement in, and responsibility for, their creation. However, such scenarios are indeed changeable, no matter how seemingly insurmountable they may appear. We may have to put ourselves through a trial by belief to get to that result, but, in the end, it *is* possible to redeem ourselves and to "rectify" whatever perceived "flaws" we've allowed to mar our creations, our behavior or ourselves. All it takes is suitable beliefs—and the conviction to see them through.

It's Never Too Late

"Crazy Heart"
Year of Release: 2009
Cast: Jeff Bridges, Maggie Gyllenhaal, Paul Herman,
Jack Nation, Colin Farrell, Robert Duvall
Director: Scott Cooper
Screenplay: Scott Cooper
Book: Thomas Cobb, Crazy Heart

Once many of us pass a certain age, we begin to think that the pattern of our life is largely set, if not intractably fixed. That can be great if things are going well, but those who embrace this fatalistic view often do so because their existence has come up short in at least one area of life, if not more. They thus reconcile themselves to an outlook—and a future—based on such unwaveringly glum beliefs. But that sense of resignation need not become permanent, as evidenced in the country music drama, "Crazy Heart."

Bad Blake (Jeff Bridges) is a man down on his luck. A one-time well-known country singer/songwriter, Bad now plays one-nighters with pickup bands in small-town bowling alley lounges and piano bars. Besides his career problems, he's got trouble with money and with maintaining relationships that last longer than overnight. He drowns his sorrows in protracted drinking binges, a habit that's clearly taking its toll on the 57-year-old's health. He seems destined for an embittered future, a reality full of bleak times and little hope for tomorrow.

Bad's fortunes change, however, when he meets aspiring lifestyle reporter Jean Craddock (Maggie Gyllenhaal), who wants to write an article about him. As time passes, the two grow close, and Bad falls for this single mother and her young son, Buddy (Jack Nation). At the same time, Bad starts to see his career prospects rebound, thanks to the efforts of his agent, Jack (Paul Herman), and the assistance of his successful former protégé, Tommy Sweet (Colin Farrell). With things looking up, Bad faces a promising future, but the critical question is, "Will he accept it?"

Bad's circumstances are clearly the making of his own choices, a cornerstone principle of conscious creation. The decisions he's made have brought him to where he is, and his beliefs about those choices provide constant reinforcement of his lot in life. But the prospect of change brings him to a pivotal point where he must either choose to stay the course or to follow an entirely new path, one to redeem himself.

At first glance, one might wonder why Bad would even consider rejecting the windfall of assistance and good fortune being offered to him; however, given his state of mind—and how inflexible his view of life has become—it's easy for him to dismiss what's come his way. He drums up all sorts of glib reasons to conveniently justify his existence. But are such flimsy rationalizations the right path to pursue? Or are they merely keeping Bad from moving forward because he can't figure out what it takes to redeem himself (or whether he's even worthy of it)? Only Bad can answer those questions, but he must first decide whether he's getting enough out of his current life to stay locked in place.

The message of this film will no doubt resonate with anyone who can identify with Bad's situation. I believe this is particularly true for those who've experienced multiple hardships and/or those who've reached a certain age, such as Baby Boomers approaching retirement. For some, change might be refreshingly welcome; for others, however, it may seem too late to start over or to strike out in a new direction, but that need not be the case unless one intentionally holds onto beliefs confirming such notions.

I had always been told, for example, that, if you don't write your first book by the time you're 35, you never will, and, for a while, I bought into that belief in a big way. But that idea is a belief, nothing more, one that's subject to alteration, just as any such notion is. I reminded myself of that when I published my first book at the supposedly over-the-hill age of 50. It really never is too late for *any* of us to usher changes into our lives unless we block them by our own self-imposed limitations. Redemption is indeed possible.

"Crazy Heart" illustrates this sentiment quite effectively. It's one of the picture's greatest strengths, even if this theme (and the movie's overall storyline, for that matter) isn't especially original (much of the narrative is reminiscent of the award-winning film "Tender Mercies" (1983) with Robert Duvall, who also has a small supporting role in this picture). Its greatest asset, though, is serving as a showcase for Jeff Bridges, both as an actor and as a surprisingly good singer. He received much acclaim for his performance, winning an Oscar and a Golden Globe Award as best lead actor. The film also features a fine performance by Colin Farrell, again both for his acting and his very capable singing. Thankfully, these elements, along with T-Bone Burnett's excellent score (including an Oscar and a Globe for best original song), shine strongly enough to distract viewers from its greatest weakness, the seriously erroneous casting of Maggie Gyllenhaal in the female lead (despite her Oscar nomination for best supporting actress). She comes across more like an overly perky flight attendant than a serious reporter, and her perpetually breathless delivery, which was perfect for her role in "Away We Go" (see Chapter 1), is all wrong here.

For those who've seen their fair share of birthdays, it may be easy to think it's too late to make significant changes in their beliefs or in their lives. But that's a choice, not a fact. It's the wise person who has the insight to know the difference—and to proceed accordingly.

Reconciling One's Life

"Get Low"
Year of Release: 2010
Cast: Robert Duvall, Bill Murray, Sissy Spacek,
Lucas Black, Bill Cobbs, Gerald McRaney,
Scott Cooper, Lori Beth Edgeman
Director: Aaron Schneider
Screenplay: Chris Provenzano and C. Gaby Mitchell
Story: Chris Provenzano and Scott Seeke

As the end of life approaches, the time comes to wind up one's affairs. It's an opportunity to say the things left unsaid, to hear the things left unheard and to settle up all manner of outstanding accounts. But, most of all, it's a time to get one's beliefs in order, to assess what's in one's heart and mind, especially in preparation for what lies ahead—and what will carry over into the hereafter. That process can be particularly tricky if someone has lived the life of a recluse, with little or no chance to tackle these issues in the course of daily living. Such is the circumstance faced by the protagonist in the touching comedy-drama, "Get Low."

Based on a true story-turned-Depression Era folktale, the film chronicles the final days of Felix Bush (Robert Duvall), a hermit of the Tennessee backwoods who has lived in virtual isolation for 40 years. Felix is generally regarded as a mean old man who's had many a tall tale attributed to him (most of them vile and grisly). Most folks avoid him, but that's just the way he likes it, because he'd rather avoid them, too. But, with his health failing and death hovering nearby, Felix decides to come out of the woods. His reason: To make arrangements for his funeral, an event that he fully intends to attend—while still alive.

To handle the logistics of the event—which the old curmudgeon ironically envisions as a party rather than a dour ritual—Felix contacts the local undertaker, Frank Quinn (Bill Murray), a shady businessman whose funeral home is on its own deathbed. Frank is a bit perplexed at Felix's request, as is his idealistic young associate, Buddy (Lucas Black), who sees the request as inappropriate. But, when Felix pulls a huge wad of cash out of his pocket, all apprehensions suddenly vanish, and plans for his funeral celebration begin in earnest.

The main reason Felix gives for wanting to attend his own funeral is that he wants to hear what others have to say about him. Given all the tales that have been told about him over the years, he invites everyone who has a story to share to attend the event. To entice guests, he even announces plans to hold a drawing for his land. But, as the time for the event draws near and his health failing further, Felix realizes that the most important story that needs to be told is his own, one that he finds difficult to recount. He seeks the support of others to help him out with this, most notably a woman from his past (Sissy Spacek) and a longtime friend and preacher (Bill Cobbs). But Felix soon realizes that telling his own story is a task that he alone must undertake, not only to set the record straight but also to get himself ready for that ultimate redemption, one that's quickly impending.

With the end in sight, the need to "get low"—to get serious about one's personal business, as Felix calls it—is important for a variety of reasons. Unburdening oneself of excess emotional baggage to achieve redemption, by way of personal confession, is perhaps the most obvious purpose. Such acts generally ease the suffering of those who are about to be left behind, providing much-needed closure. They also leave the one about to depart "lighter of heart," a condition said to make one's transition into the afterlife smoother, a notion that was considered so vital in ancient times that the Egyptians even ritualized it, literally, in the weighing of the heart ceremony after one's death. To alleviate the anxiety of his own transition, Felix obviously needs to follow suit, even if only figuratively.

Getting one's emotional and belief affairs in order is also important from a conscious creation perspective. Many who are well-versed in this subject, including some who have had near death experiences, contend that the beliefs we hold at the time we pass on carry over into the afterlife, helping to frame the experiences we encounter once we arrive on the other side. It's a concept that has been explored widely in sources as diverse as the writings of author Jane Roberts, the filmmaking of director Jay Weidner (particularly in his documentary "Infinity: The Ultimate Trip—Journey Beyond Death," see Chapter 13) and even the metaphysics of the ancient Egyptians, who believed that the main purpose of this life was to prepare for the next one. So, if Felix is to get what he wants after traversing the barrier between realities, he had better put the redemptive beliefs into place now that he wants to unfold later, advice that we'd all be wise to follow.

"Get Low" effectively evokes a wide range of emotions and reactions, from laughter to sadness to warmth and compassion. It features a stellar portrayal by Duvall, easily the best work he's done in years and an effort that should have received, but failed to get, serious awards consideration. Murray, Spacek, Black and Cobbs also turn in fine performances, successfully breathing life into supporting characters whose development gets a little shortchanged at times by an occasionally underwritten script (the overall strength of the story notwithstanding). Its period piece production values and soundtrack are top-notch, too, capably enhancing all of the film's other fine attributes.

Reconciling one's life is something we all have to face one day if we truly wish to be redeemed. Most of us would probably prefer to do so on our own terms, too, even if we don't necessarily know how. Felix's example, for what it's worth, gives us some inspiration to draw upon, at least theoretically speaking. But it's advice that could prove highly useful for the time when each of us must learn how to get low.

12

TRANSFORMATION

We all undoubtedly know someone (perhaps ourselves) who's gone through a radical life change, a modification so profoundly different from the prior phase of his or her existence that it's almost hard to believe it's the same person. Yet, despite the sweeping nature of such a change, it nevertheless represents an outcome that, like all other probable manifestations, arose through the conscious creation process. Such is the stuff of *transformation*.

Transformation can take many forms, both "good" and "bad." Those who fall from grace obviously experience the negative aspects of this phenomenon, while those who engage in meaningful acts of redemption (see Chapter 11) or who blossom into the full flower of their potential see the realization of transformation's positive attributes. But, again, no matter what qualities characterize the results, they still all emerge from the same basic metaphysical process.

What helps to define transformation as a conscious creation principle is the *magnitude* of alteration that takes place. Whether we experience personal growth in modest increments or quantum leaps, the belief-based process we employ is fundamentally the same in both instances; the degree of change, of course, depends on the caliber of the particular beliefs involved. But, when we witness someone go through a major shift in his or her life, we can thus see just how transformative beliefs really are.

All of the films in this Chapter focus on characters in transition who transform themselves in radical ways. Through the experiences of a widowed economics professor, an immigrant seeking a new life, a teenager abandoned by his family, an ex-convict seeking atonement and a civil servant charged with an unenviable task, we see how the process of transformation can reveal magnificent new horizons, ushering them into lives that they never could have imagined but that the law of attraction has nonetheless helped them realize.

If ever we doubt what's possible in our lives, we need only remember what transformation can accomplish. The only limits lie with what we believe is ultimately achievable.

A Stranger No More

"The Visitor"
Year of Release: 2008
Cast: Richard Jenkins, Haaz Sleiman,
Danai Gurira, Hiam Abbass
Director: Tom McCarthy
Screenplay: Tom McCarthy

Ever feel like a stranger in your own skin, unable to tap into "the real you"? You might even see yourself as a "visitor" to the confines of your own being. Figuring out how to reach that elusive inner self can be a wrenching personal task, but it's one many of us must undertake to transform ourselves and find real happiness in life. It's just such a journey that's the focus of the emotionally charged drama, "The Visitor."

Walter Vale (Richard Jenkins) is a lonely widower and bored economics professor in a Connecticut college town. When asked to present a paper at a conference in New York, he initially drums up excuses to try to get out of it, preferring to wallow in his rut, but, in the end, he reluctantly agrees. He thus sets off for the city in which he once spent much of his time, his only real connection these days being an apartment he keeps there. But his journey is ultimately more than just a business trip; it's also a transformative excursion into the depths of his soul.

Upon his arrival in New York, Walter finds his apartment occupied by an immigrant couple, Tarek (Haaz Sleiman), a Syrian drummer, and his girlfriend, Zainab (Danai Gurira), a Senegalese jewelry designer. Walter is appalled at the intrusion until he learns

Chapter 12: Transformation

that Tarek and Zainab are the unwitting victims of a fraudulent rental scam. They initially agree to leave, but, when Walter sees their plight, he extends them an invitation to stay, an uncharacteristic gesture of empathy, generosity and openness for the long-withdrawn protagonist. A new web of friendships is thus born, one that will change Walter in ways that he can hardly begin to imagine, allowing his true self to emerge.

To say more would reveal too much of the story, but suffice it to say that Walter's involvement with his new acquaintances launches him down an unexpected path of self-discovery and personal fulfillment that he never could have envisioned before coming to New York. The experience re-energizes his spirit, filling him with an uncharacteristically fiery passion that should serve to inspire us all, particularly when it comes to matters of justice, fairness, compassion and personal freedom. He becomes a new person because of this experience, his nature transformed in profoundly moving ways.

Walter's awakening seemingly comes out of left field. But, considering the fog he's been languishing in for a long time, there's some part of him that's desperately ready for change. After the death of his wife, he withdrew into himself, living an increasingly smaller existence. Over time, though, he's come to realize on some level that, if he doesn't alter his circumstances soon, he might as well hang things up for himself, too. As a relatively young and still-vital man, he's clearly not ready to depart this world, so he's faced with the daunting but necessary task of figuring how to return to it as a reborn soul.

Confronted with the need to rewrite the script of his life (and the underlying beliefs that drive it), Walter must draw to himself the catalysts that enable his transformation. The startling circumstances he encounters, such as the presence of his unexpected houseguests, do just that, sparking his awareness of probabilities for his life other than those to which he's grown so stagnantly accustomed. Whether or not he's *consciously* aware of the creations his new beliefs have invoked, the results he realizes from them nevertheless begin the process of aligning his actions with his new outlook, the one he knows he needs to implement to reinvent himself and his existence. By doing so, he begins to catch glimpses of his true self, bringing it forth to the surface and into being. And, before long, he flourishes like a phoenix, "the visitor" no longer feeling like a stranger in his own skin.

"The Visitor" is an engaging film, its title both literal and metaphorical. It's also a movie that inspires in many ways, most obviously in the emergence of Walter's new persona, but also in its heartfelt humanitarian messages. Through Walter's actions, we witness him symbolically issue quietly sincere, yet nonetheless zealous, rallying cries for reform to a society that needs to transform itself if it's to live up to the ideals it claims to hold so dearly, particularly for those who are new to our shores and in search of a better, fairer way of life. In this way, Walter thus unwittingly encourages society at large to go through the same kind of metamorphosis that he goes through personally, a change that, if implemented, should benefit everyone, just as his own conversion works to his own betterment.

The film features a terrific story and an excellent script, backed by a vibrant score. But the performances are the real standout here. The picture earned a very well-deserved best actor Oscar nomination for Jenkins, who gives what is probably the best performance of his career. Give kudos also to the fine supporting cast, who effectively complement the film's leading man.

Walter's story will tug at your heart, but it's also just as likely to build a fiery passion within each of us, as it clearly does for him. And, in the process, you might find out things about yourself that you never knew before (just like Walter). With a film like this to enlighten us, we need never be strangers in our own skin ever again.

Where One's Heart Is

"Amreeka" ("America")
Year of Release: 2009
Cast: Nisreen Faour, Melkar Muallem,
Hiam Abbass, Yussef Abu Warda,
Joseph Ziegler, Alia Shawkat, Jenna Kawar,
Selena Haddad, Andrew Sannie, Daniel Boiteau,
Brodie Sanderson, Glen Thompson, Miriam Smith
Director: Cherien Dabis
Screenplay: Cherien Dabis

Anyone who has ever gone hunting for a new house or apartment knows how taxing it can be to find a suitable place to hang one's hat.

Chapter 12: Transformation

So imagine what it might be like if that notion were applied on a larger scale, to find a community—or even a country—to call one's own. And, taking that idea to an even greater extreme, consider what's involved in finding oneself at home in one's very own skin. Those are some of the transformative challenges explored in the entertaining comedy-drama, "*Amreeka*."

Life on the Palestinian West Bank in 2002 is often frustrating for Muna Farah (Nisreen Faour). As a single mother separated from her philandering husband, she struggles to raise her teenage son, Fadi (Melkar Muallem), under trying circumstances. Just being a working mom is hard enough, but add in Muna's two-hour commute from her home in Bethlehem to her job as a bank officer in Ramallah in the Palestinian territory (facing intrusive scrutiny from Israeli troops at border crossing checkpoints along the way), and the routine of her everyday life becomes that much more difficult. She's also preoccupied with shedding some pounds, an undertaking in which the losses seemingly involve everything but weight. Clearly, Muna is ready for a change, and a big one at that.

That opportunity arrives somewhat unexpectedly one day when Muna receives a notice that her application for a visa to visit *Amreeka* (the Arabic word for "America") has been approved. The news comes as a surprise, since she had all but forgotten filing the application, having done so when she and her ex-husband were still together and contemplating plans for a better future. She's initially unsure what to do, but, when Fadi reminds her of all the everyday difficulties she faces, Muna agrees that a fresh start is the best course. And so Muna and Fadi relocate to rural northern Illinois to join the family of her émigré sister Raghda (Hiam Abbass) and brother-in-law Nabeel (Yussef Abu Warda).

Despite the promise of a new life, however, Muna and Fadi find that making the transition isn't always easy. For instance, Muna's job search doesn't live up to her expectations; even with her years of banking experience, she's forced into taking a job as counter help at the local White Castle. Meanwhile, Fadi struggles to fit in at his new school, where prejudiced classmates audaciously (and foolishly) show off their cultural ignorance, often to the new arrival's detriment. Even the well-meaning support of Raghda's family sometimes isn't enough, as they, too, face acceptance challenges of their own, despite having been established in the U.S. for years. But, if that weren't enough, all of the protagonists run headlong into the simmering anti-Islamic sentiments that arose in early 2003 during the opening days of the Iraq War. But this is an irony if there ever were one, since Muna and her family aren't Muslim. (Muna's religious affiliation is never definitively discussed in the film, though she does make reference to having been part of a religious minority in her Palestinian homeland. It's very likely that she's an Arabic Christian, given that her family originally hails from Bethlehem and Christian symbols periodically appear in the film.)

As time passes, however, Muna and Fadi find support to help ease their transition, most notably from Muna's nerdy co-worker Matt (Brodie Sanderson), Fadi's principal Mr. Novatski (Joseph Ziegler) and, to a certain extent, Raghda's and Nabeel's daughters (Alia Shawkat, Jenna Kawar, Selena Haddad). But the assistance of these newfound allies doesn't stem so much from what they do but from what they say and the attitudes they exhibit. They're all clearly comfortable in their own skin, and the new immigrants gradually pick up on this. The seemingly perennial outcasts, who never really felt at home in their so-called homeland and who have often felt even less at ease in their new country, begin to feel more comfortable by drawing inspiration from these empowering examples.

As their perspectives shift, Muna and Fadi realize that what they call "home" ultimately begins with them, with what they *believe* constitutes home and not just their physical surroundings (or, in Muna's case, even her own body). They grow into their new environment, making the home they want for themselves based on their beliefs, just as what anyone would do in any other conscious creation undertaking. They make their way through their own transformations, like caterpillars who become the butterflies they were destined to be.

"*Amreeka*" is a charming independent film, full of warmth, heart tugs and gentle humor. Admittedly, the movie's writing and editing could have been a little tighter in spots, but, all in all, this is an engaging and delightful little picture, a good choice for alternative viewing. The picture captured the FIPRESCI Prize of the International Federation of Film Critics at the Cannes Film Festival.

The next time you're looking for a new place, check the classifieds and the real estate listings, as you ordinarily would, but be sure to check your beliefs, too, for that's where your new home *really* gets its start. Pay particular attention to beliefs related to your innermost heartfelt feelings and emotions, because they'll help guide you to the place you're supposed to be. And, in the end, you'll find, just as Muna and Fadi ultimately do, that home truly is where one's heart is.

What You Don't See Coming

"The Blind Side"
Year of Release: 2009
Cast: Sandra Bullock, Tim McGraw, Quinton Aaron,
Jae Head, Lily Collins, Ray McKinnon,
Kathy Bates, Adriane Lenox, Sharon Morris, Omar Dorsey
Director: John Lee Hancock
Screenplay: John Lee Hancock
Book: Michael Lewis,
The Blind Side: Evolution of a Game

Often in life we think we know where our lives are headed, but then something happens that takes us down a completely unexpected path. What we don't see coming, however, can be truly transformative, taking us places we might never have envisioned (despite having drawn the conditions to us that make such events possible). Such a remarkable set of circumstances provides the basis for the touching, fact-based comedy-drama, "The Blind Side."

Based on the life story of professional football player Michael Oher (Quinton Aaron), the film recounts how this African-American teenager from the Memphis projects overcame gut-wrenchingly sad circumstances and wound up playing for the NFL's Baltimore Ravens. It's quite a moving and remarkable story indeed. But his personal metamorphosis was not the only one to take place in the film. His story touched others who underwent comparable transformations of their own.

When viewers first meet Michael, this soft-spoken gentle giant seems adrift, having been largely abandoned by his drug-addicted mother (Adriane Lenox). Yet Michael also has a strong survival instinct and a unique wisdom (despite apparent learning difficulties), qualities that ultimately prove to be his saving graces. With the help of a friend (Omar Dorsey), he first gets enrolled in an upscale private school. And then one night, through a seemingly chance encounter, he connects with an unlikely ally, one who would help him turn his life around in unimagined ways.

At first glance, Leigh Anne Tuohy (Sandra Bullock) might not seem like the type to take in a homeless kid from the poor side of town. As a successful designer happily married to her well-heeled college sweetheart (Tim McGraw) and the mother of two bright kids (Jae Head, Lily Collins), Leigh Anne has lived a charmed life of affluence and privilege; in fact, she openly admits to never having visited the part of Memphis where Michael grew up. However, something about Michael's circumstances inexplicably compel Leigh Anne to welcome him into her home, giving him things he never had—security, a family and a future. She quickly becomes an impassioned advocate for his success, helping to open doors for him that were once previously closed.

One of the doors that opens widely for Michael involves football, a game for which his ample physique makes him an ideal candidate. But it's also a sport about which he knows almost nothing. This is another way in which Leigh Anne's influence comes into play. As a former college cheerleader who married a one-time basketball star, she has a long history of involvement in sports, so who better to introduce Michael to the game at which he was destined to excel? Thanks to the guidance and catalytic spark Leigh Anne provides, coupled with Michael's considerable natural talent, the young man's abilities as a football player soar, first at the high school level, then in the collegiate ranks and eventually in the pros. The kid from the streets transforms himself, materializing abilities he never knew he had. But, more than that, with Leigh Anne's support and encouragement, Michael begins to believe in himself, manifesting a life that at one time he only could have dreamed of. And, in the process, he also gives Leigh Anne something to brag about.

By focusing on the magical, synergistic interaction between Michael and Leigh Anne, "The Blind Side" shows us how their connection allows each of them to grow and develop in ways neither of them thought possible. They were both "blindsided," to use a football analogy, by the impact that they would have on one another, but that unanticipated contact enables personal transformation for both of them in ways beyond measure. And, in reaching that point, the protagonists demonstrate how to make effective use of a number of transformative conscious creation principles, including:

* how we can formulate (or change) our beliefs to create better-than-expected outcomes, thanks to the beliefs that we have in ourselves and that others have in us, thereby enabling transformation on a grand scale;

* how having the courage to live heroically—particularly by taking chances that have the potential to pay off handsomely—can yield rewards beyond our wildest expectations;

* how charting the evolution of our beliefs about ourselves over time can lead to the development of skills and expertise we never knew we had; and

* how all aspects of our individual and shared realities are intricately connected and how we can benefit from such connectedness, both personally and collectively, in countless transformative ways.

"The Blind Side" is also a thoughtful treatise on values, especially those having to do with qualities like kindness, compassion, charity and humanity. It sheds light on the results such ideals can yield, especially when we form suitable beliefs that enable those notions to come to fruition, providing benefits both to those who hold them and to those toward whom they're directed.

Some viewers were critical of the film at the time of its release, claiming it to be a fundamentalist propaganda piece, given its candid portrayal of the Tuohys as a family of devout Christians who aren't afraid to openly practice their religion or to allow their faith to permeate their everyday lives. As seen in the film, they attend church regularly, enroll their kids in a private Christian academy and attempt to live lives that reflect the noble values noted above. Leigh Anne and her family obviously have tremendous conviction behind these beliefs, too, as evidenced by the degree of success they achieve with them. Their power is so great that it truly works wonders, even miracles of transformation, both for practitioners and beneficiaries alike.

But the claims of the detractors raise an interesting question: Since when do authentically depicted acts of sincere kindness, compassion, charity and humanity automatically equate to self-serving missives of Christian propaganda? These are qualities we'd *all* be wise to emulate, no matter what religious affiliation (or lack thereof) we may have. Such values arise from the *beliefs* that the Tuohys hold, and they have merit in and of themselves, *regardless* of whether they're enacted in a religious context or otherwise. Indeed, Christians have not cornered the market on kindness, so cynical attempts at characterizing the film in such a spurious way is patently unfair, to say the least. If more of us acted as charitably as the Tuohys do, even without any religious connotations in our efforts, we'd all be in a much better state these days.

"The Blind Side" is a thoroughly entertaining film. Its well-written script combines just the right amount of humor with a judiciously tempered sense of sentimentality that keeps the picture from becoming overly schmaltzy. The protagonists' stories are well told, though Leigh Anne's character development might have benefited from a little more back story (at the very least to the same degree afforded Michael's character). Bullock and Aaron are terrific in their respective roles, and they have an unusual but affecting chemistry together. In fact, Bullock's convincing performance earned her an Oscar and a Golden Globe for best lead actress, while the film itself received an Academy Award nomination for best picture.

"The Blind Side" initially appeared in theaters during the holiday season, so I tend to associate this picture with the timing of its release. Given the themes and values it promotes, the film makes a fine addition to the repertoire of holiday staples, joining the likes of such endearing classics as "It's a Wonderful Life" (1946), "Miracle on 34th Street" (1947) and "A Christmas Carol" (1951). All in all, it makes for a very nice holiday package—even if it isn't under your tree.

That which we least expect in life often provides us with the greatest degree of satisfaction, especially when it comes to exceeding our perceived limitations. Such revelations only occur, however, when we leave ourselves open to the possibilities, allowing ourselves to grow and develop in ways other than the tried and true. Indeed, letting ourselves get blindsided sometimes proves to be the best course of all.

If you doubt that, just ask Michael or Leigh Anne.

Packing a Punch

"Poor Boy's Game"
Year of Release: 2007
Cast: Rossif Sutherland, Danny Glover,
Flex Alexander, K.C. Collins, Greg Bryk,
Tonya Lee Williams, Laura Regan,
Stephen McHattie, Wes Williams,
Dwain Murphy, Carol Sinclair, Hugh Thompson,
Lee J. Campbell, Jeremy Akerman
Director: Clement Virgo
Screenplay: Chaz Thorne and Clement Virgo

When we give license to our beliefs to freely materialize their manifestations, their impact can be considerable. Indeed, they can pack quite a transformative punch, especially when they involve revolutionary notions. It's a concept fittingly depicted in the boxing world drama, "Poor Boy's Game."

Ex-convict Donnie Rose (Rossif Sutherland) faces some hard choices after serving a 10-year prison sentence. Having had a decade to consider the implications of his crimes, he returns to his home town of Halifax, Nova Scotia a changed man. But will a new life in his old haunts allow him to continue being the changed person he has aspired to become? Ultimately, it all rests squarely with Donnie and whether or not he chooses to let his transformation stick.

As it's portrayed in the film, Halifax is one of the few overtly segregated communities in a nation otherwise known for its social tolerance and acceptance of cultural diversity. This Canadian city struggles desperately with racial tensions, and few of its residents go unaffected, including Donnie. Having been raised in an openly racist white family, Donnie returns to his bigoted relatives (most notably his hot-headed brother, Keith (Greg Bryk)) after doing time for brutally assaulting a young black man, Charlie Carvery (K.C. Collins), injuring his victim so badly that he's left severely brain damaged. Donnie seeks to atone for his crime and to rebuild connections with his family, but is this volatile combination of aspirations possible? On top of attempting to strike this difficult balance, Donnie also wrestles with anger management issues, a problem that has dogged him his entire life.

Ironically, the source of Donnie's salvation could lie with something that contributed to his troubles in the first place—his proficiency as a fighter. At one time, Donnie faced a promising future in boxing had it not been for the crime that derailed his career, an incident that arose after one of his matches and was directly attributable to his anger management issues and prejudiced racial beliefs. Now, however, if he were to channel his energies for this pursuit in a positive way, he just might be able to resolve his challenges and tame his demons. But, then again, doing so also runs the risk of making them worse than ever.

Donnie's opportunity to test that theory comes when he's offered a fight against Ossie Paris (Flex Alexander), a black boxer with a stellar record and a mean right hook. The bout is more than just a boxing contest, though; it's also a grudge match. On the night of Donnie's crime, Ossie had made plans to meet his friend Charlie at a local nightclub, a meeting that obviously never happened. In offering the match to Donnie, Ossie seeks retribution for the incident. And, given the emotionally charged backdrop for the proposed event, it's easy to see why racial tensions continue to mount, both in Halifax at large and in Donnie's world in particular.

After some difficult soul-searching, Donnie agrees to the fight, a decision that puts further stress on local race relations. For starters, the contest is being promoted by Donnie's Uncle Joey (Stephen McHattie), owner of the aforementioned nightclub, which has had its own share of recent racial incidents. And, in yet another twist of irony, Donnie receives his fight training from George Carvery (Danny Glover), Charlie's father and caregiver, a former boxing coach turned dockworker. George's decision puzzles many of those close to him, but, after witnessing the many recent incendiary events (some of which were perpetrated in his son's name and fueled by Ossie's flamboyant, racially tinged grandstanding), he feels compelled to do something to help quell the increasing spiral of violence and hatred. It's a move made even more paradoxical by the fact that George was once Ossie's trainer, too.

However, despite such tense circumstances, as the story plays out, the film's principals come to realize that their old ways of addressing issues and differences no longer work; solutions that were once relied on unquestioningly are suddenly seen as ineffective and

Chapter 12: Transformation

inappropriate, and new measures are needed if things are ever to change. They try out alternative approaches, some of which don't work but many of which do. What's most important, though, is that these once-entrenched characters are willing to make the effort to explore new means for handling such matters as anger, violence, vengeance, victimhood, responsibility, tolerance and, most importantly, forgiveness. And it all gets sorted out, fittingly enough, in the boxing ring, culminating in a suspense-filled climax that will keep viewers guessing—and glued to their seats—right up until the very end.

How do such drastic transformations manifest? Quite simply, through changes of heart—and of beliefs. When it becomes painfully apparent that the prevailing mindset no longer works, it's time for change, and, when it occurs on a particularly sweeping scale (as it does here), change becomes transformation.

Donnie learned this lesson to a great extent while in prison; the beliefs driving his racist outlook, for example, were squarely put to the test from the outset when he was assigned a black cellmate, thereby initiating a process that played out over his 10 years behind bars. Donnie realized that he would have to change his views if he truly wanted to transform himself, and his beliefs drew to him the very conditions needed to make that possible.

George's opportunity to alter his beliefs (and subsequent manifestations) comes later, after Donnie's release. But, just as Donnie's cellmate assignment fueled the genesis of his transformation, Donnie's return to Halifax (and the incidents surrounding it) inspires the reevaluations that George engages in. This event, which was strongly opposed by the local black community and by George's wife, Ruth (Tonya Lee Williams), nevertheless prompts George's metamorphosis, shifting his views in ways that he clearly couldn't have envisioned at the picture's beginning.

What I find especially intriguing about this film's exploration of transformation is its willingness to examine the seemingly unthinkable. Skeptics might look at some of the picture's transformative events (especially toward the movie's end) as wholly improbable. But the picture doesn't hesitate to ask, "Well, why not?" If all probabilities for existence are equally viable, who's to say that some of the more "outlandish" options are any less valid or capable of expression than those considered more likely? The impact of this is stunning, taking the characters—and viewers—down paths that they might not have otherwise considered, providing food for thought worthy of further examination. What's more, if such solutions can be employed in a fictional context, then why can't they be implemented in everyday life, too? Thanks to their illustration here, such ideas just might see the light of day, transforming circumstances for all concerned.

Directed by filmmaker Clement Virgo (who has sometimes been called Canada's answer to Spike Lee), "Poor Boy's Game" played mostly at film festivals when it was initially released, but it is currently available on DVD and has been broadcast occasionally on cable TV. It's refreshing to see a movie in which once-intractable characters are willing to entertain new ideas. But, even more significantly, it's encouraging to see their efforts depicted *without* judgment being passed on them, even when they "fail" in their undertakings (a truly transformative take on such matters in and of itself). It also helps that this is all wrapped up in a riveting entertainment package, one that's gritty without being gratuitous and honest without stereotyping. I'm particularly impressed with the level of suspense it maintains, right up until the end, and then injecting an unexpected twist that not even the characters see coming.

It's been said that a leopard never changes its spots. But, as conscious creators know, that applies to leopards, not human beings. Our ability to form the beliefs that create our respective realities enables us to change the conditions of our existence, as well as *ourselves*. The transformations this makes possible can be quite astounding, producing effects that are nothing short of a knockout.

Becoming More Human Than Human

"District 9"
Year of Release: 2009
Cast: Sharlto Copley, David James, Jason Cope,
Mandla Gaduka, Vanessa Haywood
Director: Neill Blomkamp
Screenplay: Neill Blomkamp and Terri Tatchell
Film Short Adaptation Source:
Neill Blomkamp (director), "Alive in Joburg" (2006)

Chapter 12: Transformation

As humans, we often like to think of ourselves as a supremely compassionate, eminently hospitable species. But is this really true? Do we genuinely live up to our own hype, or do we come up short of such billing? If the latter is true, maybe we need to take a hard look at who we are and what we do and then figure out how to move *beyond* whatever degrees of attainment we've reached in this regard. We must thus look for ways to improve upon our accomplishments and transform ourselves to better reflect those qualities to which we lay claim. It's a theory put to the test in the unconventional sci-fi thriller, "District 9."

When an enormous alien mothership appears over Johannesburg in an alternate version of 1981, it raises many questions: Why here and not a more significant world capital, like Washington or Moscow? Why are there no such ships over other cities? And what is the intent behind the craft's unexplained presence? Are its inhabitants merely observing us, or are they preparing for something more nefarious, like an invasion?

After a long time with no explanation, a reconnaissance team is sent to the ship to investigate. Once inside, team members find it filled with a huge crew of emaciated insect-like beings who apparently belong to their society's worker class. Their ship, it seems, is severely damaged, which caused it to drift into Earth's air space. Their wish is simply to go home, but, given the craft's condition and the undereducated inhabitants' inability to repair it, they're stuck.

South African authorities, in an uncharacteristically charitable yet seemingly sincere act of compassion (remember, this story is initially set during the time of apartheid), agree to help the aliens, even allowing them to come down to the planet's surface. However, over time, the local residents grow leery of the off-world refugees, placing ever-greater restrictions on them until the aliens ("prawns" or "bottom feeders" as they're derogatorily called) are corralled into District 9, an urban resettlement camp similar to the infamous shantytowns that arose under the country's apartheid policy. But, eventually, even this level of segregation doesn't go far enough for the locals; they want the prawns completely removed from Johannesburg. Thus begins the process of evicting the aliens from District 9 and moving them to a new camp far outside the city, an undertaking headed by a newly promoted mid-level apparatchik, Wikus Van De Merwe (Sharlto Copley).

Wikus seems like an affable, sympathetic guy, though he clearly takes his job seriously, thoroughly committed to the by-the-book procedures he's called upon to execute. When confronted with alien resistance, for example, he doesn't hesitate to engage in friendly coercion or to willingly turn a blind eye to his support crew's brutal enforcement tactics. That all changes, however, when an incident occurs that suddenly places Wikus in the shoes of those he's charged with evicting. In a matter of hours, the once-scrupulously loyal bureaucrat begins to transform, becoming an unlikely champion for those who have no one to speak for them. With the aid of an alien named Christopher, Wikus embarks on an entirely new initiative, one that draws the wrath of the powers-that-be against the prawns—and now him.

In many respects, "District 9" is not typical sci-fi fare; it's more than just a special effects extravaganza with an oversimplified good vs. evil narrative. The film is a morality play on our humanity, particularly how we treat those less fortunate than us (and, accordingly, what we get back for our actions). The reality before the humans' eyes thus becomes a mirror of the intents they put out, a key concept in understanding how conscious creation works. In that sense, then, is it any surprise that brutality is often met with … brutality?

The movie also examines how we can become more than who we are (or, more importantly, how we can become more than who we *believe* we are). Through Wikus's actions, we see how to rise above our own limitations—*if we choose to*—to transform ourselves into different beings. These actions, in turn, elicit different responses from others (like the aliens)—reactions that mirror the fundamental changes in Wikus's outlook. So, in this way, it should come as no surprise how the protagonist's heroism and compassion evoke comparable reactions from others, ultimately enabling him to become more human than human.

"District 9" is a winner on many fronts. Besides its excellent technical effects, Copley's superb performance and the film's thoughtful narrative, the picture's unusual filming style—told largely through simulated news reports and staged, after-the-fact interviews intercut with the main story—is innovative and refreshing. To be sure, the film is not for sensitive viewers, due to its graphic violence, but, if viewed in context, such action effectively (and necessarily) lends itself to the character of the picture. "District 9" received four Oscar nominations, including best picture, and its adapted screenplay received both Academy Award and Golden Globe nods.

The next time we're tempted to congratulate ourselves for our humanity, we should pause and think about this film. In these days of myriad social challenges, when we sometimes fall short of doing all we can, even for our own species, we should think about how we might respond to those with tremendous needs far different from our own. It's something to contemplate if we truly wish to label ourselves "human."

13

TRANSCENDENCE

When we live out a particular line of probability to its conclusion, the next logical question that comes up is, "What's next?" The simple answer, of course, is that we move on to something else, keeping in line with the core concept that we're all in a constant state of becoming. But what exactly does moving on to something else mean? That's where *transcendence* comes into play.

Transcendence is, in some ways, like transformation only on steroids. It's a state of being where our beliefs take us from our current state of existence to something totally beyond anything we've typically known or experienced. And, even though the resulting reality is completely different from what preceded it, like all other creations, it, too, arose from our beliefs, whether we recognize that fact or not (though, at the time of transition, many of us do become aware of it, if for no other reason than we realize at that point that there's no going back).

Transcendent experiences can occur not only when we change dimensions or realities, but even when we adopt a totally new outlook for the way we view our current lives, again, because there's generally no going back when we do so. That's significant, because it represents a sea change in the beliefs and intents we employ to manifest the reality we experience, one in which we fundamentally change mindsets and shift paradigms. And, if we do it "right," the experiences we encounter are magnificent and indescribable.

Regardless of how we might feel about it, death is perhaps the most obvious example of a transcendent experience, but it's not the only one. To that end, many of the films in this Chapter examine this issue and what it means for us as conscious creators, both in terms of assessing what we leave behind and what we move toward. Another entry goes even further, showing us a new way of being that moves beyond our accepted notions of life and death, examining what can unfold when questions of fate and free will are factored into the law of attraction process, a scenario in which it's truly possible for all bets to be off, difficult though that might be to envision.

Transcendence moves us in utterly profound ways, and it once again demonstrates the power that our beliefs carry when it comes to conscious creation. May we each make the most of it.

Moments of Clarity

"A Single Man"
Year of Release: 2009
Cast: Colin Firth, Julianne Moore, Nicholas Hoult,
Matthew Goode, Jon Kortajarena, Ginnifer Goodwin,
Ryan Simpkins, Paul Butler
Director: Tom Ford
Screenplay: Tom Ford and David Scearce
Book: Christopher Isherwood, A Single Man

They flicker ever so briefly and then dissolve into the darkness. Moments of clarity, those all-too-fleeting flashes of intuitive insight, sparkle luminously like fireflies in the night. They provide undeniable confirmation that all is right with the world, that we're each where we're supposed to be and doing what we're intended to do. We often wish we could hold on to those shining moments forever, and some may indeed be able to do so, but, for most, even recognizing them is a miracle in itself. The fulfillment that comes from such transcendent realizations can be blissful beyond belief; it's getting there that's the challenge. Such is the message of the riveting drama, "A Single Man."

George Falconer (Colin Firth) is a desperately lonely soul. This middle-aged British transplant lives a materially comfortable but reclusive life as an English professor in 1962 Los Angeles during the Cuban missile crisis. Outwardly, he seems to have what most people want, but, internally, he's seriously disillusioned over the state of the world, with its imminent threat of Armageddon, classrooms full of increasingly materialistic students and his own intermittent health issues. But what pains George most is the unyielding sadness he feels over the tragic passing of his longtime partner, Jim (Matthew Goode), who died in a car accident. Carrying on almost seems more trouble than it's worth, so George decides to pursue what he sees as the only logical course to alleviate his unceasing anguish—he plans to kill himself.

The story follows George through what is supposed to be the last day of his life. He tells no one about his plan, but he meticulously goes about all the tasks necessary to carry out the deed, tying up loose ends and making sure that everything is done according to his wishes, right down to picking out the clothes for his own funeral. He's determined to follow through on his intent with an almost relentless efficiency.

But, as George's day proceeds, roadblocks appear. Each is distinguished by an increasing degree of distraction, drawing George's attention away from his quest. An inquisitive student (Nicholas Hoult) who seems interested in more than George's literary knowledge engages the professor in profound conversation; a handsome man of the streets (Jon Kortajarena) tries seducing George into joining him for some afternoon frolic; and George's best gal pal (and one-time romantic diversion), Charley (Julianne Moore), repeatedly phones her old friend to remind him about their previously scheduled dinner date.

So how's one supposed to kill oneself with so much going on? It's a question George is forced into asking himself, but the answer becomes increasingly elusive, especially when he realizes that such diversions prove that his world isn't such a bad place after all. Maybe the transition he had been intending to make is not the one that he should be pursuing.

So how does George specifically come to doubt his planned course of action? Quite simply, the diversions he encounters force him to deal with life in the moment at hand—neither the past nor the future, only the present. In these instances, George evaluates, and reevaluates, his beliefs, the foundation upon which he creates his reality. His beliefs are thus shaped, or changed, to suit the prevailing circumstances. And, given the joy that each of these newly created distractions provides, it becomes ever easier for George to forget about offing himself. In those episodes of enlightenment, those moments of clarity, the past and future dissolve like the firefly's flickers, leaving only the radiance of the present—the only materialization that can be experienced and enjoyed in that instant, and the only one that matters at the time, no matter how transient it might be. The revelations prove transcendent, that there's more to living than the elements that comprise everyday life.

This is a valuable lesson for those hopelessly locked into the pains of the past and the fear of the future. The past is behind us, and the future has not yet arrived, so all we have is the present, and the sooner we learn to make peace with it, the happier we're all likely to be. It's a shame that so many of us, like George, put ourselves through such torment in coming to that realization, but I believe most of us will ultimately be better off for doing so. It's what truly makes life worth living. And, one would hope, it's an experience—and a revelation—we'll all come to before it's too late.

The transcendence of such an experience is difficult to capture in words. It's an inner knowing, an intuitive realization that helps us identify our place in a vast Universe, one in which we occupy a unique and significant station, no matter how comparatively small or unimportant it might appear. So, given that, would it be wise to purposely bring about our own end, nullifying the singular position we hold in the Cosmos? Such an act is, arguably, akin to an affront against our inherently sacred nature, one that we've so eloquently co-created with our divine collaborator. Knowing that, then, how could we possibly contemplate an act of self-obliteration? There is joy to be had, as long as we allow ourselves to partake of it, an awareness that George comes to appreciate as his day wears on.

"A Single Man" is a masterful film, one of the most overlooked and underrated releases of recent years. I was particularly impressed with the presentation of the narrative as a story that's not about a gay man coping with life and loss but about a person coping with life and loss who just happens to be gay. This represents a major step forward in the portrayal of gay characters as everyday individuals who live everyday existences (kudos all around for this accomplishment). Colin Firth's performance is a knockout, too. He richly deserved all the accolades he received, turning in what I believe was 2009's best performance by an actor in a leading role, an effort that earned him both Oscar and Golden Globe nominations. On top of all that, the picture's lavish production values, from set design to costumes and makeup, as well as its magnificent cinematography, make this movie a visual delight to watch. In all, the picture earned one Oscar nomination and three Golden Globe nods, including a bid for Julianne Moore's supporting actress performance, but took home no awards.

Moments of transcendent clarity seem to come along so seldom, yet we invariably cherish them when they do. One can only hope that watching this film will help us learn how to become better at drawing them into our lives more often. And what a life that would be.

On Life's Transitions

"Biutiful" ("Beautiful")
Year of Release: 2010
Cast: Javier Bardem, Maricel Álvarez, Hanaa Bouchaib, Guillermo Estrella, Eduard Fernández, Cheikh Ndiaye, Diaryatou Daff, Taisheng Chen, Jin Luo, Ana Wagener, Lang Sofia Lin, Rubén Ochandiano, Nasser Saleh
Director: Alejandro González Iñárritu
Screenplay: Alejandro González Iñárritu, Nicolás Giacobone and Armando Bo

Sooner or later, the life we now live comes to an end. But the conclusion of this life is merely the close of a single chapter in our soul's journey, with death providing the conduit to transcend to whatever comes next. Whenever that end comes, the more at peace we are with the transition, the more we'll get out of the experience, not only of what we're going to but also of what we're leaving behind. Learning how to prepare ourselves for that time is the subject of the emotionally moving drama, *"Biutiful"* ("Beautiful").

Uxbal (Javier Bardem) is a dying man. Having been diagnosed with an advanced form of cancer, he knows his days are numbered. And the prospect of that impending death scares him, not only because of the loss it represents to him personally, but also because of the loss it would mean to the many others who rely on him. He worries that he won't be able to provide the means to adequately cover their needs for a time when he's no longer around.

Despite years of experience at navigating the dicey challenges of daily life in Barcelona's seamy underbelly, Uxbal's latest ordeal overwhelms him. Even though he's rather adept at employing a "whatever it takes" approach to get others what they need—be it work, shelter or nurturing—to fill the gaps in their lives (sometimes even at his own expense), he must now make provisions for them for the long term, not just the pressing needs of the moment. It's a tall order, and he needs to hurry.

Those who benefit most directly from Uxbal's efforts are his young children, Ana (Hanaa Bouchaib) and Mateo (Guillermo Estrella), as well as his ex-wife, Marambra (Maricel Álvarez), a flirtatious "massage therapist" who suffers from a severe case of bipolar disorder. He also works hard, in conjunction with his brother Tito (Eduard Fernández), as a sort of black market headhunter who specializes in securing employment for the illegal immigrants of Barcelona's African and Chinese communities, finding jobs for the disenfranchised while keeping the authorities sufficiently paid off. And, despite the many burdens of all these challenges, he's generally very effective at surmounting them. But, given his own changed circumstances, he now faces the biggest gap he's ever tried to fill.

In a somewhat ironic twist, Uxbal also has a special gift that many might view as a distinct advantage in approaching the circumstances he now faces—an ability to communicate with the dead. It's a skill at which he's quite proficient but one that he uses sparingly, primarily to help lost souls pass over and to provide comfort to bereaved survivors by relaying messages from deceased loved ones, almost as if it were another of his gap-filling talents. Little does he realize, however, that drawing upon this ability more fully now might also help *him* as he prepares to make peace with his own transition.

The subjects of death and transition have figured largely in many feature films in recent years, and it's been interesting to see how they've handled this subject. In nearly all cases, the approach has been more enlightening than many films of the past, stressing the transcendent nature of the experience. The end of this life is not portrayed as the end of our existence but merely as a shift from this reality to something new, a rising up to the next state of our eternal being, as it were. Such thinking is right in line with the principle that we're all in a constant state of becoming (or, as succinctly noted in the paranormal classic "Phenomenon" (1996), "Everything is on its way to someplace else").

As one of the latest offerings in the genre of enlightened films about death, "*Biutiful*" takes an approach that's a little different. While it postulates that we all move in the direction of personal transformation, it does so from the perspective of a character who fears the transition *despite* an innate knowledge to the contrary. Some might find that an odd line of probability for someone to explore, especially given Uxbal's special gift, but, as conscious creators are well aware, all expressions of existence are equally capable of manifestation, no matter how intrinsically incongruous they might seem. Such is Uxbal's challenge—to validate, and ultimately to freely accept, an outcome that he already knows to be true—and that he genuinely need not fear.

When Uxbal initially comes to terms with the path he's on, he focuses most of his attention on the welfare of others, with an emphasis on making sure that he gets everything done in time. With his health failing, however, he soon realizes that there's only so much he can do and that others must learn how to get along on their own, something they'll *have* to do once he's gone. Like Uxbal, then, they, too, must transcend the circumstances to which they've grown accustomed, and they will have to do so without their benefactor's direct assistance. Changes in these conditions thus free up Uxbal's energies, making possible a transition that occurs on *his* terms, one that allows him to let go of what's no longer relevant or feasible and that enables him to get the most out of the experience. His changed outlook thus eloquently reflects the wisdom found on a watercolor by artist B. Andreas that hangs prominently in my home: "Everything changed the day he figured out there was exactly enough time for the important things in his life."

With his time dwindling, some may question Uxbal's preoccupation with addressing the needs of others. "Why isn't he going out and enjoying what little time he has left?" they might ask. But being of service to others is clearly the essence of Uxbal's value fulfillment. His sensitivity to the plight of others is profound and no doubt based on his own past, having grown up without a father and experiencing an upbringing where his own needs often weren't met. It's inspiring that he takes this calling so seriously, providing a shining, transcendent example that we could all learn from, not only in being true to ourselves, but also in working for the betterment of humanity.

"*Biutiful*" is a captivating picture in many respects. Its style is classic Iñárritu, drawing upon elements and approaches that the director used in earlier works, like "Babel" (2006) (see Chapter 8) and "21 Grams" (2003), but incorporating new touches, especially in such areas as cinematography and editing, that allow this film to stand out on its own. Bardem's Oscar-nominated performance is phenomenal, arguably his best work to date and well worth the many accolades he received for it. The film's haunting soundtrack completes the package, providing the perfect ethereal backdrop to a masterfully crafted piece of cinema. In addition to his best actor Academy Award nomination, Bardem took top honors in this category at the Cannes Film Festival. "*Biutiful*" also earned Oscar and Golden Globe nods for best foreign language film, as well as a *Palme d'Or* nomination at Cannes.

The soul may be eternal, but its embodiment in flesh is not. Which is why it's so important that we make the most of the time we have in it, especially when the end draws near, for those who find it in themselves to do so will discover just what a transcendently "*Biutiful*" experience it can be.

The Eternal Frontier

"Infinity: The Ultimate Trip—Journey Beyond Death"
Year of Release: 2009
Cast: Neale Donald Walsch, Gregg Braden,
Dannion Brinkley, Alberto Villoldo, John Holland,
Stanislav Grof, Robert Thurman, Brian Weiss,
Dzogchen Ponlop, Renate Dollinger
Director: Jay Weidner
Concept: Alberto Villoldo and Jay Weidner

CHAPTER 13: TRANSCENDENCE   263

All of us have undoubtedly wondered what lies beyond the end of this life. Is it a journey to a realm of eternal bliss? A trek into our worst fears realized? An adventure that fulfills our wildest dreams? Or is it something else entirely, combining all, some or none of the foregoing? These are among the many questions explored in the engaging documentary, "Infinity: The Ultimate Trip—Journey Beyond Death."

Like many metaphysical documentaries released in recent years, "Infinity" features a panel of noted experts offering their views on the subject at hand, presented in monologue format. Their observations are intercut with stunningly beautiful photography, inventive visual effects and ethereal music to enhance the relevance of their ideas. And the result is a captivating exploration of the transcendent reality to be found beyond Earthly existence.

Some of the speakers address afterlife issues from philosophical, metaphysical or scientific perspectives. Others discuss their ideas based on anecdotal incidents, such as near death experiences, reincarnational explorations and meetings with spirit guides (both on the Earthly plane and in the hereafter). Most of them also address the concept of life reviews, experiences that allow the departed to see what lessons they've learned and what effects they've had on others, for better or worse. (Many are also quick to add that the deceased not only relive their life histories, but also experience all the associated emotions—again, for better or worse—from the vantage point of those with whom they interacted in those lifetimes, a revelation that can be truly eye-opening for many souls.)

But, regardless of the angle from which the experts approach the subject, nearly all of them agree on one important point that has tremendous implications for conscious creation practitioners: the time to prepare for the afterlife is while we're still living, for the creations of this life and the beliefs that we carry over at the time of passage will have much influence on what transpires once we reach the other side. For example, expectations about what results after crossing over are likely to play out as anticipated. Moreover, our creations in this life will have considerable impact on what we experience during the aforementioned life review process.

With that in mind, then, it would appear that law of attraction principles transcend the barrier between realities, something that we should all think about while shaping our beliefs, setting our intentions and manifesting our materializations, both during and at the ends of our lives. That's a notion that our ancestors, like the ancient Egyptians, knew quite well, but it's a concept many contemporaries have long since forgotten. All of which makes it especially important for us to understand that *now* is the time to get things right.

So how, exactly, do we go about this? In large part it involves us developing a clear awareness of the immortal nature of the soul, realizing that leaving behind this life is little more than exchanging one set of external clothes for a new one, a process that many of us have likely done countless times before (even if we don't recollect it during waking life). It also has to do with understanding the infinite nature of the afterlife, a reality in which all possibilities are at the ready, based on the choices we make, just as we do as conscious creators in waking life. But then that shouldn't come as a surprise, given that the afterlife's manifestation, like that of physical existence, is merely the creation of another—albeit different—reality, one that unfolds from our thoughts, beliefs and intents. It's even possible to catch glimpses of this new realm of existence, such as in the dream state, where the prevailing limitless conditions mirror those of life on the other side. Bringing those experiences into everyday waking life—the act of "practicing infinity," as author Neale Donald Walsch puts it in the film—goes a long way toward helping us prepare for that ultimate journey.

What that all enables in the end is the ability to step out of a world restricted by such Earthly limitations as time. Moving into a world of timelessness, where we're no longer hindered by temporal constraints or physical limitations, opens up worlds of possibilities we had never before envisioned. Imagine the ability to step into a realm where we're once again surrounded by departed loved ones or where we're even able to maintain meaningful connections with those we thought we'd left behind. The ability to conceive of such notions is especially relevant these days, given the increased attention being paid to the prophecies of spiritual texts and indigenous cultures, both of whose legends have been interpreted by some to mean that we're on the brink of a breakthrough in understanding such ideas, marking the dawning of a new expression of consciousness and the beginning of a new era for mankind. (Now *that's* a trip.)

Director Jay Weidner has created a remarkably thoughtful and visually engrossing piece of filmmaking. The monologues are mesmerizing, and the gorgeous cinematography is a sight to see, especially its brilliantly colorful kaleidoscopic graphics. It's likely to move you in ways you hadn't imagined going in. Admittedly, the editing is a bit choppy at the outset, but, once all of the speakers and their areas of expertise are introduced, the film flows beautifully, its narrative presented in a compellingly fascinating way.

The eternal frontier is a prospect that many of us have traditionally viewed with angst, doubt or skepticism. But such reactions need not hold sway over us, especially in light of the insights and reassurances offered in this film. "Infinity: The Ultimate Trip—Journey Beyond Death" shows us that life beyond life need not be feared but, instead, should be celebrated for the joyful and adventurous homecoming that it truly is.

Meditation on a Common Fate

"Hereafter"
Year of Release: 2010
Cast: Matt Damon, Cécile de France, George McLaren, Frankie McLaren, Derek Jacobi, Jay Mohr, Bryce Dallas Howard, Richard Kind, Steven R. Schirripa, Thierry Neuvic, Marthe Keller, Jean-Yves Berteloot, Lyndsey Marshal, Rebekah Staton, Declan Conlon, Niamh Cusack, George Costigan
Director: Clint Eastwood
Screenplay: Peter Morgan

What happens when we die? That's one of the most intriguing, mystifying and, for some, frightening questions that we face in life. And, given that death is the one common fate we all share, it's a question that's understandably important, even if it's one that some of us would rather ignore. All angst aside, however, coming to terms with the afterlife would seem to be an increasingly crucial concern for the mass consciousness considering how many recent films have addressed this subject. These pictures have done an exemplary job of exploring the issue, too, but one that examines this transcendent experience in a comprehensive, highly considered way is the thoughtful drama, "Hereafter."

"Hereafter" tells three stories that deal with different aspects of death and the afterlife and how such considerations ultimately play out in the characters' lives:

* George Lonegan (Matt Damon) desperately wants to find his life. He's a factory worker in San Francisco who takes night classes in the culinary arts. But most of his time is spent alone, quietly brooding about his circumstances. It wasn't always like that, though. For years, George worked as a professional psychic with the ability to help connect the living to their departed loved ones, a talent that brought him abundance and notoriety. But, while most people saw George's ability as a gift, he saw it as a curse, one that affected his relationships and his outlook on life. He had difficulty reconciling how to live a life whose primary focus was on death. Nevertheless, even though such realizations helped him discover what he *didn't* want, they brought him no closer to finding what he *did*, and so now he searches endlessly, looking for answers that perpetually elude him.

* Marie LeLay (Cécile de France) is a highly successful French television journalist. She has a great job and a devoted beau (Thierry Neuvic). Life is good. But that all changes one morning. While on vacation in the South Pacific, Marie is swept up in the enormous wave of a destructive tsunami that strikes the island paradise. She's carried away by the powerful surge, drowning and losing consciousness, eventually lapsing into a near death experience. Remarkably, she's rescued and resuscitated, but she's no longer the same person she was before, a challenge she wrestles with in the aftermath of the tragedy and upon her return to Paris. She struggles to find her place in a scheme of things she no longer sees the same way. Her search for answers and understanding thus begins in earnest.

* Jason and Marcus (George McLaren, Frankie McLaren) are identical twins living with their drug-addicted mother (Lyndsey Marshal) in a gritty London neighborhood. Despite being identical twins, the siblings are not totally alike. Jason is a courageous, gregarious, take-charge young man, while Marcus is

a quiet, reserved lad ever in search of guidance, support and self-confidence, most of which he gets from his twin brother. So it should come as no surprise that Marcus is devastated when Jason is killed in a tragic accident, a problem that becomes compounded when he's placed in foster care while his mum undergoes rehab. Marcus longs to find his departed brother, but what he really needs to do is find himself.

Not surprisingly, all three stories eventually intertwine, culminating in London as a result of an intriguing string of synchronicities. And it's through such interactions that answers are at last provided, offering the possibility of new beginnings for all concerned.

As the stories unfold, viewers are treated to a rich tapestry of ideas on the nature of death. Perhaps the most notable of these is the idea that death is an inherent part of life. It's woven into the fabric of our everyday experience, because it's the one eventuality that we all share. But, as this notion is depicted in the film, death isn't some horrific, dreadful occurrence to be feared but a transcendent experience to be seen for what it is—a transition from one state of being to another, another expression of the principle that we're all constantly evolving. The transition that death provides, then, is the means for making that transformative state of becoming possible.

Since death is a part of life, and since it's essentially an embodiment of the concept of transcendence beyond our current circumstances, it's also apparent, as seen in the film's three stories, that we all die a little each day in our waking life pursuits, sometimes literally, sometimes figuratively. One door closes, and another opens, with the death of the former giving birth to the latter. Of course, how we respond to the new circumstances that arise is ultimately what's most important, for, as every conscious creation practitioner knows, the outcome we experience will depend on the beliefs we hold going in. We get what we concentrate on, even when making transitions like this.

The intrinsic connectedness of all things—even those that seem permanently separated by the wall between the worlds—is another conscious creation theme addressed in this film. Our connections to the departed may be less obvious than when our loved ones were still incarnate, perhaps taking on forms that are more metaphorical, symbolic or synchronistic than literal. But those connections are tangible nonetheless, especially when we make the effort to make ourselves aware of them. In that sense, then, we need never feel as though we've lost those we love; it simply means we may need to connect with them in ways we never thought of before, an acquired skill that is itself transcendent in nature. Buying into beliefs that enable this obviously make this possibility easier to realize, too.

And then, of course, there's the character of the afterlife itself, which, as explained in the picture, sounds like a law of attraction practitioner's dream come true, a metaphysical playground where the limitations of physical existence are removed and the potential for creative expression knows no bounds. It's a joyful way of being that makes monodimensional reality seem mundane by comparison. Think of it as an amusement park for your consciousness, and you'll have an idea of what the departed are talking about—and what we have to look forward to.

"Hereafter" is a beautiful meditation on its subject matter, presented in a quiet, subtle, deftly layered package. It's not the kind of picture one might readily associate with Clint Eastwood, but the director has turned in a fine effort with this offering, by far his best work behind the camera. In particular, Eastwood's efforts at getting emotion out of his characters (and evoking it from viewers) easily set this picture apart from his prior works, which I've often found leave much to be desired in that regard. I was also blown away by the realism of the tsunami sequence, a phenomenal technical accomplishment, one that earned the picture an Oscar nomination for best visual effects. I especially liked the film's use (or, in some cases, absence) of sound in this sequence (and elsewhere in the film for that matter), some of the best work I've ever heard in this area. The film's pacing at times is, admittedly, a little slow, but, as the picture progresses and viewers are drawn into its three stories, that issue dissipates completely.

When it comes to life, none of us is going to get out of it alive. But then maybe that's a blessing, for, if we never died, we'd never grow and evolve, either, stagnating in an existence of stifling sameness. "Hereafter" helps us appreciate the value of transition and transcendence, both in our daily life and for the one that awaits us. And, for that, we should all be eternally grateful.

By Default or Design

"The Adjustment Bureau"
Year of Release: 2011
Cast: Matt Damon, Emily Blunt, Terence Stamp,
Anthony Mackie, John Slattery, Michael Kelly
Director: George Nolfi
Screenplay: George Nolfi
Story: Philip K. Dick, The Adjustment Team

Is the reality we experience predetermined? Or are the lives we lead up to us? Or is it possible that existence consists of some symbiotic combination of both? Developing an appreciation and understanding of how things *really* work is a profound, transcendent experience, one that gives us new insights into the nature of our very being and our place in the Universe, themes addressed in the captivating metaphysical thriller, "The Adjustment Bureau."

Congressman David Norris (Matt Damon), one of the youngest members ever elected to the House of Representatives, appears poised to make a quantum leap in his career. As the front runner in the New York Senate race, the feisty, charismatic young Brooklynite would seem to be on the verge of yet another political breakthrough. However, the brashness that made him such a popular contender in the first place also has its downside, and that personal shortcoming catches up with him in the waning days before the election. The revelation of an embarrassing incident from his past derails his campaign at the last minute, a disheartening prelude to a bitter loss.

While practicing his concession speech on election night, David has an unexpected, and quite unusual, encounter with a beguiling, enigmatic free spirit, Elise (Emily Blunt). They share insights, and a kiss, resulting in an instant, undeniable attraction, the kind that includes, but ultimately transcends, romance. However, all magic of the moment aside, circumstances force a hasty separation, one that keeps them from even being able to exchange contact information. Despite the brevity of their encounter, though, Elise's liberated thinking leaves quite an impression on David, helping to remind him of what an ardent individualist he really is. It even prompts him to scrap his planned remarks and give a candid, off-the-cuff speech that further distinguishes his outspoken style, signaling the voting public that the maverick lives and that his political career is far from over.

With the election behind him and his Congressional seat lost, David needs to find work, so he takes a job in the private sector with his longtime friend and advisor, Charlie (Michael Kelly). He still thinks fondly about his encounter with Elise, but, since he has no way to contact her, he tries to focus on other pursuits, such as work and a future run for office. And, thanks to the behind-the-scenes efforts of a team of shadowy, clandestine operatives, that's just the way it's supposed to be.

Or is it?

As David heads off to work one morning, he has another unexpected encounter with Elise, one that largely picks up where they left off. Unlike their first meeting, however, this one *wasn't* supposed to happen. That's because one of the operatives charged with ensuring that events unfold "according to plan," Harry Mitchell (Anthony Mackie), failed to prevent it from happening. With "scripted" events now threatening to fall apart, the operatives hurriedly step in to "correct" matters, but, in doing so, they also inadvertently make David aware of their existence, complicating their task even further.

The operatives' leader, Richardson (John Slattery), refers to his team of agents as "the Adjustment Bureau," a group of specially trained, specially gifted individuals responsible for seeing that human destiny plays out as it's "supposed" to. Richardson warns David not to deviate from the plan any further or to reveal the Bureau's existence to anyone. But, being the fighter that he is, David refuses to let others dictate his fate. He thus vows to take on the Bureau and to live the life he wants, a tall order given their many amazing talents. He manages to hold his own, too, eventually necessitating the intervention of one of the Bureau's toughest operatives, Thompson (Terence Stamp), to rectify matters. But, as this battle of wills plays out, a number of burning questions arise as well—for viewers and characters alike—such as why does the Bureau exist? Why is it so vital for David (or any of us, for that matter) to stick to "the plan"? Can it be changed? And, perhaps most importantly, who wrote this plan in the first place?

As conscious creators are well aware, we create our reality in conjunction with our divine collaborator. We put forth our intentions and then let the Universe take over, providing us with physical manifestations that embody our intangible impulses. Both the metaphysically inclined and even some in the quantum physics community view this collaborative process as the means by which existence comes into being.

But is this assessment accurate? Isn't it possible, as the Bureau asserts, that everything is predestined and out of our control? But, if that's the case, then how is it possible for outcomes to deviate from their predetermined paths, necessitating "adjustment"? And, if such intervention is indeed necessary, doesn't that mean "the plan" is not absolute, that's it's subject to alteration? If so, who's capable of altering it and how? Do we have a say in how things play out, that we can circumvent what's supposedly set in stone? And, if so, doesn't that mean things truly *aren't* set in stone?

In light of this, "The Adjustment Bureau" raises the all-important question, is our reality the product of destiny by default or destiny by design? It also draws attention to the duel of fate vs. free will, begging the question, which one will ultimately win out?

Conscious creators will no doubt want to place their bets on free will as it's one of the cornerstone principles of this philosophy and practice. But is that the wisest wager? After all, even those of us who are adept at using this skill have been thwarted in manifesting our creations from time to time, producing results far off the mark from what we thought we intended. Incidents like that might even cause the philosophy's staunchest followers to question its validity and viability.

But what if those seemingly misdirected results are *exactly* what we're supposed to manifest? Perhaps they arise because of a confused concoction of beliefs, some of which we're aware of and some of which we're not. Maybe such incidents are meant to serve as lessons as part of our learning curves, taking us through "failures" that make us aware of "faulty" beliefs and that help us refine our intents to produce desired successes. And, as these events unfold, perhaps the people, circumstances, synchronicities or materials we encounter in connection with them are meant to serve as our own personal versions of "the adjustment bureau," manifestations that doggedly keep us on the paths on which we're *supposed* to be to realize the outcomes we seek.

Such elements might *seem* like the product of capricious acts of fate, materializations that arise from beyond our control. And good arguments could be made in favor of that case, especially when the outcomes involve elements that strike us as patently unfair or utterly demoralizing. In light of that, one might even contend that free will is nothing but a pie-in-the-sky illusion.

But, as noted above, what if we draw such elements to us as part of our learning process, even if they don't *seem* like they're for our benefit at the time? Such a realization wouldn't negate the concept of free will, but it certainly would give us a new understanding of—and appreciation for—it. Such awareness could conceivably strip away all notions that any kind of a duel between fate and free will even exists, enlightening us to the fact that what we perceive as the cruelty of fate may be nothing more than a well-camouflaged aspect of free will, one that's often integral to the progression of our individual learning curves. It could also bring about a transcendent understanding of the conscious creation process itself, especially the breadth of its power and the need for managing it responsibly. And, perhaps most importantly, it ultimately might help to shed light on just who really writes "the plan" of our lives to begin with, an answer that might surprise in more ways than one.

The results of our manifestation experiences make us aware of the role we play as creators of our destiny. They also provide us with a new understanding of how the process unfolds, particularly when it comes to the nature of our relationship with our divine collaborator. It's been suggested that All That Is created us so It could come to know parts of Itself that It was fundamentally incapable of experiencing any other way. That circumstance thus places tremendous power and responsibility in *our* hands as we carry out our divine mission as apprentice gods, representatives of our Maker who serve as explorers of consciousness and reality and seek experiences not only for our own education, but also for the enlightenment of that from which we came. In a relationship such as that, it thus becomes apparent that God needs us as much as we need God.

To that end, then, the creation of reality is in many ways a product of *both* "default" and "design," and however it unfolds is how it's

CHAPTER 13: TRANSCENDENCE   273

supposed to manifest, regardless of which collaborator is seemingly in the driver's seat. The more we have faith in that process, the more we'll realize that things manifest just as they should, filling us with a new understanding of ourselves, our divinity and our place in the Universe.

Now *that's* transcendence.

I enjoyed this movie immensely. It comes across like a fusion of the "Bourne" series of thrillers and such sci-fi offerings as "Inception" (2010) (see Chapter 10) and "Open Your Eyes" ("*Abre los ojos*") (1997) (the Spanish film on which the Hollywood release "Vanilla Sky" (2001) was based). The story is captivating, and its translation to the screen is riveting, keeping viewers guessing how it will turn out right up until the end. The cinematography is excellent, beautifully showing off New York for the city that it is. Admittedly, the dialogue could have been a little stronger in some of the sequences, but the performances cover it well, especially those offered up by Bureau members Stamp, Slattery and Mackie.

If the goal of our lives is to ultimately rise above and move beyond our current selves, we must develop an awareness that we truly are more than we seem to be. Such personal growth requires us to discover the vast power and miraculous abilities we possess, skills that we're largely unaware of but that have the capability to serve us—and our divine partner—in ways beyond measure. Realizations like that may necessitate making some adjustments in our beliefs and overall perspectives, but the transcendent rewards afforded by those changes can take us to places exceeding our wildest dreams.

EPILOGUE

As should be apparent by now, the intent behind understanding conscious creation is to become more proficient at manifesting the reality we experience. By grasping and making effective use of the specific principles involved, we have a tremendous opportunity to shape an existence to our liking and fulfillment. And there's much to be said for that.

But, as I noted routinely throughout this book, as well as in the Epilogue of *Get the Picture*, what if we were to employ this process for a greater purpose, namely, creating a better world that benefits us all? Wouldn't it be terrific if we could all bask in the bountiful blessings that this practice can make possible? It would be a very different world indeed.

Given the current state of our planet, however, I believe this has become an increasingly important priority for us all. I'm not one to be a fear monger by any means, but I believe the global challenge ante has been upped significantly in recent years, urging us to pay more attention to this notion. In virtually all areas of life, from social justice to economics to the environment to world peace, we face significant challenges desperately in need of being addressed, and the clock is ticking.

The circumstances associated with these challenges have changed drastically in the six years since I first addressed them in the closing pages of *Get the Picture*. In the Epilogue to that book, I raised the idea as a sort of "what if" proposition, one worthy of thoughtful, meritorious consideration. However, given prevailing conditions, I believe it would behoove us to significantly step up our game. What may have once been a proposal for evaluation has now become a call to action—and one that would be in our best interests to heed. Consider my discussion of "the 'Avatar' effect" (see Chapter 6), and you'll see what I mean.

The task need not be seen as overwhelming, however. We have the capability to make meaningful alterations to our world as long as we believe we can. And, thanks to the movies, we have many good examples to draw upon for inspiration and enlightenment. As this book's entries clearly show, we have plenty of offerings available to us that illustrate the principles that make conscious creation work. What's more, unlike what was available at the time *Get the Picture* was written, we now have many more releases to draw from that offer us practical, nuts-and-bolts advice on how to proceed. Films like "The Quantum Activist," "Samsara," "Something Unknown Is Doing We Don't Know What," "I Am" and "People v. The State of Illusion" all provide valuable guidance. Give these pictures a look; I'm sure you'll find it time well spent.

The prospects afforded by the law of attraction should excite every last one of us. All we need do is make the effort to put it into practice. If we do, though, with the right intentions in mind, I'm certain we'll be thrilled with the results. And, if not, we always have an infinite range of other possibilities available to try out as alternatives. Indeed, as I observed at the end of Chapter 5, such is the true beauty of conscious creation—and everything that it makes possible.

Now, let's get to work.

INDEX OF ARTISTS

On-screen Performers:

Aaron, Quinton ("The Blind Side")
Abbass, Hiam ("*Amreeka*"; "The Visitor")
Abu Warda, Yussef ("*Amreeka*")
Adams, Amy ("Doubt"; "Julie and Julia")
Ait Benboullah, Sfia ("Babel")
Ait El Caid, Boubker ("Babel")
Akerman, Jeremy ("Poor Boy's Game")
Akerman, Malin ("Watchmen")
Akhzam, Mohamed ("Babel")
Alexander, Flex ("Poor Boy's Game")
Alonso, Laz ("Avatar")
Álvarez, Maricel ("*Biutiful*")
Ameri, Christian ("The Intouchables")
Anderson, Gillian ("The X-Files: I Want to Believe")
Anderson, Ray ("I Am")
Andrews, Anthony ("The King's Speech")
Andrews, David ("Fair Game")
Anvar, Cas ("Source Code")
Arden, Michael ("Source Code")
Argentero, Luca ("Eat Pray Love")
Arianda, Nina ("Higher Ground"; "Midnight in Paris")
Arkin, Adam ("A Serious Man")
Astin, Skylar ("Taking Woodstock")
Austin, Michele ("Another Year")
Ayala, Jimena ("*Malos Hábitos*")
Azmi, Seema ("The Best Exotic Marigold Hotel")
Badie, Mina ("Greenberg")
Bae, Doona ("Cloud Atlas")
Bagdassarian, Serge ("Midnight in Paris")
Baklini, Amy ("People v. The State of Illusion")
Bakula, Scott ("Source Code")
Bana, Eric ("Star Trek")
Banderas, Antonio ("Ruby Sparks")
Bara, Abdelkader ("Babel")
Barasch, Marc Ian ("I Am")
Bardem, Javier ("*Biutiful*"; "Eat Pray Love")
Barks, Coleman ("I Am")
Barraza, Adriana ("Babel")
Bates, Kathy ("The Blind Side"; "Midnight in Paris")
Behaire, Nicole ("The Express")

Bell, Kristen ("Safety Not Guaranteed")
Bellugi, Alba Gaïa ("The Intouchables")
Belushi, James ("The Ghost")
Bening, Annette ("The Kids Are All Right"; "Ruby Sparks")
Berenger, Tom ("Inception")
Bergere, Jenica ("Safety Not Guaranteed")
Bernthal, Jon ("The Ghost")
Berry, Halle ("Cloud Atlas")
Berteloot, Jean-Yves ("Hereafter")
Best, Eve ("The King's Speech")
Biel, Jessica ("Hitchcock")
Bill, Leo ("Alice in Wonderland")
Billingsley, John ("2012")
Black, Lucas ("Get Low")
Blanchard, Tammy ("Rabbit Hole")
Blanchett, Cate ("Babel")
Bloom, Claire ("The King's Speech")
Blunt, Emily ("The Adjustment Bureau")
Boiteau, Daniel ("*Amreeka*")
Bonham Carter, Helena ("Alice in Wonderland"; "The King's Speech")
Boseman, Chadwick ("The Express")
Bouchaib, Hanaa ("*Biutiful*")
Braden, Gregg ("Infinity: The Ultimate Trip—Journey Beyond Death")
Bradley, David ("Another Year")
Breitmayer, Peter ("A Serious Man")
Bridges, Jeff ("Crazy Heart")
Brinkley, Dannion ("Infinity: The Ultimate Trip—Journey Beyond Death")
Broadbent, Jim ("Another Year"; "Cloud Atlas")
Brody, Adrien ("Midnight in Paris")
Brolin, Josh ("Milk")
Brosnan, Pierce ("The Ghost")
Brown, Rob ("The Express")
Bruni, Carla ("Midnight in Paris")
Bryk, Greg ("Poor Boy's Game")
Buck, Joan Juliet ("Julie and Julia")
Budig, Rebecca ("Please Give")
Bullock, Sandra ("The Blind Side")
Buric, Zlatko ("2012")
Burrows, Saffron ("Shrink")
Butler, Paul ("A Single Man")
Butz, Norbert Leo ("Higher Ground")
Buy, Margherita ("We Have a Pope")
Caine, Michael ("Inception")
Camargo, Christian ("The Hurt Locker")
Campbell, Lee J. ("Poor Boy's Game")
Campbell, Owen ("Conviction")
Campbell, Tobias ("Conviction")
Cano, Aurora ("*Malos Hábitos*")
Cao, Chi ("Mao's Last Dancer")
Cardós, Raúl ("*Malos Hábitos*")
Carey, Helen ("Julie and Julia")
Cattrall, Kim ("The Ghost")
Challen, Mairi Ella ("Alice in Wonderland")

Index of Artists

Chang, Tseng ("2012")
Chaplin, Geraldine ("The Impossible")
Charhi, Liraz ("Fair Game")
Chassler, Zach ("Greenberg")
Chastain, Jessica ("The Tree of Life")
Chau, Osric ("2012")
Chen, Joan ("Mao's Last Dancer")
Chen, Taisheng ("*Biutiful*")
Chernus, Michael ("Higher Ground")
Cho, John ("Star Trek")
Chomsky, Noam ("I Am")
Cluzet, François ("The Intouchables")
Cobbs, Bill ("Get Low")
Collette, Toni ("Hitchcock")
Collins, Clifton, Jr. ("Babel")
Collins, K.C. ("Poor Boy's Game")
Collins, Lily ("The Blind Side")
Conlan, Declan ("Hereafter")
Connolly, Billy ("The X-Files: I Want to Believe")
Coogan, Steve ("Ruby Sparks")
Cooper, Scott ("Get Low")
Cope, Jason ("District 9")
Copley, Sharlto ("District 9")
Costigan, George ("Hereafter")
Cotillard, Marion ("Inception"; "Midnight in Paris")
Cross, Ben ("Star Trek")
Crudup, Billy ("Eat Pray Love"; "Watchmen")
Csokas, Marton ("Alice in Wonderland")
Cusack, John ("2012")

Cusack, Niamh ("Hereafter")
Dacosta, Yaya ("The Kids Are All Right")
Daff, Diaryatou ("*Biutiful*")
Damon, Matt ("The Adjustment Bureau"; "Hereafter")
Daniels, Jeff ("Away We Go")
Dano, Paul ("Ruby Sparks"; "Taking Woodstock")
D'Arcy, James ("Cloud Atlas"; "Hitchcock")
David, Keith ("Cloud Atlas")
Davis, Viola ("Doubt"; "Eat Pray Love")
de France, Cécile ("Hereafter")
De Grandpré, Frédérick ("Source Code")
de Haro, Elena ("*Malos Hábitos*")
de la Tour, Frances ("Alice in Wonderland")
De Van, Adrien ("Midnight in Paris")
Dean, Loren ("Conviction")
Dench, Judi ("The Best Exotic Marigold Hotel")
Denham, Christopher ("Sound of My Voice")
Depp, Johnny ("Alice in Wonderland")
Desae, Tena ("The Best Exotic Marigold Hotel")
Di Fonzo Bo, Marcial ("Midnight in Paris")
DiCaprio, Leonardo ("Inception")
Dispenza, Joe ("People v. The State of Illusion")

Dollinger, Renate ("Infinity: The Ultimate Trip—Journey Beyond Death")
Dominczyk, Dagmara ("Higher Ground")
Donovan, Conor ("Conviction")
Dorsey, Omar ("The Blind Side")
Dosa, David ("Something Unknown Is Doing We Don't Know What")
Dossey, Larry ("Something Unknown Is Doing We Don't Know What")
Doupé, Tony ("Safety Not Guaranteed")
Driver, Minnie ("Conviction")
Dubey, Lillette ("The Best Exotic Marigold Hotel")
Duchovny, David ("The X-Files: I Want to Believe")
Duncan, Lindsay ("Alice in Wonderland")
Dunne, Brenda ("People v. The State of Illusion")
Duplass, Mark ("Greenberg"; "Safety Not Guaranteed")
Dutton, Charles S. ("The Express")
DuVall, Clea ("Conviction")
Duvall, Robert ("Crazy Heart"; "Get Low")
Eastoe, Madeleine ("Mao's Last Dancer")
Echevarría, Emilio ("*Malos Hábitos*")
Eckhart, Aaron ("Rabbit Hole")
Edgeman, Lori Beth ("Get Low")
Ehle, Jennifer ("The King's Speech")
Eisenberg, Jesse ("The Social Network")
Ejiofor, Chiwetel ("2012")
Ejogo, Carmen ("Away We Go")
Ellis, Aunjanue ("The Express")
Ellis, Nelsan ("The Express")
Elmaleh, Gad ("Midnight in Paris")
Emmerich, Noah ("Fair Game")
Emond, Linda ("Julie and Julia")
Eppler, Laramie ("The Tree of Life")
Esposito, Giancarlo ("Rabbit Hole")
Esquivel, Robert "Bernie" ("Babel")
Estrella, Guillermo ("*Biutiful*")
Etura, Marta ("The Impossible")
Fanning, Elle ("Babel")
Faour, Nisreen ("*Amreeka*")
Farmiga, Taissa ("Higher Ground")
Farmiga, Vera ("Higher Ground"; "Source Code")
Farrell, Colin ("Crazy Heart")
Fernández, Eduard ("*Biutiful*")
Fernandez, Karina ("Another Year")
Fiennes, Ralph ("The Hurt Locker")
Finkel, Fyvush ("A Serious Man")
Firth, Colin ("The King's Speech"; "A Single Man")
Fleurot, Audrey ("The Intouchables")
Fogler, Dan ("Taking Woodstock")

Index of Artists

Ford, Arielle ("Something Unknown Is Doing We Don't Know What")
Ford, Debbie ("People v. The State of Illusion")
Foster, Joseph, II ("Doubt")
Francis, John ("I Am")
Franco, Dave ("Greenberg")
Franco, James ("Eat Pray Love"; "Milk")
Frewer, Matt ("Watchmen")
Fry, Stephen ("Alice in Wonderland")
Fuller, Kurt ("Midnight in Paris")
Gaduka, Mandla ("District 9")
Gaffigan, Jim ("Away We Go")
Gallagher, Peter ("Conviction")
Gamble, Nathan ("Babel")
Gambon, Michael ("The King's Speech")
Gandini, Giuseppe ("Eat Pray Love")
Garber, Victor ("Milk")
García Bernal, Gael ("Babel")
Garfield, Andrew ("Never Let Me Go"; "The Social Network")
Garner, Kelli ("Taking Woodstock")
Garrido, Joaquín ("The Kids Are All Right")
Gatehouse, Kyle ("Source Code")
Gecks, Eleanor ("Alice in Wonderland")
Geraghty, Brian ("The Hurt Locker")
Gerwig, Greta ("Greenberg")
Gilmore, Alexie ("World's Greatest Dad")
Gleeson, Domhnall ("Never Let Me Go")
Glover, Crispin ("Alice in Wonderland")
Glover, Danny ("Poor Boy's Game"; "2012")
Gobbi, Gianluca ("We Have a Pope")
Godley, Adam ("The X-Files: I Want to Believe")
Gold, Daniel Eric ("Taking Woodstock")
Good, Rebecca ("Something Unknown Is Doing We Don't Know What")
Goode, Matthew ("A Single Man"; "Watchmen")
Goodman, Henry ("Taking Woodstock")
Goodwin, Ginnifer ("A Single Man")
Gordon-Levitt, Joseph ("Inception")
Goswami, Amit ("The Quantum Activist")
Gould, Elliott ("Ruby Sparks")
Grabeel, Lucas ("Milk")
Grant, Hugh ("Cloud Atlas")
Gray, David Barry ("Game Change")
Graynor, Ari ("Conviction")
Greenwood, Bruce ("Mao's Last Dancer"; "Star Trek")
Gretsch, Joel ("Shrink")
Grof, Stanislav ("Infinity: The Ultimate Trip—Journey Beyond Death")
Groff, Jonathan ("Taking Woodstock")

Gugino, Carla ("Watchmen")
Guilbert, Ann ("Please Give")
Gummer, Mamie ("Taking Woodstock")
Guo, Chengwu (Mao's Last Dancer")
Gupta, Rajendra ("The Best Exotic Marigold Hotel")
Gurira, Danai ("The Visitor")
Gyasi, David ("Cloud Atlas")
Gyllenhaal, Jake ("Source Code")
Gyllenhaal, Maggie ("Away We Go"; "Crazy Heart")
Hackforth-Jones, Penne ("Mao's Last Dancer")
Haddad, Selena ("*Amreeka*")
Hakim, Christine ("Eat Pray Love")
Haley, Jackie Earle ("Watchmen")
Hall, Rebecca ("Please Give")
Hall, William, Jr. ("Safety Not Guaranteed")
Hamilton, Josh ("Away We Go")
Hammer, Armie ("The Social Network")
Han, Chin ("2012")
Hanks, Tom ("Cloud Atlas")
Hardcastle, Diana ("The Best Exotic Marigold Hotel")
Hardy, Tom ("Inception")
Harrelson, Woody ("Game Change"; "2012")
Harris, Ed ("Game Change")
Harrison, Nicola ("The Impossible")
Hart, Mickey ("The Other Dream Team")
Hartmann, Thom ("I Am")
Hassell, Eddie ("The Kids Are All Right")
Hathaway, Anne ("Alice in Wonderland")
Haussmann, Alexandre ("2012")
Haussmann, Philippe ("2012")
Hawkes, John ("Higher Ground")
Hawkins, Sally ("Never Let Me Go")
Haywood, Vanessa ("District 9")
Head, Jae ("The Blind Side")
Heathcote, Steven ("Mao's Last Dancer")
Heck, Yves ("Midnight in Paris")
Helberg, Simon ("A Serious Man")
Hemsworth, Chris ("Star Trek")
Henson, Darren Dewitt ("The Express")
Herman, Paul ("Crazy Heart")
Hiddleston, Tom ("Midnight in Paris")
Hirsch, Emile ("Milk"; "Taking Woodstock")
Hoang, Ferdinand ("Mao's Last Dancer")
Hoffman, Philip Seymour ("Doubt")
Holbrook, Boyd ("Higher Ground")
Holland, John ("Infinity: The Ultimate Trip—Journey Beyond Death")
Holland, Tom ("The Impossible")
Holliday, Polly ("Fair Game")
Hopkins, Anthony ("Hitchcock")
Hopkins, John ("Alice in Wonderland")

Index of Artists

Hoptman, Ari ("A Serious Man")
Horne, Deborah ("World's Greatest Dad")
Hornsby, Bruce ("World's Greatest Dad")
Hoult, Nicholas ("A Single Man")
Howard, Bryce Dallas ("Hereafter")
Huang, Wen Bin ("Mao's Last Dancer")
Huppert, Isabelle (*Amour*)
Huss, Toby ("World's Greatest Dad")
Huston, Danny ("Hitchcock")
Huston, Jack ("Shrink")
Hutcherson, Josh ("The Kids Are All Right")
Hutton, Timothy ("The Ghost")
Hyde-White, Alex ("Game Change")
Ifans, Rhys ("Greenberg")
Imrie, Celia ("The Best Exotic Marigold Hotel")
Irwin, Bill ("Higher Ground")
Jacobi, Derek ("Hereafter"; "The King's Speech")
Jahn, Robert ("People v. The State of Illusion")
James, David ("District 9")
James, Geraldine ("Alice in Wonderland")
James, Liam ("2012")
James, Pell ("Shrink")
Janney, Allison ("Away We Go")
Jason Leigh, Jennifer ("Greenberg")
Jenkins, Richard ("Eat Pray Love"; "The Visitor")
Jiao, Gang ("Mao's Last Dancer")
Jindachote, Ploy ("The Impossible")
Johansson, Douglas ("The Impossible")
Johansson, Scarlett ("Hitchcock")
Johnson, Jake ("Safety Not Guaranteed")
Jones, Justin ("The Express")
Jones, Tad ("People v. The State of Illusion")
Jordan, Chris ("I Am")
Joslin, Samuel ("The Impossible")
Kang, David ("A Serious Man")
Kang, Soogi ("The Ghost")
Kawar, Jenna (*Amreeka*)
Kazan, Zoe ("Ruby Sparks")
Keener, Catherine ("Please Give")
Keller, Marthe ("Hereafter")
Kelly, Michael ("The Adjustment Bureau"; "Fair Game")
Keltner, Dacher ("I Am")
Kennedy, Mimi ("Midnight in Paris")
Kidman, Nicole ("Rabbit Hole")
Kikuchi, Rinko ("Babel")
Kind, Richard ("Hereafter"; "A Serious Man")
King, Kaitlyn Rae ("Higher Ground")
Kirby, Chris ("Mao's Last Dancer")
Klathaley, Tor ("The Impossible")
Knightley, Keira ("Never Let Me Go")
Kortajarena, Jon ("A Single Man")

Krasinski, John ("Away We Go")
Kulkarni, Neena ("The Best Exotic Marigold Hotel")
Kurtinaitis, Rimas ("The Other Dream Team")
LaBelle, Rob ("Watchmen")
Lam, Alvin ("Sound of My Voice")
Lampley, Jim ("The Other Dream Team")
Landecker, Amy ("A Serious Man")
Landsbergis, Vytautas ("The Other Dream Team")
Lang, Stephen ("Avatar")
Larson, Brie ("Greenberg")
Le Ny, Anne ("The Intouchables")
Lee, Brody Nicholas ("Cloud Atlas")
Lee, Christopher ("Alice in Wonderland")
LeFevre, Adam ("Fair Game")
Lennick, Sari ("A Serious Man")
Lenox, Adriane ("The Blind Side")
Leo, Melissa ("Conviction")
Leonard, Joshua ("Higher Ground")
Lerner, Michael ("A Serious Man")
Levy, Eugene ("Taking Woodstock")
Lewis, Juliette ("Conviction")
Lilly, Evangeline ("The Hurt Locker")
Lily, Morgan ("2012")
Lin, Lang Sofia (*Biutiful*)
Lindahl, Melanie ("People v. The State of Illusion")
Loggia, Robert ("Shrink")
Lowe, David ("Midnight in Paris")
Lu, Lisa ("2012")
Lucas, Matt ("Alice in Wonderland")
Luna, Diego ("Milk")
Lundh, Daniel ("Midnight in Paris")
Luo, Jin (*Biutiful*)
Lynch, Jane ("Julie and Julia")
Lynskey, Melanie ("Away We Go")
Macchio, Ralph ("Hitchcock")
Mackie, Anthony ("The Adjustment Bureau"; "The Hurt Locker")
MacLachlan, Kyle ("Mao's Last Dancer")
MacNicol, Peter ("Game Change")
Madison, Bailee ("Conviction")
Mahon, Sean ("Higher Ground")
Mailer, Stephen ("Rabbit Hole")
Makkar, Sid ("The Best Exotic Marigold Hotel")
Malik, Xola ("Safety Not Guaranteed")
Maltman, Oliver ("Another Year")
Mamet, Zosia ("The Kids Are All Right")
Mandell, Alan ("A Serious Man")
Mandvi, Aasif ("Ruby Sparks")
Mankuma, Blu ("2012")
Manville, Lesley ("Another Year")

Mara, Rooney ("The Social Network")
Marčiulionis, Šarūnas ("The Other Dream Team")
Marling, Brit ("Sound of My Voice")
Marquez, Ramona ("The King's Speech")
Marshal, Lyndsey ("Hereafter")
Martin, Demetri ("Taking Woodstock")
Martin, Evan ("World's Greatest Dad")
Martin, Justin ("The Express")
Martínez, Alma Sofía ("*Malos Hábitos*")
Masten, Gordon ("Source Code")
Mazzello, Joseph ("The Social Network")
McAdams, Rachel ("Midnight in Paris")
McCall, Mitzi ("World's Greatest Dad")
McCarthy, Tom ("2012")
McCormick, Michael ("People v. The State of Illusion")
McCracken, Hunter ("The Tree of Life")
McCraty, Rollin ("I Am")
McDonald, Kevin ("People v. The State of Illusion")
McFadden, Davenia ("Sound of My Voice")
McGill, Bruce ("Fair Game")
McGraw, Tim ("The Blind Side")
McGregor, Ewan ("The Ghost"; "The Impossible")
McHattie, Stephen ("Poor Boy's Game"; "2012"; "Watchmen")
McKinnon, Ray ("The Blind Side")
McLaren, Frankie ("Hereafter")
McLaren, George ("Hereafter")
McManus, Jessica ("A Serious Man")
McRaney, Gerald ("Get Low")
McTaggart, Lynne ("I Am")
Meikle-Small, Isobel ("Never Let Me Go")
Melamed, Fred ("A Serious Man")
Mendy, Cyril ("The Intouchables")
Menjou Cortes, Vincent ("Midnight in Paris")
Mennell, Laura ("Watchmen")
Meritte, Dorothée Brière ("The Intouchables")
Messina, Chris ("Away We Go"; "Greenberg"; "Julie and Julia"; "Ruby Sparks")
Messmer, Michele ("Conviction")
Meyers, Christy ("Sound of My Voice")
Miller, Omar Benson ("The Express")
Minghella, Max ("The Social Network")
Mirren, Helen ("Hitchcock")
Mistry, Jimi ("2012")
Mitchell, Edgar D. ("Something Unknown Is Doing We Don't Know What")
Mohr, Jay ("Hereafter")

Möhring, Sönke ("The Impossible")
Mollet, Clotilde ("The Intouchables")
Monaghan, Michelle ("Source Code")
Montaño, Cynthia ("Babel")
Moore, Joel David ("Avatar")
Moore, Julianne ("Game Change"; "The Kids Are All Right"; "A Single Man")
Moore, Thomas ("People v. The State of Illusion")
Moretti, Nanni ("We Have a Pope")
Morgan, Jeffrey Dean ("Watchmen")
Morris, Sharon ("The Blind Side")
Morrison, Jennifer ("Star Trek")
Morse, David ("The Hurt Locker")
Muallem, Melkar ("*Amreeka*")
Mulligan, Carey ("Never Let Me Go")
Mullin, Chris ("The Other Dream Team")
Murphy, Cillian ("Inception")
Murphy, Donna ("Higher Ground")
Murphy, Dwain ("Poor Boy's Game")
Murray, Bill ("Get Low")
Myer, Nancy ("Something Unknown Is Doing We Don't Know What")
Nabawy, Khaled ("Fair Game")
Nation, Jack ("Crazy Heart")
Ndiaye, Cheikh ("*Biutiful*")
Nelson, Donnie ("The Other Dream Team")
Nelson, Roger ("Something Unknown Is Doing We Don't Know What")
Neuvic, Thierry ("Hereafter")
Newton, Thandie ("2012")
Nicholas, Thomas Ian ("Please Give")
Nicholson, Lorraine ("World's Greatest Dad")
Nighy, Bill ("The Best Exotic Marigold Hotel")
Nikaido, Satoshi ("Babel")
Nimoy, Leonard ("Star Trek")
Novotny, Tuva ("Eat Pray Love")
O, Henry ("2012")
Ochandiano, Rubén ("*Biutiful*")
O'Connell, Jack ("Doubt")
Oestermann, Grégoire ("The Intouchables")
Oh, Sandra ("Rabbit Hole")
O'Hara, Catherine ("Away We Go")
O'Hare, Denis ("Milk")
O'Malley, Mike ("Eat Pray Love")
Page, Ellen ("Inception")
Pais, Josh ("Please Give")
Pally, Adam ("Taking Woodstock")
Palmer, Keke ("Shrink")
Parrott, Roger ("The King's Speech")
Patel, Dev ("The Best Exotic Marigold Hotel")
Paulson, Sarah ("Game Change")
Pearce, Guy ("The Hurt Locker"; "The King's Speech")

Pearl, Eric ("Something Unknown Is Doing We Don't Know What")
Peet, Amanda ("Please Give"; "2012"; "The X-Files: I Want to Believe")
Pegg, Simon ("Star Trek")
Peña, Michael ("Babel")
Pendergast, Oaklee ("The Impossible")
Pendleton, Austin ("Game Change")
Penn, Sean ("Fair Game"; "Milk"; "The Tree of Life")
Perry, Tyler ("Star Trek")
Pert, Candace ("People v. The State of Illusion")
Peters, Russell ("Source Code")
Pettie, Darren ("Taking Woodstock")
Piccoli, Michel ("We Have a Pope")
Pickup, Ronald ("The Best Exotic Marigold Hotel")
Pierson, Geoff ("World's Greatest Dad")
Pigott-Smith, Tim ("Alice in Wonderland")
Pileggi, Mitch ("The X-Files: I Want to Believe")
Pill, Alison ("Midnight in Paris"; "Milk")
Pine, Chris ("Star Trek")
Pitt, Brad ("Babel"; "The Tree of Life")
Place, Mary Kay ("Julie and Julia")
Platt, Oliver ("Please Give"; "2012")
Plaza, Aubrey ("Safety Not Guaranteed")
Plemons, Jesse ("Shrink")
Pohl, Avery ("Sound of My Voice")
Ponlop, Dzogchen ("Infinity: The Ultimate Trip—Journey Beyond Death")
Portnow, Richard ("Hitchcock")
Postlethwaite, Pete ("Inception")
Pounder, CCH ("Avatar")
Powell, Jemma ("Alice in Wonderland")
Preece, Tim ("The Ghost")
Pugh, Robert ("The Ghost")
Purnell, Ella ("Never Let Me Go")
Puthoff, Hal ("Something Unknown Is Doing We Don't Know What")
Quaid, Dennis ("The Express")
Quinn, Daniel ("I Am")
Quinto, Zachary ("Star Trek")
Rabourdin, Olivier ("Midnight in Paris")
Rachidi, Mustapha ("Babel")
Radin, Dean ("I Am"; "Something Unknown Is Doing We Don't Know What")
Rajskub, Mary Lynn ("Julie and Julia"; "Safety Not Guaranteed")
Rampling, Charlotte ("Never Let Me Go")
Ramsey, Laura ("Shrink")
Rao, Dileep ("Avatar"; "Inception")

Regan, Laura ("Poor Boy's Game")
Remnick, David ("The Other Dream Team")
Renner, Jeremy ("The Hurt Locker")
Rennie, Callum Keith ("The X-Files: I Want to Believe")
Reyes Spíndola, Patricia ("*Malos Hábitos*")
Ribisi, Giovanni ("Avatar")
Riccardi, Emilio ("The Impossible")
Rickman, Alan ("Alice in Wonderland")
Rickman, Allen Lewis ("A Serious Man")
Rintoul, David ("The Ghost")
Riseborough, Andrea ("Never Let Me Go")
Riva, Emmanuelle ("*Amour*")
Rivera, Victor ("*Malos Hábitos*")
Roberts, Dallas ("Shrink")
Roberts, Julia ("Eat Pray Love")
Rockwell, Sam ("Conviction")
Rodriguez, Michelle ("Avatar")
Rolland, Sonia ("Midnight in Paris")
Rosen, Beatrice ("2012")
Rosenman, Zvi Howard ("Milk")
Ross, Chelcie ("The Express")
Rostain, François ("Midnight in Paris")
Roukhe, Driss ("Babel")
Roukis, Mike ("Doubt")
Rowe, Charlie ("Never Let Me Go")
Rubinek, Saul ("The Express")
Rudolph, Maya ("Away We Go")
Ruffalo, Mark ("The Kids Are All Right")
Rush, Deborah ("Julie and Julia")
Rush, Geoffrey ("The King's Speech")
Ryder, Winona ("Star Trek")
Sabara, Daryl ("World's Greatest Dad")
Sabonis, Arvydas ("The Other Dream Team")
Sahmi, Wahiba ("Babel")
Sahtouris, Elisabet ("I Am")
Saldana, Zoë ("Avatar"; "Star Trek")
Saleh, Nasser ("*Biutiful*")
Sanderson, Brodie ("*Amreeka*")
Sannie, Andrew ("*Amreeka*")
Sarandon, Susan ("Cloud Atlas")
Savage, Martin ("Another Year")
Sayegh, Christopher ("The Hurt Locker")
Schirripa, Steven R. ("Hereafter")
Schlitz, Marilyn ("I Am")
Schneider, Paul ("Away We Go")
Schreiber, Liev ("Taking Woodstock")
Schull, Amanda ("Mao's Last Dancer")
Schwartz, Gary ("Something Unknown Is Doing We Don't Know What")
Schwenke, Taylor ("Higher Ground")
Segal, George ("2012")
Selby, David ("The Social Network")
Senge, Peter ("People v. The State of Illusion")

Index of Artists

Seydoux, Léa ("Midnight in Paris")
Shadyac, Richard ("I Am")
Shadyac, Tom ("I Am")
Sharma, Kunal ("The Kids Are All Right")
Sharma, Vishnu ("The Best Exotic Marigold Hotel")
Sharp, Hannah ("Never Let Me Go")
Shaw, Fiona ("The Tree of Life")
Shawkat, Alia ("*Amreeka*"; "Ruby Sparks")
Sheen, Michael ("Alice in Wonderland"; "Midnight in Paris")
Sheen, Ruth ("Another Year")
Sheldrake, Rupert ("Something Unknown Is Doing We Don't Know What")
Shepard, Sam ("Fair Game")
Sheridan, Jamey ("Game Change")
Sheridan, Tye ("The Tree of Life")
Shetty, Bhuvash ("The Best Exotic Marigold Hotel")
Shimell, William ("*Amour*")
Shivers, Elizabeth ("The Express")
Shmulenson, Yelena ("A Serious Man")
Simmons, Henry ("World's Greatest Dad")
Simpkins, Ryan ("A Single Man")
Sinclair, Carol ("Poor Boy's Game")
Singh, Rushita ("Eat Pray Love")
Skagford, Brent ("Source Code")
Slattery, John ("The Adjustment Bureau")
Sleiman, Haaz ("The Visitor")
Smith, Kurtwood ("Hitchcock")
Smith, Lois ("Please Give")
Smith, Maggie ("The Best Exotic Marigold Hotel")
Smith, Miriam ("*Amreeka*")
Solivéres, Thomas ("The Intouchables")
Song, Brenda ("The Social Network")
Soni, Karan ("Safety Not Guaranteed")
Spacek, Sissy ("Get Low")
Spacey, Kevin ("Shrink")
Spall, Timothy ("Alice in Wonderland"; "The King's Speech")
Speirs, Greg ("The Other Dream Team")
Spoto, Yves-Antoine ("Midnight in Paris")
Stamp, Terence ("The Adjustment Bureau")
Staton, Rebekah ("Hereafter")
Staunton, Imelda ("Alice in Wonderland"; "Another Year"; "Taking Woodstock")
Steele, Sarah ("Please Give")
Steen, Suzie ("Mao's Last Dancer")
Stern, David ("The Other Dream Team")
Sternhagen, Frances ("Julie and Julia")
Stiller, Ben ("Greenberg")
Stoll, Corey ("Midnight in Paris")

Streep, Meryl ("Doubt"; "Julie and Julia")
Stroh, Kandice ("Sound of My Voice")
Studi, Wes ("Avatar")
Stuhlbarg, Michael ("A Serious Man"; "Hitchcock")
Stuhr, Jerzy ("We Have a Pope")
Sturgess, Jim ("Cloud Atlas")
Subiyanto, Hadi ("Eat Pray Love")
Sundberg, Jan Roland ("The Impossible")
Sundberg, Johan ("The Impossible")
Sutherland, Rossif ("Poor Boy's Game")
Suzuki, David ("I Am")
Swank, Hilary ("Conviction")
Sy, Omar ("The Intouchables")
Tahir, Faran ("Star Trek")
Tarchani, Said ("Babel")
Tart, Charles ("Something Unknown Is Doing We Don't Know What")
Teller, Miles ("Rabbit Hole")
Temple, Juno ("Greenberg")
Tenney, Jon ("Rabbit Hole")
Tharaud, Alexandre ("*Amour*")
Thay, Lee Hong ("The Ghost")
Thomas, Craig ("Source Code")
Thompson, Glen ("*Amreeka*")
Thompson, Hugh ("Poor Boy's Game")
Thompson, Jack ("Mao's Last Dancer")
Thompson, Sophie ("Eat Pray Love")
Thongruang, La-Orng ("The Impossible")
Thurman, Robert ("Infinity: The Ultimate Trip—Journey Beyond Death")
Timberlake, Justin ("The Social Network")
Tomlinson, Eleanor ("Alice in Wonderland")
Toure, Absa Dialou ("The Intouchables")
Traylor, Susan ("Greenberg")
Treviño, Marco ("*Malos Hábitos*")
Trintignant, Jean-Louis ("*Amour*")
Trucks, Toni ("Ruby Sparks")
Tucci, Stanley ("Julie and Julia")
Turner, McKenzie ("Higher Ground")
Tuttle, J.B. ("People v. The State of Illusion")
Tutu, Desmond ("I Am")
Urb, Johann ("2012")
Urban, Karl ("Star Trek")
Urbanski, Douglas ("The Social Network")
V., Tony ("World's Greatest Dad")
Valančiūnas, Jonas ("The Other Dream Team")
Vandermark, Michael ("People v. The State of Illusion")
Vergotis, Camilla ("Mao's Last Dancer")
Vicedo, Elisa ("*Malos Hábitos*")
Vicius, Nicole ("Sound of My Voice")

Index of Artists

Vickers, Austin ("People v. The State of Illusion")
Vidal, Gore ("Shrink")
Vidal, Milagros ("*Malos Hábitos*")
Villoldo, Alberto ("Infinity: The Ultimate Trip—Journey Beyond Death")
Wagener, Ana ("*Biutiful*")
Wallach, Eli ("The Ghost")
Walsch, Neale Donald ("Infinity: The Ultimate Trip—Journey Beyond Death")
Walton, Bill ("The Other Dream Team")
Wang, Shuang Bao ("Mao's Last Dancer")
Wasikowska, Mia ("Alice in Wonderland"; "The Kids Are All Right")
Watanabe, Ken ("Inception")
Watts, Naomi ("Fair Game"; "The Impossible")
Weaver, Sigourney ("Avatar")
Weaving, Hugo ("Cloud Atlas")
Webber, Mark ("Shrink")
Weiss, Brian ("Infinity: The Ultimate Trip—Journey Beyond Death")
Wever, Merritt ("Greenberg")
Wharton, Richard ("Sound of My Voice")
Whishaw, Ben ("Cloud Atlas")
Whitehouse, Paul ("Alice in Wonderland")
Wiest, Dianne ("Rabbit Hole")
Wight, Peter ("Another Year"; "Babel")
Wilkinson, Tom ("The Best Exotic Marigold Hotel"; "The Ghost")
Williams, Jermaine ("World's Greatest Dad")
Williams, Olivia ("The Ghost")
Williams, Robin ("Shrink"; "World's Greatest Dad")
Williams, Tonya Lee ("Poor Boy's Game")
Williams, Wes ("Poor Boy's Game")
Wilson, Freya ("The King's Speech")
Wilson, Owen ("Midnight in Paris")
Wilson, Patrick ("Watchmen")
Wilton, Penelope ("The Best Exotic Marigold Hotel")
Wincott, Michael ("Hitchcock")
Windsor, Barbara ("Alice in Wonderland")
Wisden, Robert ("Watchmen")
Wolff, Aaron ("A Serious Man")
Wolff, Alexander ("The Other Dream Team")
Woll, Deborah Ann ("Ruby Sparks")
Woodcock, Fagin ("The X-Files: I Want to Believe")
Worthington, Sam ("Avatar")
Wright, Jeffrey ("Source Code")
Wu, Constance ("Sound of My Voice")
Wyner, George ("A Serious Man")
Xzibit ("The X-Files: I Want to Believe")
Yakusho, Kôji ("Babel")

Yelchin, Anton ("Star Trek")
Yeo, Josh ("Hitchcock")
Young, Aden ("Mao's Last Dancer")
Young, Karen ("Conviction")
Yue, Xiu Qing ("Mao's Last Dancer")
Yunt, Catherine ("Something Unknown Is Doing We Don't Know What")
Zhang, Su ("Mao's Last Dancer")
Zhou, Xuo ("Cloud Atlas")
Ziegler, Joseph ("*Amreeka*")
Zinn, Howard ("I Am")

Directors:
Abrams, J.J. ("Star Trek")
Allen, Woody ("Midnight in Paris")
Batmanglij, Zal ("Sound of My Voice")
Baumbach, Noah ("Greenberg")
Bayona, J.A. ("The Impossible")
Beresford, Bruce ("Mao's Last Dancer")
Bigelow, Kathryn ("The Hurt Locker")
Blomkamp, Neill ("District 9")
Bross, Simón ("*Malos Hábitos*")
Burton, Tim ("Alice in Wonderland")
Cameron, James ("Avatar")
Carter, Chris ("The X-Files: I Want to Believe")
Cervine, Scott ("People v. The State of Illusion")
Cholodenko, Lisa ("The Kids Are All Right")
Coen, Ethan, and Joel Coen ("A Serious Man")
Cooper, Scott ("Crazy Heart")
Dabis, Cherien ("*Amreeka*")
Dayton, Jonathan, and Valerie Feris ("Ruby Sparks")
Eastwood, Clint ("Hereafter")
Emmerich, Roland ("2012")
Ephron, Nora ("Julie and Julia")
Farmiga, Vera ("Higher Ground")
Fincher, David ("The Social Network")
Fleder, Gary ("The Express")
Ford, Tom ("A Single Man")
Fricke, Ron ("Samsara")

Index of Artists

Gervasi, Sacha ("Hitchcock")
Goldthwait, Bobcat ("World's Greatest Dad")
Goldwyn, Tony ("Conviction")
González Iñárritu, Alejandro ("Babel"; "*Biutiful*")
Hancock, John Lee ("The Blind Side")
Haneke, Michael ("*Amour*")
Holofcener, Nicole ("Please Give")
Hooper, Tom ("The King's Speech")
Jones, Duncan ("Source Code")
Lee, Ang ("Taking Woodstock")
Leigh, Mike ("Another Year")
Liman, Doug ("Fair Game")
Madden, John ("The Best Exotic Marigold Hotel")
Malick, Terrence ("The Tree of Life")
Markevicius, Marius ("The Other Dream Team")
McCarthy, Tom ("The Visitor")
Mendes, Sam ("Away We Go")
Mitchell, John Cameron ("Rabbit Hole")
Moretti, Nanni ("We Have a Pope")
Murphy, Ryan ("Eat Pray Love")
Nakache, Olivier, and Eric Toledano ("The Intouchables")
Nolan, Christopher ("Inception")
Nolfi, George ("The Adjustment Bureau")
Pate, Jonas ("Shrink")
Polanski, Roman ("The Ghost")
Roach, Jay ("Game Change")
Romanek, Mark ("Never Let Me Go")
Scheltema, Renée ("Something Unknown Is Doing We Don't Know What")
Schneider, Aaron ("Get Low")
Shadyac, Tom ("I Am")
Shanley, John Patrick ("Doubt")
Slade, Renee, and Ri Stewart ("The Quantum Activist")
Snyder, Zack ("Watchmen")
Trevorrow, Colin ("Safety Not Guaranteed")
Tykwer, Tom, Andy Wachowski and Lana Wachowski ("Cloud Atlas")
Van Sant, Gus ("Milk")
Virgo, Clement ("Poor Boy's Game")
Weidner, Jay ("Infinity: The Ultimate Trip—Journey Beyond Death")

Screenplay/Teleplay Writers:

Allen, Woody ("Midnight in Paris")
Anaya, Ernesto, and Simón Bross ("*Malos Hábitos*")
Arriaga, Guillermo ("Babel")
Batmanglij, Zal, and Brit Marling ("Sound of My Voice")
Baumbach, Noah ("Greenberg")
Black, Dustin Lance ("Milk")
Blomkamp, Neill, and Terri Tatchell ("District 9")
Boal, Mark ("The Hurt Locker")
Briggs, Carolyn S., and Tim Metcalfe ("Higher Ground")
Butterworth, Jez, and John-Henry Butterworth ("Fair Game")
Cameron, James ("Avatar")
Cholodenko, Lisa, and Stuart Blumberg ("The Kids Are All Right")
Coen, Joel, and Ethan Coen ("A Serious Man")
Connolly, Derek ("Safety Not Guaranteed")
Cooper, Scott ("Crazy Heart")
Dabis, Cherien ("*Amreeka*")
Eggers, Dave, and Vendela Vida ("Away We Go")
Emmerich, Roland, and Harald Kloser ("2012")
Ephron, Nora ("Julie and Julia")
Ford, Tom, and David Scearce ("A Single Man")
Fricke, Ron, and Mark Magidson ("Samsara")
Garland, Alex ("Never Let Me Go")
Golder, Ted ("The Quantum Activist")
Goldthwait, Bobcat ("World's Greatest Dad")
González Iñárritu, Alejandro, Nicholás Giacobone and Armando Bo ("*Biutiful*")
Gray, Pamela ("Conviction")
Hancock, John Lee ("The Blind Side")
Haneke, Michael ("*Amour*")
Harris, Robert, and Roman Polanski ("The Ghost")
Hayter, David, and Alex Tse ("Watchmen")
Holofcener, Nicole ("Please Give")
Kazan, Zoe ("Ruby Sparks")
Leavitt, Charles ("The Express")
Leigh, Mike ("Another Year")
Lindsay-Abaire, David ("Rabbit Hole")
Malick, Terrence ("The Tree of Life")
Markevicius, Marius, and Jon Weinbach ("The Other Dream Team")
McCarthy, Tom ("The Visitor")
McLaughlin, John J. ("Hitchcock")
Moffett, Thomas ("Shrink")
Moretti, Nanni, Francesco Piccolo and Federica Pontremoli ("We Have a Pope")
Morgan, Peter ("Hereafter")

Index of Artists

Murphy, Ryan, and Jennifer Salt ("Eat Pray Love")
Nakache, Olivier, and Eric Toledano ("The Intouchables")
Nolan, Christopher ("Inception")
Nolfi, George ("The Adjustment Bureau")
Orci, Roberto, and Alex Kurtzman ("Star Trek")
Parker, Ol ("The Best Exotic Marigold Hotel")
Provenzano, Chris, and C. Gaby Mitchell ("Get Low")
Ripley, Ben ("Source Code")
Sánchez, Sergio G. ("The Impossible")
Sardi, Jan ("Mao's Last Dancer")
Schamus, James ("Taking Woodstock")
Scheltema, Renée ("Something Unknown Is Doing We Don't Know What")
Seidler, David ("The King's Speech")
Shadyac, Tom ("I Am")
Shanley, John Patrick ("Doubt")
Sorkin, Aaron ("The Social Network")
Spotnitz, Frank, and Chris Carter ("The X-Files: I Want to Believe")
Strong, Danny ("Game Change")
Thorne, Chaz, and Clement Virgo ("Poor Boy's Game")
Vickers, Austin ("People v. The State of Illusion")
Wachowski, Lana, Tom Tykwer and Andy Wachowski ("Cloud Atlas")
Woolverton, Linda ("Alice in Wonderland")

Book, Story and Source Material Creators:

Arriaga, Guillermo, and Alejandro González Iñárritu ("Babel," story)

Belón, María ("The Impossible," story)

Blomkamp, Neill ("District 9," film short adaptation source, "Alive in Joburg")

Briggs, Carolyn S. ("Higher Ground," book, *This Dark World*)

Carroll, Lewis ("Alice in Wonderland," source books, *Alice's Adventures in Wonderland* and *Through the Looking Glass*)

Carter, Chris ("The X-Files: I Want to Believe," TV series source material, *The X-Files*)

Cobb, Thomas ("Crazy Heart," book, *Crazy Heart*)

Dick, Philip K. ("The Adjustment Bureau," story, *The Adjustment Team*)

Fricke, Ron, and Mark Magidson ("Samsara," concept)

Gallagher, Robert ("The Express," book, *Ernie Davis: The Elmira Express*)

Gilbert, Elizabeth ("Eat Pray Love," book, *Eat Pray Love: One Woman's Search for Everything Across Italy, India and Indonesia*)

Harris, Robert ("The Ghost," book, *The Ghost*)

Heilemann, John, and Mark Halperin ("Game Change," book, *Game Change: Obama and the Clintons, McCain and Palin, and the Race of a Lifetime*)

Isherwood, Christopher ("A Single Man," book, *A Single Man*)

Ishiguro, Kazuo ("Never Let Me Go," book, *Never Let Me Go*)

Jason Leigh, Jennifer, and Noah Baumbach ("Greenberg," story)

Lewis, Michael ("The Blind Side," book, *The Blind Side: Evolution of a Game*)

Li, Cunxin ("Mao's Last Dancer," book, *Mao's Last Dancer*)

Lindsay-Abaire, David ("Rabbit Hole," play, *Rabbit Hole*)

Mezrich, Ben ("The Social Network," book, *The Accidental Billionaires*)

Mitchell, David ("Cloud Atlas," book, *Cloud Atlas*)

Moggach, Deborah ("The Best Exotic Marigold Hotel," book, *These Foolish Things*)

Moore, Alan (author), and Dave Gibbons (illustrator) ("Watchmen," graphic novel, *Watchmen*)

Powell, Julie ("Julie and Julia," source book, *Julie and Julia*), and Julia Child and Alex Prud'homme ("Julie and Julia," source book, *My Life in France*)

Provenzano, Chris, and Scott Seeke ("Get Low," story)
Reardon, Henry ("Shrink," story)
Rebello, Stephen ("Hitchcock," book, *Alfred Hitchcock and the Making of Psycho*)
Roddenberry, Gene ("Star Trek," TV series source material, *Star Trek*)
Shanley, John Patrick ("Doubt," play, *Doubt*)
Tiber, Elliot, and Tom Monte ("Taking Woodstock," book, *Taking Woodstock: A True Story of a Riot, a Concert and a Life*)
Villoldo, Alberto, and Jay Weidner ("Infinity: The Ultimate Trip—Journey Beyond Death," concept)
Wilson, Joseph ("Fair Game," source book, *The Politics of Truth: Inside the Lies that Led to War and Betrayed My Wife's CIA Identity: A Diplomat's Memoir*), and Valerie Plame Wilson ("Fair Game," source book, *Fair Game: My Life as a Spy, My Betrayal by the White House*)

OTHER WRITINGS BY BRENT MARCHANT

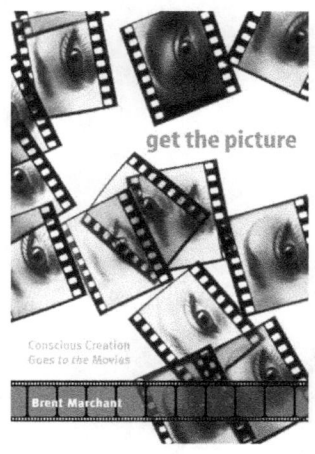

Get the Picture: Conscious Creation Goes to the Movies
(ISBN 978-1-930491-12-0)
(Moment Point Press, 2007)
Cover design by Kathryn Sky-Peck

Brent Marchant

Official Web Site of Brent Marchant
www.BrentMarchant.com

Featured Contributor, Arts & Entertainment
VividLife magazine
www.VividLife.me

Featured Contributor
Smart Women's Empowerment
www.smartwomensempowerment.org

www.ingramcontent.com/pod-product-compliance
Lightning Source LLC
Chambersburg PA
CBHW051627170526
45167CB00001B/83